What people are say

Answering Avalon's Call
The Mystical Odyssey of an Earth-Healer

Carol's extraordinary memoir will lead you back home to your own soul. She is a wonderful storyteller, in tune with the mystery. Her book is a unique blend of spiritual teaching, poetry, and simple life wisdom.

Molly Harvey, CEO Harvey Global, Corporate Soul Woman. Molly is a transformational business thinker and author. www.MollyHarvey.com

Glastonbury has been a place of myth and legend for many hundreds of years and this book beautifully captures the ways that these mysteries can reveal themselves. Carol's writing style creates a lyrical bridge, inspiring the reader to come along and explore with her the secrets long held in an ancient landscape which is still very much alive with the pulse of sacred living.

Mano Mannaz is a Visionary Light-worker, artist, writer, and poet, residing in Glastonbury, UK. Author of *The Truth Sings in Circles* [M. Warren]. https://avalongrailcode.wordpress.com/

An intriguing blend of reminiscence, real events and storytelling. The author's sibylline style connects us to realms beyond the mystical.

Peggy Spencer Behrendt is the Co-Founder and Creative Director of Shawangunk Nature Preserve in Cold Brook, New York. www.ShawangunkNaturePreserve.com

Carol Ohmart Behan's spiritual-growth memoir resonates with my soul. Her guidebook provides hope, inspiration, and encouragement for people to explore their inner universe of infinite possibilities and for readers who search for further spiritual awareness, health and healing. She courageously delves into her own soul and shares her unique human experience with us.

Mari L. McCarthy, Founder and Chief Inspiration Officer of CreateWriteNow. Author of *Journaling Power: How To Create The Happy, Healthy Life You Want To Live*. www.CreateWriteNow.com

Carol is an enchanting storyteller and writer whose tales, though mysterious, are true. She will take you to other times and introduce you to other beings, all entwined with the present and to that mysterious place called Avalon. You just may find yourself not only intrigued but opened to new possibilities and a new world.

Rosemary Dowling, Educator and Spiritual Pilgrim

It was with great joy that I reconnected with my high school friend Carol after 40 years to find we were on the same spiritual, writing, and history-seeking path. As a result of this reconnection I was able to travel to Glastonbury with Carol and share in some of the stories she relates in her book. To read this book is to be transported to Glastonbury and to other realms where so many mysteries and their answers still thrive.

Kathie Bishop, PhD, author of *Whistling up the Wind*. Kathie's professional career was in Gerontology with a specialty in Aging with Developmental Disabilities. Among the many honors she has received is the Seneca Falls Women's Wall of Fame Plaque honoring her advocacy for older women.

Answering Avalon's Call

The Mystical Odyssey of an Earth-Healer

Answering Avalon's Call

The Mystical Odyssey of an Earth-Healer

Carol Ohmart Behan

BOOKS

Winchester, UK
Washington, USA

First published by O-Books, 2017
O-Books is an imprint of John Hunt Publishing Ltd., Laurel House, Station Approach,
Alresford, Hants, SO24 9JH, UK
office1@jhpbooks.net
www.johnhuntpublishing.com

For distributor details and how to order please visit the 'Ordering' section on our website.

Text copyright: Carol Ohmart Behan 2016

ISBN: 978 1 78535 508 0
978-1-78535-509-7 (ebook)
Library of Congress Control Number: 2016944523

A CIP catalogue record for this book is available from the British Library.

Design: Stuart Davies

Printed and bound by CPI Group (UK) Ltd, Croydon, CR0 4YY, UK

We operate a distinctive and ethical publishing philosophy in all
areas of our business, from our global network of authors to
production and worldwide distribution.

Other titles by the author:

Point of Departure (2002) Trafford Publishing
Downstream (2006) Trafford Publishing

For Earth-Pilgrims everywhere...

May your journeys be blessed with
days of delightful travel
in both outer and inner landscapes,
excellent companions,
and heart-opening encounters
in abundance.

Namaste'

Preface

From the moment we enter this world, we are constantly companioned by Gaia, our beautiful Mother Earth. I was wonderfully fortunate to enjoy a carefree country childhood so this vibrant connection with the living Earth was never muted or lost as it is for many. Reaching young adulthood in the turmoil of the late 1960s, the stark realities of Her distress led to an abiding commitment to environmental activism. Bringing the first Earth Day to reality on my college campus is a cherished memory. The forms my involvement took following that were various and modulated by whatever else was demanding attention in my life at the time. The *constant* was seeking steady connection with Her through all sorts of outdoor activities with my young family at our own rural home. And whenever possible I cherished the times I could spend alone in nature.

By some fortunate synchronicity, I came to know that Gaia's resonant heart-source, her Heart Chakra, was to be found Glastonbury, England, where the mists of Avalon hold ancient secrets and stories. And as is true for so many, from the time I first knew of this, I felt a strange and strong pull to go there. Shortly after the arrival of the New Millennium, a surprising opportunity came to attend a writer's retreat there. Without doubting for one minute that I was to go, I registered for what would be a pilgrimage of soul and heart, and personally transformative beyond my wildest imaginings. The story that follows picks up at that point so all these details await.

Gaia is in no less distress in these tumultuous times than was true in the 1960s. It is heartening to celebrate the gains made over these decades, but at every turn daunting threats remain to Her and our well-being. Wendell Berry's words shape much of my present focus and work: "The care of the Earth is our most ancient and most worthy, and after all our most pleasing respon-

1

sibility. To cherish what remains of it and to foster its renewal is our only hope."

I am certain that most of you reading this think of yourself as Earth-lovers. But we are called upon to be more if we can, to be Earth-advocates and even Earth-warriors... to raise our voices and take action on Her behalf. It is a mutually-beneficial, heart- and spirit-nourishing alliance. Beautiful Gaia, the ineffable Spirit of our Earth-home, offers her vital presence everywhere but particularly radiantly and powerfully on Avalon's ancient isle.

There are innumerable people to thank for the nearly countless ways that they have contributed to this whole grand and ongoing evolutionary-journey of mine. Many of you and your stories are woven into these pages.

Truly endless thanks to the several dozen of you Glastonbury Pilgrims who over the years took me up on the offer to be your guide on your own pilgrimage journeys to Avalon and to other sacred sites in Southwest England. The adventures and extraordinary experiences we've had together are memorable beyond the telling, though I've attempted to fashion some of the stories to share in these pages.

On my first trip to Glastonbury I was blessed to meet Mano Mannaz whose visionary insights, generous spirit, and abiding friendship, have been and are such sustaining grace for this still unfolding journey. Her poem "Daring to Dream" sets the stage for the story that follows.

Immeasurable inspiration and courage to follow my heart came through studying with Dr. Jean Houston and Peggy Rubin as part of their marvelous Mystery School program. Their profound and soul-expanding teachings nudged and often pushed me to release all sense of limitations and to be "fierce with my own reality." And so many within the Mystery School community offered their marvelous and enthusiastic support for my various quests. A special acknowledgement to Betty Rothenberger, member of the Mystery School faculty, whose loving enthusiasm for all my Glastonbury work has been a deep well of guidance and inspiration. Her focused, thoughtful reading of the book's draft helped to shape it to its fullest potential.

In addition to thanking Mano Mannaz for her poem, I am deeply grateful to two other writers who gave permission to use their luminous poetry to enrich these pages: to Lauren de Boer for his poem, "The Small Song," and to Jill Stephanie Morgyn for her poem, "Bone-singers."

Thank you too to the fine people of John Hunt Publishing and their O-Books Imprint who entered this journey more recently. I am honored that you saw the merit in this story and wished to help share it with the wider world. If the "past is prologue" (thank you, W.S.), by any stretch of the imagination we're in for a fine collaboration.

Finally, and in no way reflected by saving you for last, truly endless thanks and gratitude to a special crew of creative co-collaborators and adventuresome-instigators who have cheered me on all along the way: Mari McCarthy, Michelle Gallant, Carol Williams, Mary Kay McGraw, Laraine Waterbury, Nancy Fanara, Dawn Kirk, Cheryl Resler, Diana Rankin, Rosemary Dowling, Ruth Elliott, Cathleen Kelly, Bonita Shear, Nandini Weitzman, Pam Rosati, and Dorothy Abrams. And of course, always, to my adventuresome offspring, Justin Behan and Sarah Robarge, and granddaughter, Brianna Nicole Behan, who joyfully explored the magick Isles with me in 2013. Avalon sings in all of you too.

COB
Lightspring Glen
June 2016

Daring To Dream

Sitting in the apple tree
With the west wind swaying
My thoughts move to wandering
There are Prayer Ribbons sighing
And dragonflies hovering
With recollections murmuring
Ancient chants singing
And River Songs calling
A chorus of remembering
With Invocations seeking
Their Dreamers finding
Ancestral Keepers responding
Their melodies emerging.
~ *Mano Mannaz*

Chapter 1

The Path leads on, I must depart
to hidden places of the heart.
~ COB

Our plane made its final turn and lumbered onto the runway at JFK, slowly starting to pick up speed. In the window seat beside me my new friend, Sue Southward, said quietly, "Oh, no..." I turned towards her expecting that the imminent take-off was frightening her.

"You okay?" I asked.

She nodded and grinned. "Oh sure. It's just that I've only ever taken two adult ed courses in creative writing. I have no idea why I'm here!"

The plane was now thundering forward. I patted her arm. "Don't worry. It's all going to be just fine."

And with that the pilot throttled up and we lifted off into the bright July evening, the sun setting in a brilliant blaze behind the New York City skyline. As we came around in a sweeping turn, for a long moment the Twin Towers loomed above all else and then the plane circled further up heading out over the Atlantic towards England. If there was anything certain in that moment, it was my knowing that I was poised on the brink of what was likely to be the greatest adventure of my adult life. Two quite incredible pieces of it were set to come together in the ten days ahead.

Sue and I, along with nineteen other women, were headed for a 10-day writing retreat in Glastonbury where we aimed to tap into the energies of ancient Avalon to fuel our creative fires. Our eminently capable workshop leader, Emily, had taken other groups there and several women were returning for more of its magic. A dozen or so of us, including Sue and me, were blissfully excited to be experiencing it all for the first time.

2001 had already been a magical, amazing year. I was nearing completion of my first novel, *Point of Departure*, aiming for its publication by the next Spring. Calling myself a Writer and working towards that goal had become an increasingly important focus in the last few years. Getting to this place in my journey was so often unbalanced with pressing family matters, but I never gave up the long view. Some of the thornier challenges and obstacles were at last clearing, at least a bit. And to my delight, I was finding my fifth decade a place with *open spaces* and room to start spreading the wings I'd always sensed I had.

One such *open space* that came my way was "Remember the Magic," a week-long gathering for women writers (and creative Spirits!) held each August at Skidmore College in Saratoga Springs, New York. It was sponsored by the International Women's Writing Guild, a wonderful organization with the purpose of empowering women through their writing. I'd been an active member for a while and without question had grown increasingly confident of claiming my identity as a Writer. Among the inspiring instruction and wonderful connections the annual conference offered, I had the good fortune of meeting workshop-leader Emily Hanlon the previous Summer. Through her considerable influence another long-dormant seed sprang into life.

It was a very summery August morning when I took a seat in her seminar packed with at least 40 other enthusiastic women-writers. She had us put something meaningful on an altar space on the floor in the center of our large circle, and soon pens, jewelry, and crystals made for a glittery offering. The exercise that began the hour was motivating and delightful though its details are lost in time. It was what she said next that remains as clear as a bell.

She smiled brightly around at all of us, announcing that in the coming Summer of 2001 she would be taking a group on a writing retreat to Glastonbury, England, also known by its ancient name, Avalon. As she started to say, "If any of you are interested…" my hand shot up seemingly of its own volition. With a grin, she nodded across the circle at me and finished, "… stop and talk with me after class." Oh yes, indeed I did!

I came back home from that empowering week claiming myself fully as a writer and thrilled beyond words at the prospect of the Avalon Writer's Retreat. My regular life claimed my attention, work as a substitute teacher interwoven as often as possible with my writing, primarily revision work of the novel's manuscript. Like a jewel, the Glastonbury retreat glowed on the horizon. I had faith that somehow I'd manage the cost and when a check for $800 arrived out of the blue in November… a life insurance dividend… it thrilled and delighted me to realize that some Divine force was underwriting my Avalon adventure.

In January Emily sent out several e-mails full of delightful details of what we'd be doing and all sorts of intriguing infor-mation on Glastonbury. Our retreat would overlap with the quite famous annual Glastonbury event, "The Goddess Conference." As soon as I read this I knew a lovely intersection of my spiritual explorations and my writing enthusiasms was set to blossom.

The past decade had found me on a path of exploring spiritu-ality through my membership at the Unitarian Universalist Church in Utica, New York. From the start I'd enjoyed their open-minded approach encouraging exploration of spiritual truths, especially as viewed with one's inner light. From the beginning I'd loved the UU symbol of the chalice with its bright flame. The ritual lighting of the chalice at the beginning of each Sunday's service always moved me. Things I couldn't express about it were to take on deeper meaning as I was drawn ultimately to know more about the Sacred Feminine.

A group of women joined together to study several books on Feminine Spirituality. A number of us were deeply stirred by what we discovered in the readings and knew we wished to go further. And so we formed the WISE group, *Women in Spiritual Encounter*. Together we explored and practiced the ancient traditions of seasonal celebrations, supporting each other in our spiritual growth, especially as it related to the Goddess and women's wisdom. Our monthly gatherings over three years were devoted to studying books on the Divine Feminine, exploring the ancient heritage of women's mysteries, and practicing Earth-honoring ceremony and ritual. It was an extraordinary odyssey for all of us.

One book in particular mesmerized me, Jean Shinoda Bolen's heart-opening book, *Crossing to Avalon: A Woman's Midlife Pilgrimage*. Emblazoned on each chapter's opening page was the symbol of the Vesica Piscis from the cover of the Chalice Well in Glastonbury, England. Its archetypal mystery dove deep the first time I looked upon it and did so all the more as I pored over the pages of this marvelous and somehow unsettling book.

So on that starry July night winging our way across the Atlantic, my first trip out of the country, and at fifty-two years of age, I was so very much embarking on my own Midlife Pilgrimage. We'd be spending time the very first morning at Chalice Well Garden, and it gave me goosebumps every time I thought about seeing the Well and its ornately-carved cover for the first time. Chalice Well… echoing the UU chalice I was so familiar with… what might I be shown about that?

I closed my eyes hoping for some sleep, vaguely aware of something else. Echoing in my inner ear were the lines of a poem that had come to me quite mysteriously early in my writer's journey. At that point I had been still quite focused on my teaching career along with the *everything else* that was part of my forties. It would be a while until I completely claimed my writer's-mantle, but I did enjoy nurturing the teenage writers among my high school students. One year a spirited group created the After School Poetry Society and I much enjoyed being their advisor. Thanks to them and their earnest efforts at writing poetry, I made a recommitment to my own writing, so frequently set aside for life's other demands.

One evening at home, my Muse quietly but insistently whispered this mischievous couplet in my Inner Ear:

Trouble's a-foot—but who's to know?
There's nowhere else for me to go.

I knew enough to dash up the stairs to my desk and jot it down at once in my notebook. Something about the lines ran a shiver up my backbone, especially when the single couplet quickly expanded to its finished form. I wrote rapidly filling the page, then sat in wonder, reading it over several times.

A voice calls out, the words I hear.
And though I look, there's no one near.
But close at hand, a door, a key...
And no one dare inhibit me.
The path runs true, I must depart
To hidden places of the heart.
No less than this, a pilgrim's prayer
Anoints the one who sojourns there.
Misty dawn conveys its grace
On hearts which dwell in sacred space.

I knew this was a special treasure and that its spontaneous arrival portended further mystery and magic. Before the end of the term, I got up the nerve to share it with the After School Poets, and they were delighted, offering me high praise. I still smile remembering how sweet that was. So along I went on my writer's journey, this mysterious poem tucked carefully away. At odd moments some of its words and images would pop up, tantalizing me anew but most always still withholding fuller meaning.

Here I was now aboard this England-bound plane doing my

best to get comfortable in my less-than-comfortable seat, and most certainly following my Muse's insistent summons to Glastonbury. Beyond my human companions I was keenly aware of *other* unseen traveling companions, my Spirit-Guides and Teachers. Their voices and presence I'd come to know and trust in the past several years. Indeed, for months they had been enthusiastically helping me prepare for the experiences and adventure that awaited in England.

An avid and longtime journaler, I kept a variety of journals and notebooks, some centered on the ups and downs of my mid-adult life, one devoted to dream-work, and some for spiritual exploration and musings. No matter what was happening in the outer world, there was always welcome refuge within the covers of these journals. Sometimes messages appeared on the page *arriving* from unknown Sources that I couldn't identify but that I had grown to trust completely. Earlier that Summer, contemplating the approaching Avalon adventure, this short message came: *Now there is beginning a subtle shifting of gears, a setting of the sails to embark on a magical and marvelous path.*

Earlier, in mid-Spring, on the edge of overwhelm with family difficulties, I posed this question in my Spirit Journal. "It has been a long journey of late – what is it you wish me to hear?" Soon my pen began to record an answer:

Dear One,

Despite the difficulties, you are coming closer all the while. Despair comes too easily to you. Fraught though your path is with what you perceive as burdens, these are not so. Come closer now so you can truly hear unencumbered in the day's light. Spirit smiles and wishes you well. Fortitude resides in others even if the appearance seems otherwise.

Set aside this role of motherhood and devote yourself now to the fullness you have been heading for. Missions of your lifetime emblazoned in the stars, seeing through the thickets to the Tree Spirit who resides below the house; a beneficent Friend who is joyous you found this site; labyrinth Over Soul and adventuring there. So much to broadcast to the world! People begin their "walk" towards you. You will so benefit them on their separate journeys—and you have one to go on this summer (to England!), as you know. Magical moments full of the deepest significance. Few will be able to resist what you have to share. Many will entrust themselves to your work. Keep to the course—hold to this Path. There is a crest ahead with a magnificent view—so happy to share this in advance with you—(perhaps the view from the Tor?!).

Spirit's reassurance in this message was such a comfort in regard to the burdens mentioned. There had indeed been some easing to them, but no magic wand had swept them clear away. The friendly Tree-spirit… the huge maple beside the house… kept his steady vigil, always a comfort. All my life Nature had offered such lively company and support. Other parts of Spirit's message were harder to decipher. Was it my book that was to be "broadcast to the world"? What did it mean that *People begin their "walk" towards you…*? Towards me? Really??

It was true. There was a definite theme running through many messages of late that I was going to be sharing something "irresistible" with the world sooner or later. The closer the trip to England came, the more I sensed the answers to these questions would be revealed there in Avalon when I reached that *crest* and looked out on that magnificent view. It might be a figurative one or a literal one, but there was no doubt I would *know* when I reached it.

Chalice Well, the mysterious hill known as The Tor, the ruins of Glastonbury Abbey, our visit to Stonehenge. All of these lay ahead of us, mere hours away, as our plane flew swiftly and steadily towards the dawn.

Chapter 2

What would happen if one woman told the truth about her life?
The world would split open.
~ Muriel Rukeyser

Our cheerful flight attendants roused us in the last hour of the flight to serve us a hot drink and a warm muffin. Outside the cabin windows the morning sun beamed a welcome as we flew steadily towards London. Sue and I oohed and ahhed at glimpses of the English countryside passing below at a steady clip. Enchantment! My first international flight, other than short on sleep-time, was a fine beginning of this grand adventure ending with a smooth landing at Heathrow's huge airport.

A first-time international traveler, I was so grateful to be with people experienced at the process of going through Customs, claiming our luggage, and then wending our way through the crowded, cavernous halls to our waiting bus, the Avalon Coach. Our smiling driver gave us a hearty greeting and saw to our getting comfortable for the four-hour drive to Somerset.

I did my best to stave off impending jet lag, too excited to want to close my eyes as many did for the first part of the drive. As we left London behind I could scarcely believe I was looking out at England's countryside on this bright Summer's day. Even before we reached Glastonbury our adventures would begin with an hour's stop at Stonehenge which was on the way there. Stonehenge! Jet lag or not, I was primed to plunge into whatever experiences were awaiting me there.

And as I was to soon learn, when someone chooses to make a journey to Avalon, *off-the-charts* experiences show up almost at once.

At some point my eyes closed and I dozed for a little while which proved to be important minutes of restorative rest. I knew that not only the Stones awaited, but something possibly even more mysterious weaving their way through the Circle: *ley lines.* What I understood was that these were currents of something like electromagnetic energy that "traveled" through the landscape in stable pathways and that where they intersected it produced often palpable sensations, an energy "source." And what excited me in particular was learning that Stonehenge was a virtual powerhouse of ley lines coming in from all directions.

It was quite a hot Summer's afternoon as we pulled into the parking area and stepped off the bus onto the ground of the Salisbury Plain. As a tour group we were thankfully able to bypass the longer lines of other tourists and make our way through the turnstiles. We entered a short tunnel that passed beneath the roadway and then up a short incline to where, as if by powerful magic, the silent megaliths of the Stonehenge Circle appeared in their considerable presence, the sense of them heightened all the more by jet lag, no doubt. There's no way to describe how that first sight felt to me.

Of course there were literally hundreds of others slowly traversing the walkway that runs all around the Circle, pointing, snapping photos, commenting in excited voices in all sorts of languages. I found a bit of an open place and stood awestruck gazing at the Circle for several long minutes. Then I consciously surrendered to my inner-guidance letting it lead me along. I moved along in the crowd of tourists, glancing at the stones through the wall of people standing at the low chain fence. Then up ahead I saw a group of people a little way off the main path standing in something of a double line a few feet across from each other. Most of them were looking down at the ground. I felt my first England-shock-of-recognition... I knew why!

I hurried over and found a place to stand in one of the rows, catching a bit of conversation. Yes! A ley line was right here! Someone reached down to the ground and exclaimed, "Oh!" I did the same and inches from the ground felt a shockingly strong flow of chilly air moving out from the Circle. On that hot July afternoon, it felt like someone had opened a refrigerator door. I put my hand back down a second time into the air current to be sure of what I'd felt. As I straightened up with what I'm sure was a look of delighted surprise, several near me nodded and smiled. Even writing this years later, this shared experience carries such a sense of wonder. And I'd been in England only a few hours.

Sorry to not have more time to linger there, I rejoined the slowly moving tourist-crowd, and drifted around the rest of the Circle. Stopping when it felt right, gazing across the short grass to the silent Standing Stones, and being open to whatever energy and messages they wished to convey to me.

Back on our Avalon Coach we headed towards Glastonbury, now only an hour away. I worked on keeping my sleepy eyes open, eager for my first sight of the Glastonbury Tor, the enigmatic, steep-sided hill that rises above the town, dominating the landscape for miles around. Jean Shinoda Bolen had written eloquently of seeing it for the first time, of how it had immediately captured her imagination and telegraphed its significance.

Once we passed through the village of Shepton Mallet, I knew this first sight was only minutes away. And then, rounding a bend in the road, the Tor's mysterious and compelling bulk rose into magnificent view ahead of us, St. Michael's Tower standing tall on its summit. A jolt of its powerful energies came straight into my heart, literally taking my breath away. I treasured every glimpse of it as it appeared and disappeared those last few miles, at last coming into town along its steep flank. I certainly wasn't the only one awed by its presence.

And then another surprise. When we stepped down from our Avalon Coach onto the ground of Avalon... as I was to find out later... three of us had a distinct sensation not of arriving for a "first time" in 21st century Glastonbury, Somerset, but of a vivid sense of *home-coming*.

With travel fatigue setting in, this was just a faint awareness in that moment, but it was definitely "there." When my roommate, Jennifer, and I entered the room we'd be sharing for the next ten days, we crossed to the window and gasped at the same time. Before our eyes lay a completely magical scene, the ruins of Glastonbury Abbey just over the back wall of the Abbey House lawn. We'd learn that guests of the Abbey House had nearly unfettered entry to the ancient grounds, something I would take full and happy advantage of. After I got home I remember describing to people how totally incredible it was to be greeted each morning by this enchanting view. It was like waking up in a fairy tale… again and again!

Emily had planned a brilliant itinerary to support the activation of our deep creative Selves and fuel our writer's fire. After a night of marvelously restorative sleep, we ventured out through the East Gate, the original one of Glastonbury Abbey, and set off along Chilkwell Street to Chalice Well Garden. Our ten-minute walk brought us to the gateway where we were greeted by a full-sized replica of the Vesica Piscis. A blessing ceremony was to come first, and then we'd have the chance to explore the rest of the Garden and the first opportunity to be at the Holy Well.

If the Garden is not too crowded, the sound of flowing and falling water fills the air. The sacred red-tinged waters rise in their constant flow into the Holy Well and then down through the gardens. It tumbles down a marvelous natural waterfall into the Healing Pool of Arthur's Court, and then dances down the flow-forms into the shallow Vesica pools and then out of the Gardens into the town's waterway.

People come from around the world to wade in and even immerse themselves in the healing waters of the shallow pool in Arthur's Court. We paired up for a foot-washing ceremony, just as ancient Pilgrims would have done when they arrived in Glastonbury needing to wash the dust of the journey from their feet. It was a loving, invigorating ritual as Jennifer and I took turns bathing each other's feet, holding hands while one at a time we walked carefully through the cold waters of the slippery-bottomed pool, and then toweling dry one another's feet.

When at last we were invited to go and explore the rest of the Garden, I stopped first at the Lion's Head out-flow where two glasses stood ready. Several people were standing around the low-walled stone basin that's sunk into the garden space. I watched how people took turns, filling a glass in the water issuing from the Lion's mouth, taking deep swallows, then pouring a libation of thanks over the Lion before rinsing and setting the glass back on the wall for the next person.

My turn. I stepped forward for my own first ritual, picking up a glass and bending to fill it, then for a long moment studying its cold vibrant *presence* captured in the glass. I gave silent thanks for this morning and more, and then drank deep of the crystalline waters of Chalice Well. Another incredible moment.

It was just a few more steps to the Holy Well through a wrought iron gateway. And then I stood before the Well-head, the first strong impression a sense of this moment and place being not-quite real. It was down a few steps from where I stood gazing awestruck. Curved stone ledges offered seats to Pilgrims. My legs were a bit shaky but carried me safely down to where I found a place among those already sitting in quiet contemplation. The hushed and deep peace of the place settled comfortably around me.

There before me was the Vesica Piscis on the thick wooden well cover, which was leaned back against its supporting stone pillar. The bulk of it was startling somehow, or the reality of being in its presence was hard to absorb all at once. I looked and looked, bringing myself as much into the moment as I could, to be fully present.

Beneath an iron grid, the Well's shaft drew my eye down into its secret depths. The gray-stoned edge was lined with the most ethereal emerald-green moss and tiny plants, and from below the splash of the rising Waters. I allowed the enchantment to envelop me completely, the sense of linear time fading gently away. "I'm here," I told myself silently, "I'm really here."

The days followed each other filled with delightful and amazing experiences in both our writer's lives and emerging goddess-selves. With each experience that unfolded, my sense of being in an entirely new and different world to the one I had come from grew in dazzling dimension.

Avalon's enchantment in no small way also arises from the Somerset landscape and the many magical Beings which inhabit it, each new encounter thrilling me anew. Having been enthralled at my first sighting of the Tor from the bus, it was a very special experience to step onto the path that first time and clamber up along the many steps and turns leading to the now-roofless St. Michael's Tower which is all that remains of the medieval structures of the Benedictine monks of Glastonbury Abbey. The views from the Tor's 520-foot summit are worth the tired legs and labored breathing necessary to get there. One can see for easily 25 miles in all directions across the Levels, land that once was shallow ocean and salt marsh before the Romans and then the monks drained it for agricultural use. On certain mornings when the air is right, mists rise just as they did in those ancient days, obscuring the land all around the Tor and rendering it an island-in-the-mist once again. *The Mists of Avalon* as Marion Zimmer Bradley captured in her book title.

I was also completely awed by the trees. As already noted, Abbey House bordered the ruins of the ancient Abbey and it was a marvelous bonus that, as guests there, we had free access to the grounds through the huge wooden gate at the back of the yard. Apart from the haunting beauty and mystery of the tumbled and towering ruins, there are acres of verdant lawn, an apple orchard, two huge fish ponds, and dozens of incredible trees, most towering giants with impossibly huge trunks and limbs.

One quickly became my favorite, an enormous Copper Beech

not far from the gate. Its smooth gray trunk would need at least eight people to encircle it. Its many knobby roots offered seats, an invitation I happily accepted, enjoying the presence of this amazing Tree-being and the marvelous views of the Abbey grounds spread out before me. I sought the Beech's company often leaning back against its friendly bulk and closing my eyes for quiet reflection, my special retreat place for the Retreat.

Under Emily's skillful guidance, we were all happily diving deep into our creative writing depths. One afternoon she announced that she would be leading us in what promised to be, at the least, an intriguing guided meditation, possibly even a personally powerful one. We would visualize ourselves at a crossroads and see a person coming towards us who we would meet and engage in conversation. This person might offer himself or herself as a character with whom we could do further work.

We each found a spot to stretch out comfortably on the floor of our marvelous workroom, the enormous, high-ceilinged Victorian parlor of Abbey House. Telling us to take several deep, centering breaths, Emily guided us into our inner landscape.

I found myself in a country setting at the promised crossroads and knew at once that it was a long-ago time of Somerset's past. Beautiful fields bordered by low wooded hills stretched out around me on a Summer's day. The roads were empty at first glance. Then, in the distance appeared the figure of a woman coming along the lane towards me. I could see she wore a long dress or skirt. I could also see that she was looking at me with interest. Something in all of this caused me to catch my breath and every one of my senses signaled the aliveness of the unfolding scene. I felt my imaginal-self standing stock still as she drew near enough for our eyes to lock together. She was a young woman of slight but sturdy build with penetrating dark eyes and wavy dark hair to her shoulders. The air between us became charged with an unnameable energy. I felt tears pricking my eyes... my physical eyes. A few tears escaped and ran down my face as I lay there on the floor trying to not "come out" of the meditation-focus.

As the distance closed between us, a sob rose in my throat. Worried that I might disturb other people in the room, I clenched my hands at my sides trying to stay in control. It was useless. The best I could do was muffle my sobbing as she came to stand in front of me, her beautiful dark eyes offering a friendly and curious regard. We stood arm's length from each another, looking deeply into one another's face, neither saying a word. Were we both crying? By now I was gasping for breath, both my conscious and imaginal-self were weeping. If she and I spoke any words, I never heard them. I was completely engulfed with the emotions surging through me.

Somewhere in the room I heard another woman sobbing with her own fierce experience. Emily gently "called us back," and asked us to find someone to share the exercise with. The two of us who'd wept quickly found each other. Hers had been an encounter with her deceased father and I was very moved by her story. She found my meditation-encounter to be quite awesome too. I was so grateful to ground some of its extraordinary energy and excited at the prospect of working with this wonderful "character."

Glastonbury is a place of many coexisting dimensions that can be exhilarating and daunting all at the same time. It proves challenging for some... soul- and heart-expanding for others. A few years later I learned a secret to the powerful energy that supported this profound experience for my partner and myself that day. The Michael ley line runs up through the ruins of the Abbey and then passes straight through our workroom there in Abbey House. I'm rather sure Emily knew this and helped us tap into its power for the creative work we did together.

And then one more telling indicator of the validity of this *encounter* with the mysterious woman occurred just two days before the retreat's end. In our free time, we loved nothing better than exploring Glastonbury's many fascinating offerings. There was an abundance of cafés and shops that catered to the New Age-inclined visitor as well as a dizzying number of metaphysical practitioners offering everything from crystal healing to past-life regression. Several in our group spoke glowingly of their sessions with a woman at the Bridget Centre. I'd been contemplating something along these lines, though was a bit hesitant considering this sort of thing almost too far out of my comfort zone. But my powerful encounter with the young woman during the meditation convinced me to seek more information. And so I scheduled a past-life regression with Mano Warren.

A bit nervous but definitely excited, I found my way to the courtyard near the Market Cross and climbed the stairs of the Bridget Centre. Mano was gracious and welcoming and ushered me into her treatment space. She described how the session would go, reassuring me it would be, at the least, an interesting experience. Emily's similar techniques helped open me to this new experience and I felt at complete ease as I closed my eyes. Mano's guidance soon had me relaxed into a light meditative state, and we began. This was the entry I made later in my journal:

As I passed through the door in the Temple of Memory I emerged into a courtyard filled with warm sunshine, a Summer's day. The ground under my feet was dusty. I walked along a wall and then someone was walking with me—or I was that woman—long brownish skirts brushed my ankles and the top of my feet. This person later told me her name was Hannah. I/She was returning from town to her home that stood on the outskirts of the village. She was nearing 27, no longer young but not yet old. She was married but childless after nearly ten years of marriage. Her husband was a good man for which she was grateful. For a woman of her day she was somewhat independent, partly because she had no children, but also because she kept bees in their small orchard and sold the honey to her neighbors. Her skill with herbs made her also notable. Some of what she had learned of herb-lore went beyond accepted practices of the day and she guarded most of this knowledge closely. Only she knew the true reason for her barrenness—it was not God's will as some supposed, but was her own choice and doing. Though her husband had accepted the fact of their childlessness, he sorrowed over this at times. She regretted this since she loved him, but not even this would persuade her to put aside the monthly cups of strong, herbal tea.

Session complete, Mano brought me back to full awareness and helped me make notes of what I'd experienced. It had been a vivid one. I thanked her for the work and tucked this intriguing hour's adventure into my heart along with the now-countless delights of my first Avalon adventure.

An account of that first time in Glastonbury isn't complete without describing my lovely and wondrous encounters with Mary, the Holy Mother. Emily was particularly pleased to set the dates for our retreat to coincide with the Goddess Festival. While seeing women dressed in Goddess-themed clothes is a common sight at any time, the town was especially crowded with brightly-clothed conference participants.

The festival was in progress when we arrived with final events happening our first weekend. Emily had written ahead and received an invitation for us to take part in the Goddess Procession that started in the town center and ended at the Chalice Well for concluding ceremonies and celebration. So on that sunny, blessedly cooler Sunday morning we excitedly dressed in our Goddess clothes, and stood waiting at the gate of Abbey House. Soon, there they came along Chilkwell Street walking to the beat of drums and chanting... dozens and dozens of women in rainbow-hued clothes and carrying huge banners of images of the Goddess. Another moment that took my breath away.

They reached us and we stepped into the line of marchers. Women smiled their welcome. I felt transported to another Time, barely feeling my feet on the pavement. I was walking next to a woman carrying one of the banners. As we turned the next corner she asked, "Would you like to carry this?" And so I received it, hardly able to say my thanks. The eight-foot tall banner on its slender pole wasn't at all heavy and it floated gently above my head. When we reached Chalice Well, I set the pole on the ground and realized I hadn't even known what Goddess image I'd carried. I turned it towards me and there was the beautiful image of Mary, the Holy Mother, smiling at me from beneath her blue veil. Oh my…

So there I was with dozens and dozens of women, all of us dressed in our Goddess finery, circulating around the shallow Vesica pools at the bottom of the Garden. Such delightful conversations and warm greetings exchanged in all sorts of accents and languages. I wandered happily and came to a small group gathered around someone who had a camera new in that time which had an image screen to instantly display photos. I looked over someone's shoulder to see a shot she had just taken of the scene across the lower pool. In an open space was a hazy but distinct image of a blue-veiled woman standing alone looking our way, a stillness about her that felt unmistakable to me. Her veil completely covered her face, but it was clear she was regarding us. I raised my head quickly seeing people mostly as they were in the photo, but the space where the woman stood was startlingly empty. There was no sign at all of a blue-veiled woman. She could not have walked away that fast! I looked down again at the camera's display, and there she was in the photo. A shiver ran through me. Mary was here among us.

It was quite an emotional departure from Glastonbury that August morning as we headed reluctantly back to the "real world." And it was equally hard to say goodbye to one another after sharing this marvelous and incredible adventure. Bonds were formed that would continue for several years and to this day two of my dearest friends are from this special circle.

The reentry into the everyday world took some doing, something I would find true after every journey to Avalon. But I was not alone. The mysterious young woman I'd encountered in Glastonbury was busy taking up permanent residence in my life, hints of which would begin to appear in the not far-off future.

Less than a month later on the morning of September 11th I was excited to be getting my regular writing routine underway once again. So much fuel for the fire!

Then the phone rang in the bedroom down the hall.

It was our son, Justin, calling from his Boston apartment to ask if I'd heard the shocking news about a plane hitting one of the towers of the World Trade Center in New York City. Holding the phone against my ear with one hand, with the other I picked up the television remote to turn on the set. The footage of the second plane's impact was already running. And so began this most awful day when the world changed for all of us.

Sensing the enormity of what was starting, I returned to my desk and doggedly attempted to focus on my goal for the day... my writing. Later that afternoon, I left the house and walked out to sit on the hillside out in the horse pasture. Hugging my knees tightly, I gazed deeply into the peaceful beauty of the early Autumn countryside spread out so gloriously before me. New York City was to the southeast and from that direction I keenly felt the waves of grief and trauma washing over me and over the landscape. It was a long, bleak moment. But then, something stirred in my consciousness bringing a glimmer of comfort and something that felt like peace.

What came to me was the awareness that those extraordinary ten days in England had deeply charged me with spiritual energy and that this fathomless reserve would sustain and nourish me for whatever was to come in the days ahead. That reserve did not fail.

Somehow we all managed to find our way forward after that horrific day. Writing of things now, it is challenging to recall precisely how we all got through those first few days and weeks. These lines from my journal capture this: *"In the swirl of thoughts and emotions during the first few days, my sense of mission was all the sharper. As the darkness that washed over the face of the Earth splattered its malevolence everywhere, a counter-wave of Light and Love spilled forth... I have remembered how my true identity is that of a Warrior/Teacher of the Light. It is these days which call out for these positive forces."*

And Glastonbury reached out. I have a vivid dream in late September of returning to Abbey House, all my senses so alive as I stand in the foyer and look about me, my dream-self realizing that I'm not supposed to be here but so delighted that I am. I can hear through the closed door that there's a new group in our meeting room, but somehow I know that I won't be detected. A day or so after the dream it comes to me in a flash that I'd experienced my first astral-projection dream! *"I love the thought that this took place and that I will be able to return when I need the peace of this place."*

Even more marvelously, as October begins I'm able to go on a two-night retreat to The Spiritual Center in Windsor, NY, a place that had come to be a special haven since I first visited there to recharge my spirit during my mother's illness three years previously. These forty-eight hours would offer uninterrupted time to ground and sort through what the past two months have been: *"I believe I am here in part at least to reconnect with the images that came to me in Glastonbury in the guided visualization that Emily led, and in the past-life regression with Mano. There might be more and I hope to keep clear and open to what might be seeking me."*

This message from Spirit some two weeks after my Windsor retreat does offer great clarity of not only the larger landscape, but some unease that is showing itself at home.

18th October 2001: Channeled message
Start with this, Dear One, let your thoughts be untroubled. Your

dreams—yes!—have been rich with potent images. The world's stage is crowded with drama, excesses, almost beyond viewing, imagining (**9/11**). It tries the souls of all, especially Light-workers. Steadfast must you (all) be to your work. Grace awaits, abides. Persevere… the way will be shown. Disregard as much of the distraction in order to stay clear. This is so very necessary. Don't fight it—it comes at a risk and we cannot afford to lose your energy, or can the world. Your stubborn persistence helps no one, least of all you! Be with the work that has fallen your way and runs so pure, and is so needed. Do not fear to lose the path. Just stop letting things threaten to trip you up.

Stay clear. Focus thoughts and energies for steady and truly spectacular progress is soon (so very soon!) and is as certain as is our presence. You do us honor with the purity of your heart, utilizing your talents as you do. Be careful and perhaps even wary. Breathe deeply of the charged newness. Clasp hands with those who share the vision. Work on mindfulness. Partnership is power. Trust your instincts fully. You are a true daughter of the Light.

The truth—allow it to galvanize your resolve. Reach for it now!

Chapter 3

Let yourself be silently drawn
by the strange pull
of what you really love.
It will not lead you astray.
~ Rumi

Although I wouldn't encounter this wonderful poem of Rumi's until several years later, it most certainly captures what the next two years would be for me. There were times I was somewhat doubtful of the direction things were going in, but never did I resist the beautiful and *strange pull*. Not once. And most surely, beyond what I fully grasped at first, the part of my heart I'd left in Avalon (or the part rediscovered) was calling me to return. But before I could, so much of my other life was waiting…

In the first few months following the horrific events of September 11th – already shortened to its numbers, 9/11 – my own journey saw much promise of personal growth. The outer world's news was seldom good, especially with Washington-leaders' clearly-desired expansion of the Afghanistan conflict into Iraq. Though so many of us rallied in protest to this, the drumbeats of war begin their ominous vibration. I'd taken part in antiwar protests against the Vietnam War and didn't hesitate this time to add my voice when I had the chance to join the rising chorus. But otherwise I focused on my Spiritual Path, knowing this somehow contributed its positive energy to the world. So while I dutifully followed events to stay informed, I did my best to keep this chaos at the outer edge of my awareness.

Creative pursuits, primarily my writing, and the extraordinary expansion of my interior life continued through sessions with long-time Spiritual Counselor, Christine Thompson, meditation, and journaling. I heeded my Guides' messages and my own Inner Voice. And both I heard more and more clearly all the time.

Family matters still claimed a good deal of time and energy. Our daughter was now living in Ithaca and attending Cornell, doing her best to make a life for herself and two-year-old daughter, our precious grandchild. Brianna's arrival in our lives in September of 2000 was the sweetest blessing for all of us, even with the uncertainties and challenges Sarah faced. Her dad and I gladly embraced our roles as grandparents and offered what help we could in what were still challenging times for them.

With the start of 2002, my spiritual journey once more crossed paths with the labyrinth. A few years earlier during a *Remember the Magic* week at Skidmore I came across one that someone had laid out in white yarn in one of the quads. I approached it almost shyly, taking in its simple and elegant pattern on the grass knowing vaguely that this was a labyrinth. I felt how it was encouraging me to step into it. My eyes took in its circular nested circles with their inviting sensuous curves. I took a breath and took my first step in. It was a memorable time slowly walking its curving path to the center and then slowly back to where I'd entered. Just like my discovery of the Vesica Piscis, this mysterious design captured me immediately and I knew I wanted to learn more about it.

There's a saying, "When the student is ready, the teacher will appear." She did. Dr. Lauren Artress, Canon at Grace Cathedral in San Francisco, had designed a training program for people interested in working with labyrinths and becoming facilitators. Two weekend-long workshops were required along with developing and offering three labyrinth presentations. Just as I'd known about the rightness of going to Glastonbury, I knew I needed to take this course with the wonderful name, *Veriditas, The Greening Power of God*. It was a thrill to receive the news that my application had been accepted and my first training weekend took place early in the New Year. Right from the start this labyrinth work blended beautifully with my expanding spiritual journey.

After several years of determined effort, my first novel, *Point of Departure*, made its debut just before my birthday that April. The exhilaration was beyond what I'd anticipated, not only the sense of reaching this long-held goal, but I was astonished by the outpouring of exuberant congratulations of friends and family. Though there was plenty of work to do for its sales and distribution, the book signings and talks over the next year were always so gratifying.

My delighted Muse wasted little time *introducing* me to a second set of wonderful new characters who lived in a small town called Black Creek Falls. And how pleased I was to *sign on* to working with them! So another novel was underway with the working title, *Significant Lives*.

With all the public attention to my writing work, it wasn't surprising when a friend urged me to offer a creative writing class. So "Feeding Your Writer's Fire" took shape that Winter and was offered at her cozy bookstore. People signed up at once. Just as with the Edmeston ASPS, I was inspired by the adults who arrived each week with notebooks in hand ready to feed their "Writer's Fire." I drove home after the first one completely exhilarated saying, "I should be paying *them* to let me teach the class!"

Apart from the wonderful Writer's Fire group and the new novel, further revelations about the direction of my writing came at my birthday-session with Christine:

April 2002

An incredible number of Presences fill the room. Who they are – many historical personages – is beyond belief.

"Welcome to the realm of writers, thinkers, Bold Explorers and Experimenters. You are like Cortez looking out over the ocean, seeing a New Land. You share yourself with the world and we rejoice." They

offer praise for "... your positive contribution to all Creation!"
Copernicus is giving to me a Scroll containing a list of past and future
accomplishments, and a Pen, their "gift that is a divine instrument" by
which my future works will be written.

My mother appears with praise for how "You've worked
wonders" and for my growing awareness "of emerging patterns
as you walk the Bright Path."

The time is coming to visit other sacred places, they tell me.
Rapid spiritual growth "is engendered at these places." Each
place is the same but unique in how "the quickening" takes place
for you!

And... I am to write a book about my spiritual growth that
will be instructive to others for how to trust and grow, and as a
guide for how to hear their true voices.

Much food for thought, to say the least. And what was this about
visiting other sacred places? I wondered. Not that I ever doubted
the messages received in Christine's sessions, but these revelations were on the *marvelous* side, and I tucked them away for
further pondering.

So the steady and powerful flow of this year, 2002, carried me
along with positive developments in both our son and daughter's
lives when life partners appear for them both and these new
relationships take root and grow. It is heartening to be able to at
last devote more of my attention to my own creative pursuits.
There are several book-signing events, a writing workshop,
developing the labyrinth work, and working on the new novel
when I can find the time. My tech-savvy son helps me create and
launch my web site, Golden Spiral Journey, establishing a new
platform for *Point of Departure* and the increasingly joyful work
with the labyrinth.

With the first anniversary of 9/11 approaching, there were few
who weren't wondering how the day would be gotten through.
The Washington powers-that-be were milking the surge of patri-

otism for all it was worth, using it to bolster the continued US military actions in Afghanistan. It was a considerable blessing that one of my labyrinth presentations coincided with that day, clearly the work of Spirit for all concerned. It was sponsored by the Women's Group of St. Paul's UU Church in Little Falls. They'd invited women from all faith communities and the church basement where I opened my labyrinth was filled with thirty-three people. It was an evening of powerful emotion and significant healing for many. One woman took me aside and with tears in her eyes said walking the labyrinth was the first time she'd felt peace since the events of a year ago. Driving home, accompanied by glimpses of the Crescent Moon behind racing clouds, I was suffused with gratitude for what I was coming to understand about the powers of the Labyrinth.

A month later I did the final presentation for my facilitator program at a Sunday service of the Unitarian Universalist Church in Salisbury, a lovely village north of Utica. I'd led other services there in recent years and much enjoyed the people of the small congregation who were always so welcoming and appreciative of my coming to speak. Having the chance to share the labyrinth was a magical hour there.

Journal reflections

... I ended with a time for questions/feedback. Richard Carpenter, a lovely, gentle bear of a man who sat in the front row, offered his softly-spoken "observation" on the presentation. As he searched for words, his eyes moistened. We looked deeply into each other's eyes. It had been for him an hour which "brought spiritual energy" into their sanctuary and he felt filled with peace and spirit. Indeed, shortly after the service began, I sensed all of us there, some 14 or 15 souls, connecting with one another as if golden light was weaving us together... and I could nearly see it. And for a man—and such a lovely man—to respond this way, this so reinforces my confidence that I can reach out to all.

October keeps bringing incredible happenings. Just before a session with Christine, there's a Full Moon in Aries, always a special occasion. A wondrous and powerful channeled message comes from my Guides:

Message, 21st October 2002: Aries Full Moon

Dear One,

Magnificent creature of this Aries light, seeker of the Path, you are blessed with good fortune. Your energy comes from a deep and ever-flowing source. An opening exists that with time you will navigate with ease as *they* have all learned to do, those that came before. It is yours to do as well. The labyrinth carries you to center: We were watching with you, all intertwined, scarcely any boundaries. Mia Cara, you need not despair of your journey's apparent lack of purpose at the moment: We know well your puzzlement. Some of this time is sorely needed to relax and rest. Much awaits that will require tremendous focus, tasks you will well do. But for this time there is rest to have. Open to the gift. Wells of silent reflection, as Sr. Paula pointed out... sit by the well. The Light grows within, not for the adding of fuel so much as a polishing of the crystal and uncovering of the fabulous energy/fire you already possess—unfurling wings of proportion and intricate design—moving to center and great fulfillment. The goal is not fixed but fluid, part of a mosaic lovingly crafted by the Infinite, time out of mind. Your part integral and so very lovingly patterned. Others have seen, are drawn to you. Accept these Powers because they are rightfully yours. A Key is close at hand. Ask for it.

Do not cease in your requests for clarity. A host of loving Spirits is your birthright.

Go forward! Go forward! All is well.

A few days later Christine receives me into her home with her always-warm welcome. Our now several-years connection is a special one and she's cheered to hear the positive developments in my family. As much as I am, she's curious and eager to hear what my Guides will offer.

We begin. I am told that an important Spiritual Teacher will appear within two years involving me in something like "A Course in Miracles" and that this "... will be a re-membering for me," pronouncing the word clearly in its uncustomary form so I will understand. New work coming will be "... helping others to the next level" and will encompass both teaching and the writing of at least two books, maybe four.

Then Christine welcomes an entirely new Being into the session and his presence fills the room. He tells us his name, Loth-riel, of the Great White Brotherhood. He's come to give me an initiation of sorts:

I am sending a constant beam of golden light to hold you, Daughter of the Golden Robe. You have been a teacher in the other realm between lifetimes which explains your facility. Your work is of Peace and is/will be of great influence. The purpose of your humble birth rather than a greater place is becoming clearer. You will be traveling more and more.

Let it all come out, here and now, as a Daughter of the Golden Robe.

The labyrinth work and experiences had brought me to some sort of center, however etheric. As best I could I'd orchestrated some rest-and-relaxation time as Spirit had urged. The Holidays brought the usual pleasant hubbub with wee Brianna infusing it with grandchild magic for the second time.

2003 announces its arrival. The world is slipping into further turmoil led by the Bush II administration's war-mongering and saber-rattling thinly disguised by a continually trumped up, patriotic sermonizing. Every time I hear America referred to as "The Homeland" under dire threat by terrorists, I am reminded of the Nazis' use of that term in World War II. Sometimes it makes me shudder. It is a relief to mostly be able to stay in the cocoon of our house, most days cozily sequestered at my writing table with its view of the side yard and peaceful Winter landscape of the Unadilla Valley.

I seek my journal for a summing up of where it is I find myself as this new year begins.

16th January 2003: Journal notes

My favorite comic, *For Better or For Worse,* in this morning's paper showed Elly reflecting on how she worried about her kids no matter how old they were... ah, how true. And my above comment [in the previous entry] on a decade of anxiety – yes – the weight of it, has it left scars? Maybe just worn me down? That and the time of Mom's illness, her passing, the disconnect from Bartlett Road – all this I've understood, "survived," emerged from and went on to a spectacular year of my Glastonbury pilgrimage, the birth of *Point of Departure,* my odyssey with Veriditas – all of this a re-balancing. What I think I am experiencing is the perhaps "last part" of a necessary healing process. It doesn't matter if it's a healing of scars (though I am marked by this decade) or a re-balancing not yet completed. It has been a time, as Sr. Paula says, that is not one to "put myself out there." (Though that will happen soon enough: last night I got a call to do a service at the Cortland UU church.) Soon enough – soon enough! Time for the present to focus on the characters stirring in *Significant Lives,* the regular meditation practice I'm doing each morning, Taiji (an increasingly rich discipline), and even a likely upcoming Writer's Fire class.

As of this morning and coming here to write this entry, a clarity of things has come into focus accompanied by a very audible sigh of relief!

My attraction to the Moon and its monthly phases had begun a decade earlier with the WISE group and the three years of ceremonies and Sabbat celebrations we faithfully observed, so much of this based on the Moon's waxing and waning. While I was still a very novice astrologer, I did keep some track of which sign the Full Moon was visiting. The March Full Moon in Virgo is witness to peace demonstrations all around the world with cries of "No War" directed at Washington. On that windy moon-bright night I join a couple hundred people lining the streets of downtown Utica, candles in hand, registering our solidarity and heart-hopes that there will be no invasion of Iraq. It is heartening to see so many there.

The next morning I go for a walk up Davis Road's hill: *"... through the pearly light of a foggy morning. Mountain Stream is breaking free of its icy bonds. My spirit was soothed by calls of robins, killdeer, song sparrow... a gentle unfolding presence emerging, peace-engendering. Words come to me: 'Do not be transfixed by the Serpent's stare... move forward, there is work to be done.' Those forces want us to be immobilized, rendered powerless, but we need to reflect their blackness back to them. It is a transformative power that we hold. For me this comes through the labyrinth, such a generous gift from the Universe."*

Sadly and tragically the invasion takes place despite the massive outcry against it. Two weeks later this is how I see things and how I am managing to keep balance:

"A lot is happening in both inner and outward worlds. The start of aggression against Iraq is now a week behind us. I guard against hearing and seeing much of it, filtering its details mostly through e-mails from the group, Voices in the Wilderness... *There is an awful transformation in process, though its cost of world suffering grieves me. I seek out distractions of hopefully constructive work and lighter thoughts centered on Justin and Tracy's August wedding and Brianna. It's inspiring that work is being done in the cause of peace, justice, and ever-increasing international joining of hands and hearts. That shows to me the emerging communion and lifts me up on darker days."*

My dance continues between this often too-troubled outer world and the glowing inner one, a hectic tango some days, but one I am deeply devoted to and thrive in. Celebrating both my approaching birthday and the New Moon in my sign, I sit with my journal and seek this familiar and vibrant connection:

Message of 1st April 2003: New Moon in Aries

Dear Presences,

This begins a New Year with so much to come and ends one like no other. With this day's Aries New Moon energy, what do you want me to hear and to know?

Dear One, Child of Light,

Know that you are celebrated through the Life Force that fires your Soul, pathway rooted deep, significance revealed in greater and greater detail, a charge to keep thenceforth. Peace forthcoming but a sad struggle persists in minds alien to Light tho' remedies EXIST and are offered through children of wisdom/Light Beings (as you are, an Emissary of Wondrous Energy). Speaking through metaphors of Love and Journey, you unwrap/unknot the tangled thicket that some/many have made of their lives. Spider Woman, you, an incarnation of these times — gift to those who spy your Light — so, yes! Do continue your spiraled journey, releasing others to more of their hidden gifts. Things spill down and out, an outpouring of myriad blessings. Go forth with no hesitancy. Some secrets too-long smothered begin to take in their full and sublime destined dimensions. Breath of Life in you continues in answer to an echoing call. Censor not its triumphant message, for that which is to be in and through you comes forward in this year — a celebration and challenge but one you are here to do. Think not of impossibilities, since they, like so much else you feared, are simply illusions. Do not linger near them. Inner and outer Grace sustains You now and always. So be it. Blessed Be!

The Earth continues her turning and the spiral of my path unfurls, drawing me on. The energetic *tango* of that Summer includes leading a gratifyingly successful writer's retreat, the engrossing but delightful preparations for the wedding, and as much writing time as I can carve out of this which is precious little most weeks. Sarah, expecting a baby with her partner, Brian, will be eight-months pregnant at the time of her brother's wedding. They are thoroughly delighted at their family of three becoming four sometime in October.

Sharing such joy for our two children is a welcome relief in more ways than one. Ken and I look at each other sometimes and laugh at how we can be such young grandparents, but agree we wouldn't trade a moment of it. And this lovely *job* helps to smooth over the rougher moments of our marriage that have grown too common in the last few years.

After thirty-plus years together, "the wedded bliss" part is harder and harder to find. At one of the Veriditas weekends, Lauren has us in stitches when she shares a quote of Joseph Campbell's that she enjoys using at labyrinth events. *If the path before you is clear, you're probably on someone else's.* When something crops up that triggers prickly antagonism between Ken and me, these words now frequently come to mind, reassuring me of my direction at least.

One day in early August a postcard appears in the mailbox announcing an introductory weekend in October of something called Mystery School. I puzzled over this for a minute or two and then it struck me that Lauren had talked enthusiastically about Mystery School and its founder, Jean Houston. It was at one of these Mystery School weekends where she had first encountered the labyrinth. And she always spoke in glowing terms of Dr. Houston. Though I don't remember with certainty as I write this, I will wager that I felt goosebumps when this all connected. The weekend detailed on the card would be in October and take place not too far away in the Catskills. Nearly at once I knew that Spirit had indeed brought this opportunity to me for careful consideration. It's an easy decision to make. The necessary funds appear and I register for it, feeling so keenly "the strange pull of what you really love" that Rumi described. Further reflection reminds me of the message at last October's session with Christine of an important Spiritual Teacher appearing involving me in something like "A Course in Miracles." It seemed it took Jean Houston just a year to show up to help me with the *re-membering*. I was mightily excited at the prospect of learning more!

But first there is the absolutely fabulous event on August 25th: Justin and Tracy's homespun wedding. Brianna and another little girl proudly lead the way in their matching lavender dresses strewing flower petals in the hayfield setting. I could not be prouder of her and was doubly delighted that I'd made her flower girl dress. It's a very summery day with thunderstorms threatening off and on, but all goes beautifully and not a drop of rain falls on us.

The moments of Ken and I together walking our son down the slope to the assembled guests are ones that will forever glow in my mind's eye and heart. Other than it being awfully warm to much enjoy dancing, there's not a single thing anyone would have changed. A little more than six weeks later we welcome Logan Lee Robarge to the family. Sarah's labor started and stopped twice and both times I'd driven the ninety miles hurriedly down to Ithaca to be with Brianna. The second such dash was a very late evening aiming to beat an approaching tropical storm. Each time Logan apparently changed his mind. At last, five days later he finally joined us. Photos of that first meeting showed how close these two special children would be to each other right from the start. His parents were awfully pleased with their beautiful son too.

With all major family events seen to and celebrated, the spiral of my journey drew me forward and upward. And so, on a beautiful October Friday afternoon, I head towards the south-eastern Catskills and the Greenkill Conference Center in Huguenot, NY. The portal to the magic, spirit-expanding realm of Mystery School awaits with the transformative teachings of Jean Houston and those of her equally-marvelous teaching partner, Peggy Rubin. From that weekend on this becomes my Beloved Community through its final year in 2009 and ever afterward in a vital, etheric connection. Worthy of a book in itself, this simple paragraph will need to serve as testament.

Following this introductory weekend of Mystery School, I went for a session with Christine eager to hear messages from my Guides about this dazzling gathering. They are delighted in my *report*, and I can almost see Them nodding their approval. I'm urged to now spend time nurturing myself and *opening to the Light*. And where better to accomplish this than registering and attending the upcoming full year's program! And they also offer this revelation: *After Mystery School, the path will be much clearer. Until now you have often known yourself to be a Silent Watcher of the world, but more active work is coming.*

As the session nears its end I receive another revelation about my future path, this one quite unsettling. In England when something unpleasant comes out of the blue, people say with a wink "a spanner's been tossed into it." My Guides threw just such a *spanner* telling me that my marriage to Ken was likely coming to an end. As if there wasn't plenty to ponder from the Mystery School weekend, now *this*.

This sense of disconnection with my marriage partner, the father of our two wonderful kids and devoted grandparent, had been developing for some time. This could not be denied. We had coped with it a lot by ignoring it and when we couldn't, our behavior towards each other was at best regrettable and at the worst hurtful. But somehow we kept going and mostly hoped for the best. If I was to believe what Spirit revealed in that session, the permanence of our connection hoped for on the day of our wedding was fraying beyond repair.

The end of 2003 was approaching. So much to reflect on in the past months of the journey in both the Outer and Inner worlds. One of my favorite journals that I had kept for nearly ten years was close to its last pages. It was an emotional day sitting down at my writing table and opening its beautiful cover to write a final entry.

12th November 2003: Final entry of the Brown-Paisley Journal

A foggy mist clothes the hills and fields, temps back once more near 50. Yesterday's showers and chill give a reflective cast to what Canada wisely calls Remembrance Day. Met Laraine W. at the Adirondack Coffee Shop for brunch and a welcome chance to touch base – delighted at how her emergence continues – further reflection on my many single friends' lives compared to mine.

How to make meaning of our lives is, I think, the Big Question.

Sunday I spent doing some family research with Keith and Helen [my brother and sister-in-law] at Oliver and Ethel's. The focus was on Maggie and Mary Putman/Schermerhorn's time, the late 19th century. Looking at old photos, absorbed by Oliver's recollections, those times take on a meaningful shape. By now I believe I can grasp some sense of what daily life meant for them. A hundred years beyond them, they in their 45th year, likely they thought of themselves as mature women much as I regard myself at 54... an interesting point of comparison that I didn't grasp until now.

Just now I went back to the first several entries of this journal made in the Summers of 1995 and 1996 – from there to this quiet November morning in 2003... such an amazing sweep of my life's journey in these 8 years (enough for a memoir, my Muse suggests with his smile!). Certainly a time of transformation and true empowerment.

This past Saturday, November 8th, there was a spectacular lunar eclipse the night of the Full Moon. The constellations formed what was called the Harmonic Convergence, a much-heralded event by the Spirit-ed community. At the very least, though I celebrated alone here, this event occurred during a time of personal culmination. I've reached a place of level-going for a while – the anxieties, uncertainties, and traumas reflected in the early entries (and beyond) of this journal have all been lived through and nearly all comfortably resolved. None of it a "closed chapter," all of it a turbulent stretch of living. And, Goddess bless!, such marvels these 8 years have brought me of new work, incredible accomplishments, the treasure of continuing friend-ships, the arrival in my life of Brianna, Logan, Brian, and Tracy, new and special colleagues and circle of my spirit-ed tribe, nearly countless memories... "All in the loom/And oh! What patterns!"

There is nothing I would trade for all these days, even the bad ones... I have lived to tell the tale. In a weird sort of way, this present "level place" with its reflective calm and quiet is... maybe boring?! I have to laugh writing this, but there is a different pace and I've been awkwardly adjusting to it. With so much of the craziness of the past years settled, I've been asking myself if I'm resting on my laurels... but likely not. In my sessions with Christine T., I've been told the pace will be picking up, but my hope is that the challenges will be ones I'm eager to engage.

There has been such wonderful adventure in these past 8 years, age 46 to now 54. I will hope for more of this zestful living between now and my 62nd year.

Having registered for the 2004 Mystery School, I would soon be engaging in Jean Houston and Peggy Rubin's version of *zestful living*. I could hardly wait!

Chapter 4

Our life is an apprenticeship to the truth
that around every circle another can be drawn;
that there is no end in nature,
but every end is a beginning,
and under every deep, a lower deep opens.
~ Ralph Waldo Emerson

As the new year, 2004, began, I sensed how big a year it felt destined to be, but truly I had no idea just how exponentially huge this would become. The first Mystery School weekend in mid-January would prove to be a catapult to fabulous destinations in both Outer and Inner worlds. And oh my, it definitely was. Another Glastonbury-writer friend, Elizabeth, was exploring Mystery School too, and we entered in to the year of "The House of Many Mansions" with happy enthusiasm.

At Friday night's opening session each of us Mystery School first-timers were introduced to Jean. Her larger-than-life presence spoke of her Athena archetype. She took our hands warmly in hers, eyes twinkling, booming out, "Welcome to Mystery School!" Then in we all went to the auditorium, Jean stepped to the podium, and my first year with this extraordinary community was underway.

Of the many things that took root and started to grow from that very first weekend was a deepening dedication to Earth-healing work, and quite delightfully, the first glimmer of a vision of leading of Pilgrimages to Glastonbury. I was in the company of others who accepted and celebrated the presence of Guides, Spirit-helpers, and especially the important part our *entelechy*, our Higher Self, desired to play in our lives. While getting to know my Entelechy was a new experience, working with Spirit-Guides was a comfortable concept and familiar practice.

The influence of Mystery School is immediate. There's so much to take home from the weekends: incredible food for thought from Jean and Peggy's lectures, spirit-expanding practices, the vivid sense rapidly growing of this unique community of kindred spirits. There are daily e-mail messages called "Home Play" to nurture our growth between sessions. All of this to help us open to our Greater Self and embrace the Possibilities that come our way. I was in my element!

I'm delighted... and not at all surprised... when a new Spirit-Guide appears who calls himself Denahdin and tells me that he is a tree-spirit.

13th January 2004: Meditation message

Tree spirit... it would seem a fated connection not necessarily overlooked, just too often unacknowledged... but they do speak to you most audibly. Look about you! Create an altar! Begin earnest journaling. Significant breakthrough; you ARE a voice for good, for right... a labyrinth amidst the trees. Seek others to open the gates to. The way in is clearly marked.

The Goddess of the Grove seeks you and desires a conversation beyond the enchanting whimsical verses you bumped into. Look no further than the sentinels that guard your abode. S/he is rich in years and will nurture you well. Seek their advice. A joyous journey awaits you! And such magnificent traveling companions!! Let them seek you out. Some [who are] disguised wish now to step forth and simply await your invitation. Do not hesitate any longer. Do you now accept her and their invitation?

Yes! And with a glad and joyful heart!

Denahdin, your Guide and companion, rooted as you are, in ancient soils — damp, moist loam run through with vibrant tendrils reaching down deeply into the earth:

"About the trees my arms I wound/Like one gone mad, I hugged the ground!" [Edna St. Vincent Millay]

Tree-visions, tree embraces. Your life is rich with them, my Sweet

One. We have much sweet, earthy work to do! Keep your ear to the Earth Heart...

Vivid memories stirred of my Copper Beech friend in the Abbey grounds. And now a mysterious and intriguing invitation from one who calls herself the Goddess of the Grove. These are all such delightful wonders.

It is in April that more *magnificent traveling companions* appear. I learn about a group in Syracuse that's planning a Peace Gathering in October. A group of environmental activists was hard at work organizing the first Onondaga Lake Peace Festival. This once beautiful lake in central New York State so sacred to the Haudenosaunee, the Iroquois Nation, was horrendously polluted by centuries of misuse. Just maybe this is some of the *sweet, earthy work* awaiting me. So I go to one of their meetings to see what this is all about.

Though my plan was to sit quietly in the back to observe, not long into the presentation I knew without a doubt that I was to join in. I studied the faces around me of those who I will soon come to know as kindred spirits in this ambitious venture of Earth-healing and celebration.

My journal thoughts soon after are these: *"The very first time I heard about the Onondaga Lake Peace Festival I sensed strongly the call to be a part of it—the pieces of my future work are coming together. How all of this will ultimately unfold and fit together will be shown in good time. All I need to do is continue to move forward and embrace the Light."*

And also at that first meeting one very astounding connection leaps to my attention. Central to the group's work is the Haudenosaunee figure known as the Peacemaker. When he is mentioned I realize with amazement that Jean Houston identifies him as a powerful influence in her work. The legend tells how he orchestrated peace among the warring tribes of what would later become Upstate New York several centuries before the arrival of

Europeans. After successfully waging peace, he gathered the war leaders together on the north shore of Onondaga Lake where a huge hole was dug and into which all weapons were thrown. Upon them was planted a great white pine, the Tree of Peace. This peaceful and powerful Iroquois Confederacy that was thus birthed was still thriving when the New World was "discovered." And famously it offered a governing template for the founders of the fledgling United States of America.

Jean had written a book on him, *Manual for the Peacemaker: An Iroquois Legend to Heal Self & Society*. She summed up his historical and mythical legacy this way: "The figure of [the Peacemaker] carries archetypal power as a new kind of Peacemaker; his peace embraces what he calls a New Mind, a radical change in consciousness that opens itself to a new order of health, justice, and sacred power... though he knows himself to be a messenger of the Great Spirit, he invites others to help him clarify the message and carry it forward persuasively to kin and kind. As his mission proceeds, so does the peace, becoming feisty and rich!" [Introduction, *xxi–xxii*]

The potent cross-fertilization of these two new and important circles, the Peace Festival group and my Mystery School community, was gloriously underway.

Ah, and then the most incredible development of all! Word comes that Emily Hanlon is offering a 2005 Glastonbury retreat. I e-mail Mari McCarthy asking if she's considering this and she replies that she's actually planning a solo trip to England later this year. Spirit helps fan the flame of this bright ember, and within a few days she and I have teamed up to make this a joint adventure, just the two of us. By the middle of March we have our plans outlined for a week's trip in October. Wonders never cease!

Somehow I'd reached a place in my Journey where not only did I accept that such marvelous things found their way to me, but it had gotten so easy to welcome these opportunities and say,

"Yes!" If any niggling doubts surfaced, Spirit sent dazzling confirmation. Shortly before my birthday I had a wonderful dream of a tremendous snake.

5th April 2004: Snake dream

What a lovely night for a Moon Dance! And what partners the Egg Moon in Libra brought me! I was with one or two others in the yard; the day a warm and sunny one. My friend, a woman, walked around the pool and then reached down to lift up a corner of it. Out from under it to my surprise (not hers... she, a goddess?, knew it was there) came a huge and magnificent black snake. It felt like she was freeing it. It was cautious of us. I wasn't afraid. It looked at me for a long moment and then it moved away, gliding towards the river. My only words were, "Oh, it's a milk snake. They can grow quite large." And indeed it was likely eight to ten feet long and my two hands together would not have gone around it. Then we discovered a second snake practically right at my feet, coiled and still. She... so I felt... was clearly of the same huge proportion, but was a beautiful deep emerald green shading to nearly black beneath, a subtle pattern of diamonds extended from her forehead partway along her back. I was thrilled at discovering her! For some reason my friend and I wanted to move her, so she produced some sort of "snake stick" and gently began drawing the snake out to her full length. The snake seemed to accept this but wasn't in a hurry to be "teased out." I left the dream before she was fully extended. The last I saw were some odd bulges and disproportionate sections in her body, but we were confident she would soon be her full and beautiful Self!

The second weekend of Mystery School at the end of April is every bit as awesome as the first. It's wonderful to be getting to know my fellow *Mysterians* and sharing the soul-stretching experiences provided by Jean and Peggy. Jean calls it "a wondrous Kindergarten for Grownups!" Of course I shared news of the Festival with them with an excited response to have me continue to keep all informed of the progress for October 11th. Jean herself is delighted to hear and not at all surprised that this important link-up has occurred for us all.

Late Spring and Summer is a heady time. A second writer's weekend at The Spiritual Center in July ultimately attracts five enthusiastic participants including a lovely retired Rutgers professor, Ken Negus, who makes a great addition to our circle. His considerable skills as an astrologer add a lot to people's experience and he offers each of us a reading of our chart.

There are monthly meetings for the Peace Festival with its occasional leadership challenges but never any doubt of my vital involvement on behalf of the Earth. My work as an Earth-healer was blossoming from its deep roots helped hugely by the cross-fertilization of Mystery School's influence. Mari's and my travel plans were developing as well with our departure for England set for one week after the Peace Festival.

Pondering all of this incredible mix, I note in my journal how it is I've come to understand my role in what's calling me to these actions. *"It is the critical state of the Earth's environment which has called me into this life. I bring with me the skills and passions of several lifetimes to do this work."* It won't be long until the signs of this heritage become unmistakable.

My work with the labyrinth is steadily and wonderfully evolving. Out near our vegetable garden I'm constructing a 7-circuit labyrinth using recycled bricks to outline the path. It is quite labor intensive but very satisfying work. One day as I'm working I *hear* its name, *Morningside Labyrinth*. On July 17th I host a small and beautiful gathering to dedicate it and welcome its first walkers. Each person brings a rock from their land for its border creating a lovely ceremony. And there are enchanting visits from now 4-year-old Brianna, as pleased as ever to be spending time with her Pop-Pop and me. The bricks of the labyrinth make a nice choo-choo track as far as she's concerned!

19th August 2004: Journal entry

Happily anticipating next week's trip to visit Jennifer in Michigan [my Glastonbury roommate]. Beyond that some exciting times with the 3rd Mystery School weekend; preparation for the Onondaga Lake Peace Fest and the October 11th event; and then off to Glastonbury. Still hard to believe on some level that Mari and I are going to arrive on the doorstep of Abbey House on October 19th!

Pondering the happy distractions of these past two months that have drawn me away from purposeful writing and, to some extent, spiritual work. Trusting that the whole of it is *right* regardless of how things go. Listened recently to my Solar Return tape and *see* how several pieces have come to be or are unfolding. So very *right* is the process ongoing with Mystery School and Glastonbury.

Amidst all this, and especially with the upcoming return trip to Glastonbury, I scheduled a session with Christine, arriving at her door on a late September morning.

While I knew it was likely that I'd be receiving information about Mari's and my second England adventure, I was astounded by the appearance of a mighty angelic presence who Christine later called simply, "a Great Being." All my metaphysical explorations and journey had fortunately taken me far enough to fully embrace the reality of this Presence. S/he'd come with a simple but profound request. During my upcoming time in Glastonbury I was being asked to do spiritual healing work on behalf of the sacred landscape of Avalon. S/he further assured me that all I needed would be revealed when I reached England and that it would all be "easily accomplished." I was deeply humbled and awestruck but nonetheless accepted this "request" with little hesitation. Still, I felt somewhat shell-shocked when I departed Christine's house that day. Little did I know that I would be encountering another amazing Being even before I flew off to England.

With the Peace Festival approaching and much work left to

do, I set aside any misgivings about the Great Being's daunting message to focus on October 11th. A ceremony was planned to offer "healing thanks and love" to the Lake along the lines of Dr. Masaru Emoto's ground-breaking concepts for healing Earth's damaged waters. I was honored to be given the beautiful task of organizing the Water Blessing ceremony and thrilled that I would also be overseeing this the day of the festival. As promised, I let the Mystery School community know about the Water Blessing work and people began to send vials of water to me so that they could be a distant part of the ceremony. It was humbling to be the receiver of these vials and the messages that came with them.

A wondrous prelude occurred one night during my hour-long drive home following one of the final committee meetings. We were all so excited by our months of preparation and the emerging beautiful shape of the gathering now just two weeks away.

The Full Moon beamed down from the starry sky and bathed me in its glow as I drove along the quiet country highway lost in reflection of the evening's outcome. I was over halfway home when a faint singing registered in my inner-awareness. I focused my attention on it and it grew steadily louder until I heard women's voices chanting in a language I didn't know. The chant began again and I hummed along, utterly entranced, somehow still managing to drive and continue "tuning in." All at once I knew what to do: I silently sent a message to them. "I am sorry, but I do not understand what you're singing. Please translate the words into English." Abruptly the singing stopped and there were a few moments' silence. Then the chant began again in English and every word clearly sung! I joined them, singing along as I drove, rapt with joy. "Children of the Earth, gather round in a circle. Join hands in this sacred Circle now…" I was so conscious of these women reaching across to me from some most special place, Native Americans, yes, and no doubt in a parallel reality whose dimensional threshold had opened between us.

I finally pulled off the road for a few minutes so I could concentrate better, wanting to commit this to memory, so aware of the gift I was being given and not just for myself but to be shared with others. The Voices gradually faded once they felt I'd received it complete, and when I reached home I dashed into the house and wrote down the words, making notations of the tune as well. With grateful thanks I went up to my bedroom and fell into a deep sleep. When I woke the next morning I was elated to find that none of this had slipped away in the night.

A cool, cloudy Autumn day greeted us the morning of October 11th as we gathered at Long Branch Park at the northern end of Onondaga Lake. We began the day by joining in a large circle, nearly sixty of us, with ceremony calling the Sacred Directions, giving thanks to the Beings of the Land, thanking and acknowledging the Peacemaker. And most especially we called upon the Lady of the Lake to hear us and receive the healing energy we were raising for Her in our work together that day.

There was music from several wonderful groups, speakers, informational booths, a labyrinth to walk, and a children's activity area, all focused on celebrating the Lake and honoring the Earth. And everyone was encouraged to spend some time during the day at the simple altar we'd devised for the Water Blessing. A wooden stool held a white and blue enameled basin into which people poured their offerings of water blessed by their prayers of Love and Thanks. The four directions were marked with rows of yellow gourds so people could choose the place that felt right to come and stand with their offering and then pour it into the basin. Many had brought small bottles with water from a body of water that was special to them, springs, streams and rivers, the ocean, lakes, even from their own wells. And for those who hadn't known about this ahead of time, a pail of the Lake's water rested on the ground next to the stool from which they could dip up a cupful. It was my privilege to oversee this all that day, standing nearby to answer any questions, but mostly to "hold the energy" of this beautiful ceremony.

All day the humble basin received people's water-offerings, each one infused with blessings and messages of *Love and Healing for the Water*. And of course there were a dozen and more water offerings and messages from the larger Mystery School community and I reverently added and gave voice to each one.

Late in the afternoon the much-blessed water was poured carefully into a five-gallon bucket which was brought into the center of our closing circle. Over one hundred people held hands and we sang a last blessing to the gathered water. Then it was carried down to three canoes and the half-dozen people waiting to carry it out from shore and offer our day-long efforts to the Lady of the Lake.

With everything finished at last, I drove off into the evening dusk somewhat weary from the long day, but so marvelously elated. I was driving along the Parkway on the Lake's east shore when an unmistakable summons came. "Find a place to stop and come down to the water." Moments later a pull-off appeared and I turned into it, shut off the engine, and got out. It was only a short walk down to the water, not yet too dark to see my way clearly. I had no idea what to expect, only thrilled at what was unfolding. Then I stood at the water's edge, the peaceful Lake stretching out before me, mirroring the moving golden string of car-lights driving along the highway on the west side.

There was a stirring out on the water not far from shore. Transfixed, I saw a shadowy shape rising and begin moving towards me. Now in total awe I knew at once it was the Lady of the Lake. It was She who had called me to stop and come down to the water. She came to within perhaps a dozen feet of the shore and stopped, hovering above the water, clearly pleased that I had come and that I could see Her. I felt more than saw Her smile and nod to me. I received her thoughts, a gentle message of thanks to all of us who had gathered that day and for what it was we had done and created together. Then, unmistakably, these words were clearly spoken to me in the dusk, "We are healing one another... we are healing one another. Please share this with the others." I told her I would and again She nodded, smiled, and slipped away into the night. I remained there at the water's edge for several long moments suffused with the Grace of this visitation, then made my way back to the car and drove home.

I shared all of this with Michelle, my sister-in-Spirit, always pleased to welcome my musings and to give back confirmation and her deep wisdom. The angelic-crafted work awaiting in Glastonbury, the wonderful and extraordinary events at the Peace Festival, the still almost-unbelievable fact I was getting to go back to England... "Carol," she tells me in her cheery voice, "you're off on *your* quest this time!"

Yes... this was indeed my true pilgrimage journey.

Waiting to board the plane at Logan Airport and awaiting my traveling companion, Mari, I pulled out my journal from my backpack and recorded these thoughts:

18th October

And then I had my session with Christine – blimey! And then there's the Mystery School selection for today, words of HD Thoreau: *There after harvest could I glean my life—a richer harvest reaping without toil, and weaving gorgeous fancies at my will in subtler webs than finest summer haze.* And for tomorrow's arrival in England, Peggy's choice of Quantum Partners, Rhiannon and Bird Goddesses.

Ecstatic weavings these. Sr. Elizabeth last Thursday responded to my request and reason for visiting The Spiritual Center to receive their/her blessing, "Well, honey, of course you have it. But what you really came to get was the blessing from the Land."

It is here tonight in Logan Airport that the total message and import of this clarifies. The Great Being who came to Christine's session told me that part of my work in Glastonbury is to facilitate human connection with the land… at-one-ment. In this next week I will spend as much time as possible *solitudo*, "Nature" in Latin.

And so Mari and I flew through the night, doing our best to get some sleep. My eyes opened with perhaps an hour to go before landing. I raised the window shade a little and was treated to the marvelous beauty of the stunning pink and orange band of light widening all along the curved horizon ahead of us. A moment of scarcely believing this all was real, and then a strong sense of some Presence touched my awareness. A gentle voice spoke to my inner hearing. "Welcome! Welcome home again, Carol. We're so glad at your return." I breathed this in with deep delight knowing its source… I was being hailed and welcomed by the Spirit of the Land. There was no doubt of that.

So down we came at Heathrow Airport, made our way confidently through Customs, and hopped aboard the Express Bus to Bristol with the final leg of the journey *home* aboard the First 376 bus into Glastonbury. Then there we were knocking on the door of Abbey House officially beginning our second shared adventure in Avalon. It was our intent to stay again at Abbey House where we'd been for our marvelous 2001 writer's retreat. David Hill, the Warden, was happy to welcome us back but sorry not to have rooms available for the whole of our stay. Searching the Internet for options, we found a wonderful-sounding place, Jacoby Cottage, a B&B exclusively for women. And making it all the more intriguing, it was one of the three "Slipper Chapels" built to welcome medieval pilgrims visiting Glastonbury Abbey. Coming down the steep hill from Wells with the Abbey's buildings just ahead, they would enter the chapel to remove their shoes and wash their feet before continuing barefoot to the Cathedral. Somehow it had survived the Dissolution and the tyranny of Henry VIII in the 16th century becoming a 21st century B&B.

If there was any doubt that my Spirit allies would be about, the third day at Abbey House brought this channeled message:

There is an inner harbor, in faith and love — Ulaythio —

For more of what ails this troubled land, look no further. The signs of it are starkly apparent. You have not missed them, yet on the horizon hope glimmers like the dawn-edged sky into which you flew four days ago, confident of your purpose. No matter what the cause, the outcome is somber and sobering but not inevitable. There are others at work within, and you, moving amongst them as you do, [help] create an unseen current of rising Light energy to which they turn, unknowing.

Half-a-globe away others linger awaiting the same signs. You, Spirited One, must not fail in your faithfulness — Light Bearer — others see, sense, apprehend. This calls forth hope, and goodness follows. Symbolic healing precedes the stirring of notable progress. Grant as you need signs for others to follow. Conclusive signs will soon cheer many more. Ah, how faithful you are to what we recently asked of you. Convincing some will not be easy, but you know that. And not all will or need to awaken. It is Earth's beauty, joy, peace that slowly emerges.

So go now, in such peace and tender love of us towards you, our Beloved, as you extend to all around you. Beware of certain ones whose hearts and minds cannot change soon or at all. Do not exhaust yourself on their behalf.

All will be and is well. We rejoice in You.

(22nd October: Channeled message at Abbey House)

It had been revealed to me that when I arrived in Glastonbury I must ask for and then would receive a prayer which I was to write down. I would then be led to various places where I was to quietly say the prayer aloud. That was all there was to it… yes, "easily accomplished." One thing that had given me pause was Spirit's insistence that I not let others know what I was doing, and at times this solitary task felt uncomfortably large. Once I'd settled in to being back in beautiful Abbey House, I sought the Copper Beech.

Entering through the wooden gate into the Abbey grounds, I

smiled at the sight of the huge tree and hurried towards him. An electrifying energy of welcome washed over me and I began to weep, rushing forward to sink down on his roots, falling against his wonderful trunk. I felt how he held me, hugged me. I heard his voice, "Welcome home again, Dear One." So I had his grand company for refuge and soon I knew his name, Carnaphon. And almost at the same time, another promised companion made himself known, a Tree-being named Joseph whose voice with its delightful country accent and his nearly-physical presence accompanied me on all my walks.

I no longer recall where I was when the prayer came, but the Glastonbury Angel, as I'd come to know her, ultimately delivered the wording with patient clarity while I wrote it down on a slip of paper. The mid-October weather was brisk with occasional rain showers. So I tucked the paper into the pocket of my rain jacket, reasonably confident that all I needed to do now was await Spirit's guidance as to where I should go.

When our days at Abbey House concluded, Mari and I made the move to Jacoby Cottage around the corner so to speak, and part way up Bovetown Road where we were warmly greeted by Michou Godfrey. We were totally smitten upon first setting foot inside this ancient and very *alive* dwelling. I took up residence in the room called "The Angel Retreat." The original beams from the Slipper Chapel, some 450 years old, formed a ledge along the side of the room and the small window looked out on the street. Michou told us that this was the original road from Wells, the very one that long-ago pilgrims followed as they made their way to the wonders of Glastonbury Abbey.

There simply was not a better place than Jacoby Cottage, and none more awe-inspiring in its simple yet profound presence, from which to carry out the spiritual mission I'd been summoned to do. Two journal entries capture something of what this beautiful yet daunting task was for me. Every day brought an ever-evolving sense of what it all might mean.

Sunday, the 24th: Jacoby Cottage

In a week's time it is Samhain. The veil has begun to thin.

So is my purpose here mostly the sacred work I was summoned for? Is any writing work of very little importance? There is something of resentment, at least a little, as I get sent out to "Walk around some more," assured each time that I spread the Light of my prayer. Yes, yes, how could this not be important?

And I am disturbed by the stress level felt by cars/progress/21st century intrusions. I see, hear, feel, sense this damage. But then I have great Carnaphon's presence and my deep emotional reactions there with him. Something of long ago rises up in me there.

And now I've come to be in this ancient chapel, Jacoby Cottage, a place I know...? The hill and its garden are energetic places. A time there this afternoon brought two voices: Joseph, my Guide-Protector, as I move about Glastonbury. He speaks in a "country accent" and has a humorous take on things. Then a woman's voice, Lyllia, perhaps the Angel of the garden. She intends further communication. I fully expect more from each one.

Early morning, Tuesday, the 26th

Accepting this work with grace has proven easier than I'd expected. The allied forces of the Glastonbury Angel, Joseph, and Lyllia, don't feel overwhelming, nor does any of this feel too unimaginable. I know the reason I'm drawn out-of-doors so much is to do the work. I am now mostly content that whatever writing should come from this time here will be done eventually.

A big lesson still is staying in the moment, over and against the sense I carry of otherworldliness. The helpful terms for these from Bill Plotkin's *Soulcraft* are survival dance and soul dance. So it's a matter of moving between these two.

This quote I found yesterday...

Don't ask yourself what the world needs. Ask yourself what makes you come alive and then go do that... because what the world needs is people who have come alive.
~ Harold Thurman Whitman

A short aside in the telling of this, and paralleling my ever-deepening connection with Avalon, was a synchronistic encounter one afternoon with Mano Warren who had given me my past-life regression in 2001. We literally bumped into each other on the street when I was going back to Jacoby Cottage and she was on her way downtown. We both knew at once the importance of this encounter and set up a time to meet for tea and further conversation. The next day found me knocking on her door and soon I was sitting across from her in her lovely small courtyard. She was delighted to hear about this second journey to Glastonbury. Conversation flowed wonderfully between us as we got to know each other. I learned that she'd changed her surname to *Mannaz* at her Guides' urging, a protective move to allow her to work more safely within the less-friendly energies of Glastonbury. It was an eye-opening thing to hear and I appreciated her openness. Still, respecting my own Spirit's guidance, I chose not to speak about the prayer-work I was doing during my visit. Saying farewell and thank you at her door, we hugged and I went back up to Jacoby Cottage feeling much renewed for the final part of the stay. And further warming me was the sense of a marvelous friendship begun in that hour's time together.

On our last full day, I was "sent out" for a final walk, directed to climb the Tor one last time, stop in at Chalice Well Garden, walk down through town and then up Wearyall Hill to the Holy Thorn. It would be several hours all told. Rough weather was due by evening, the tail end of a hurricane coming in from the Atlantic. I set out dressed as warmly as possible, the prayer's much-folded paper tucked securely in my pocket.

The further I went, the more exhilarating it all became. On my way up the Tor the already very strong wind buffeted me, but thankfully it was not yet that cold. Nearing the top, I had a unique encounter that I recorded in my journal the next day on the plane flying home to America.

There on the walkway so high up on the side of the Tor, a small brown-furred caterpillar was making her way across the path. I would have just stepped carefully around her, but others were on their way up behind me. And so I bent down, and with my cold fingers carefully picked her up. For a moment I saw her many-footed underside curled up against this intrusion, and felt the soft bristly coat in my curled fingers. I spoke to her that this was best to make her safe, and tossed her up into the grass out of harm's way. How startling to find this small creature there—but it was what she has let me know here on this plane, speeding down over Newfoundland, speaking to me of my own transformation, its progress and its promise, and no doubt amazing and endless surprises.

Perhaps two hours later I reached the foot of Wearyall Hill and started up the path towards the Holy Thorn. The wind was beginning to reach gale force. Absolutely nobody else was about. My thoughts bordered on *"I must be a bit crazy."* Nonetheless I smiled to myself and continued my climb. When I reached the Thorn, how glad I was for the protective iron railing around its trunk. Only by clinging to it did I stay on my feet when the stronger gusts thundered past. Though I knew the prayer almost by heart, I didn't want to get a single word wrong saying it this final time. So I took out the much-folded paper, clutching it tightly to keep it being blown from my grasp, and shouted the words a last time into the wild gale.

Once more I folded it and slid it back into my jacket pocket where it remained for a couple of years. I'd sometimes feel its folded shape when I reached into my pocket, but only once opened and read it again. Perhaps it was a talisman needed for my further journey that confirmed I'd answered that peculiar and wonderful Call and had followed the guided path through

Avalon's landscape in company with such marvelous Friends. It did my heart such good every time, and at some point the paper with its prayer simply vanished.

Then I let the wind blow me back down the hill, managing to beat the drenching rain into the Blue Note Café where I savored a most-welcome mug of hot cocoa. I've never had a more delicious cocoa before or since.

By morning the storm had mostly departed and I arose very early to spend some time outdoors before our bus's departure to Heathrow Airport. Standing in Michou's garden this morning, dawn-light growing gently behind the Tor, I sought the Moon behind the swiftly passing clouds, the air still full of the energy of last night's storm. Above me Ursa Major tipped out its energies to me. Orion raised his arms in the southern sky signaling to planes in-bound to London. I looked towards the Tor's dawn-dark outline and felt a gentle touch on my shoulder. I turned and the brilliant Moon beamed itself at me, incandescent in the West. So I called the Directions a last time, so keenly aware of mighty presences — AA Michael, Rhiannon, Sophia, the Glastonbury Angel who called me, and that dear one, Joseph. Time to say a final thank you and know in the sadness of parting that he and Carnaphon are near to each other – and some comfort to know that Denahdin is waiting my return.

And so a final Taiji form, only a little wobbly in the still dim light, but grounded by Michou's terraced garden underfoot, the coming sun and departing Moon on either hand, and the Somerset Levels coming to view in the growing light.

I went down to the Cottage to find Michou preparing our breakfast a last time. We talked of the night's beauties and that we stood together on this morning of the momentous Grand Quintile. Looking out her window early, the Moon sailing still bright and the Light growing over the Land, she felt a profound difference in the landscape. Some change, some shift had happened, the lightening of a burden. "I felt an optimism and positiveness that I haven't felt since as far back as the first Gulf War." She looked amazed as she said this, and so happy and relieved. Perhaps it was something of the work I'd come to do, and perhaps even more given this day's astrological magnitude.

What came to me as I stood in the garden was the Land's deep gratitude to me for my work of this past week, such a profound dimension to this. And Joseph as a final service helped me to take it all in and accept it for exactly what it was. There is no other to share it with – a promise – how is it I could have done this? And yet I did; carried it here, carried myself here too, and willingly surrendered to the work. It felt something like what parts of the October 11th work was at Onondaga Lake, especially the heights of the ceremony, watching people come to the humble altar, my holding the energy while they offered prayers and gifts of water. And later, standing by the Lake, and hearing the words of benediction and blessing from the Lady of the Lake. This was what carried me to Glastonbury, and what I brought with me to pass on.

In the end, there was little doubt about any of it. And when the enormity of it seized me, Joseph was always there to steady me… and also Carnaphon, gentle giant.

Chapter 5

The Earth is still new in this day as am I,
departing from the ordinary to this likely limitless adventure. I've
answered its call, and I vow to be true to what awaits, to whose voice
emerges.
~ Jacoby Cottage, Journal, last morning

So my pilgrimage and quest concluded with the flight home
under the cosmic convergence of the Grand Quintile... the Moon,
Saturn, Jupiter, Pluto, and Uranus arranging themselves in a
heavenly pentagon. A solar eclipse took place within hours,
followed in days by the presidential election that saw
progressive, environmental champion, Al Gore, edged out by he-
who-shall-not-be-named... much more than a tongue-in-cheek
reference for me. Neither event can I say I fully understood but
both sent seismic waves through all of us, though I dare say the
cosmic gathering drew much less attention. GW II's return to the
White House along with his dark-energy cronies was so terrible
that I shut off the news with increasing frequency. Preserving the
powerful vibes I'd brought back with me from England was what
mattered most.

For weeks I just allowed all of those eight days to lie quiet
within me for whatever initial internal processing-work needed
to happen. My journals held little new though those entries
written while I was in Glastonbury fairly smoldered within their
covers. There were *regular life* events to tend to and enjoy
including making up for lost time with my two lively grandkids,
four-year-old Brianna and toddler Logan.

December arrives with the pleasant prospect of family holiday
plans. Seeded and nurtured at Mystery School sessions, I'd also
begun the first exciting steps for offering a Glastonbury
Pilgrimage perhaps by 2006. On the 13th, an ordinary enough

day, I sat at the kitchen table after lunch "on hold" with the NYS Department of Taxation. I'd brought down a Glastonbury book to look at during the wait. As I started leafing through it a dream I'd had during the night but had forgotten blazed into my awareness. I sat stunned, its very tangible images replaying themselves. As soon as I was freed from the call, I hurried to my writing desk.

13th December 2004: Dream

Avalon dream of last night:

I am on a hill with others I know. Dusk is approaching. As I gaze out on the beautiful landscape, I see water rising as if a gentle flooding is taking place. I watch silently for a minute and then suddenly realize where I am and what is happening. I am standing on the Tor and I am witnessing the sea-tide flooding the Levels. I run to another high place and look out. I am very excited! Yes! The waters are rising here too! I yell to my companions telling them to look. I can scarcely believe I am back here again and I'm filled with joy. The scene changes and we are now down near the water. A man appears in a long, narrow wooden boat. I get in and sit at the front. I'm not sure if there's a particular destination as we start off. The man knows the channels and easily and smoothly propels us forward. We glide between trees and little hills, sometimes amazing me that there's an opening large enough to pass through. We reach a small, wooded "island" and the boat comes to rest on the shore. I am excited and happy, a sense of being on a magical journey or adventure.

It is still early in my understanding of Glastonbury and its long history stretching back into the mists of time. With each journey I make there, I discover new and intriguing information. It enchants me when I learn that, before the Romans and others arrived to drain and otherwise subdue the landscape around the

Tor, it was a vast tidal marshland exactly as shown to me in the dream of that December night! And later on in conversation with Angeline and our growing trust of each other, she tells me of the Old Ones, quite possibly one of whom served as my Guide.

It's an easy decision to sign up for a second year of Mystery School with its absolutely perfect theme, "The Mystery of Destiny and Purpose." With the first year so marvelously completed, I felt all the more capable and at ease in embracing the work Jean and Peggy presented to us. A key piece in these new sessions was seeking our Quantum Partner with whom we would journey through our year of study. This special Being arrived just before the end of January in a meditation session at home where he gave me his name, Bar'antha, and then this first message:

Late January 2005

I sense you very near, Bar'antha. Are you seeking me? What is this energy? What work?

Filled with Spirit, let this work begin. You are building a bridge, yes, to the past that dwells within you, but also very much into the future. It is for now a delicate dance, but given your willingness to trust this Guidance, whisperings... heed the call... and long-dormant heart energies take wing in and through you. Listen. Listen well to these heart sounds... disparage none of this. Your trust will be so very richly rewarded... a conduit of both joyful and painful rememberings that lie hidden but are now seeking your gentle but fearsome presence. Remember the hawk in the garden [at Jacoby Cottage], its fierce beauty—how this all fits together and falls into place—the weavings of Spirit, netting together mind and heart. Ineffable pleasures. Yes, call me Bar'antha. It is enough for now. Go forth with Faith and trust your strong and good heart. Namaste'

And when February's New Moon in Aquarius came calling, I was by then eagerly and happily welcoming his presence. The Mystery School "Home Play" message for that day offered the tantalizing message that this was "... *time for planting revolutionary seeds of change that support evolutionary growth... am I living what I believe?"*

8th February

I looked back at last April 14th's entry with its powerful images of fire and magic embodied in my Snake dream. Within these ten months I have become evermore the magician and enchantress, transmuting energies and accepting the fire's power... There is simply nothing I can't do or take on... nothing!

The New Moon found its depths at 5:39PM. I have felt its resonance all day and return to contemplate some more here. When I finished this morning's entry, I meditated for a while bringing back images of water and some sense of baptism. There was last Thursday's dream of the Lake – and right after this meditation, contact again from the Being of Light called Bar'antha. This time answering questions through the pendulum, informing me S/he is my quantum partner for Mystery School and the vital connection to my Glastonbury character. The Moon card's assurance that I can draw aside the veil... Bar'antha is showing me the gateway to the inner vision of this past life. It is time to go there.

11th February: Meditation message

Declare these truths, Wind-walker. Clouds part, gliding above these rain-washed plains, then down to rest on brothers' arms, gliding still earthward. Safe passage again home to kin who await your word. Alliances forged in ancient forests when Old Ones borrowed your swift wings for Seer's journeys, sky-born paths. Cognizant now are few of these ancient ways. Voices echo in glens 'neath the north hill. Walk with purpose. Others will know and follow.

"Others will know and follow"... I knew in part this was a reference to my Glastonbury character who was beginning to make her presence known once more. This new presence and

Guide, Bar'antha, left little doubt of that. Not that I had forgotten her… hardly that. The fabulous ferment of "everything else" had made it easy to nudge her and her reality aside for long stretches of time. But that sort of evasive maneuvering was starting to come to an end.

As Winter gave way to Spring that year, my life felt in a fiery but fabulous ferment of personal work and developing events. There was my ever-expanding writing for the new novel, *Significant Lives*, Mystery School-inspired metaphysical growth and birthing the 2006 Pilgrimage, and the joys of the June wedding of our daughter and her partner, Brian. And there were many intriguing and powerful hints and signs that a destiny was calling not only for my *larger work* as it was referred to in Mystery School, but for my self-development physically, emotionally, and spiritually.

Mari and I kept a lively connection through weekly phone calls where we shared the latest in our creative-doings and cheered each other on. Perhaps to no surprise, we knew that we *absolutely needed* to return to Glastonbury together for another shared adventure. When Mari contacted Michou Godfrey at Jacoby Cottage, she replied with the incredible question, Would we be interested in house-sitting for two weeks in October while she and her partner went on vacation? You can imagine how little time we took to say, "Yes!" A third pilgrimage to Avalon… Yes!!

14th April 2005: Birthday message!

Dear One,

A day of celebration and joy among all the rest—happy tidings of love and Light for your good, joyous, and fulsome Life. Remember always to celebrate daily. Your breath celebrates and exalts this fire and your Aries nature befits to a "T" your magnificence. There is much to do, work that is a celebration of en-spirited shape and intent. Some learning still before the full dimensions of this year's coming Journey to Glaston, but revelations are approaching. Watch for them and remain alert.

Allies are in good number—nearly all of marvelous benefit, and some come in nonhuman form. Keep to the path you have espied—not all will be on it with you. Honor those things which allow for you to dance unencumbered, for then will your Soul Work a-light with all the brilliance it is meant to have.

Breathe into your soul and spirit-flame and the doubt that you sometimes allow in will cross your path less and less. The world needs the full force of your spirit's energy and yearning. Unbridle these passions... allow the Magic. Know that any needed protection is within as well as without.

Yes, "dancing unencumbered" was becoming a stronger and stronger desire. I knew who Spirit meant by saying *not all will be on [the path] with you.* With plans for Sarah's wedding happily unfolding, it felt we were at last coming to a place of family harmony and happiness. Yet the bond between Ken and me was increasingly fraught, something I dearly hoped wouldn't cast its shadow on our daughter's happiness. Spirit's guidance at last brought an opportunity for the two of us, Ken and me, to have a heart to heart discussion one day not long before the wedding, and together we made the decision to seek marriage counseling.

So it is a marvelous day that summery Saturday when Brian and Sarah exchange vows in the fairytale setting of the Taughannock Falls Overlook near Ithaca. Apart from it being one of the hottest June 25ths ever, it is a day of celebration and also healing. The day before we celebrated Brianna's 5th birthday making sure it was a special celebration in the midst of the wedding hoopla. The guests assembled on the shady steps and ledges and Peggy Spencer began to strum the strings of her Celtic harp. I came down the steps on the arm of one of the groomsmen and gasped at the magical setting. Logan happily enjoyed every-thing though being the ring bearer (with his Uncle Justin's help) was a bit confusing. It was a delightful part of their delightful ceremony, and other than the steamy temperatures, it matched

Sarah's long-held vision of her wedding day.

It will be nearly three months more until Mari and I set off together once more for Avalon, so I settle into a relatively quiet summer of gardening, writing work on the novel, and the start of our marriage counseling sessions. The immediate effect of these is a welcome lessening of the tension that had hung in the air for such a long while. Ken and I are both very grateful for that.

In August I spend a marvelous week "farm-sitting" at Justin and Tracy's place that they'd named Cottonhill Farm. It's very peaceful there with its lovely fields and wooded hillside. I reveled in having it all to myself going off on rambling walks with the dogs, doing the daily chores of tending the hens and ducks, and having uninterrupted hours for working on *Significant Lives* and journaling. I'm seeing important insights and connections in the lives of these characters, especially as is represented in Luke, a troubled Vietnam war veteran.

13th August 2005: Journal entry

I am working with characters I know so well and the lives they lead. The growing reconnection/relationship of Luke and Maggie is one I think I understand. Luke's haunted past is one I trust I can give special respect to. It has been made all the more so as I live through the awful mess in Iraq and witness the destruction of lives and harm at every turn. The other night I sat and listened to Crosby, Stills, and Nash ask the questions again as only they can do, challenging us to *keep awake* and pursue peace and justice.

This is in part what I'm pursuing with my work, a type of social artistry that facilitates the inner development of others so that they will be "awake and aware," and therefore empowered and vocal. More distinctly now I sense a call to facilitate Earth-healing directly through personal practice and then enlivening that same passion in others. Somehow this Glastonbury character/person I'm going to be working with is similarly called.

Things are developing rapidly and all the more so as

September 14th (our departure date for England) draws nearer. This suddenly occurred to me – that part of not pushing myself to complete *Significant Lives* is knowing that what lies behind it is this potent new/old story. *Go deeper, go deeper*, I'm being told.

There's a stirring weekend of Mystery School to attend and enjoy with all its delights, and I'm given an enthusiastic send-off by many for this next Avalon adventure. I've been particularly enjoying a connection with two delightful women at this year's sessions. Molly Harvey is coming all the way from Liverpool, England to attend the weekends with her American friend, Louise Griffith. My first interaction with Molly came when we paired up for an early-morning exercise. We sat down together on the floor and introduced ourselves. After I told her a few things about myself, she studied me for a moment, then nodded and said in her charming Irish accent, "Carol, I can see you're one of the Old Ones." A special friendship and connection was born.

At last the morning of September 13th arrives. Brimming with excitement, I head out on the road to Mari's home south of Boston for our flight the next evening from Logan Airport. Mari has upgraded us to Business Class so it's quite a comfortable flight. We toast each other with wine in our miniature glasses, and do our best to get some sleep. With two other such flights under my belt, I feel quite the veteran, and love how I can focus on simply enjoying all of it.

And then at about the same distance from England as was true last year, an hour out from Heathrow, the gentle, warm welcome of the Land comes once again. "Welcome home, Carol." I close my eyes in quiet bliss, wondering what other marvels await in the days ahead. Oh yes, marvels were awaiting indeed.

Again we forge through the gauntlet of Customs and bus connections until, four hours later, the Tor rises from the Levels as the 376 First bus lumbers down the Mendip Hills into Wells. If anything it is even more thrilling to see it and feel its welcome, like a lighthouse of the Spirit. Then we step down at the top of the High Street and smile through our travel-weariness. We pull our suitcases up Bovetown Road to the ancient door of Jacoby Cottage. Michou is waiting with warm hugs along with her beautiful greyhound, Gaston, wagging his tail in recognition. She and her partner, Linda, are getting ready to depart and there are two other guests staying on for a bit. But in just a couple of days, Mari and I will have Jacoby Cottage entirely to ourselves for a whole two weeks. We settle in to the Angel Retreat Room in total bliss.

Knowing of my writing intentions, Michou takes me up to the top of the garden to show me the cozy shed that will serve well as a place to work. It's set up as a kitchen for guests staying in the yurt nearby and there's ample room for writing space with a window looking out across Bushey Coombe towards Chalice Hill. I decide to call it my Writer's Camp.

After a night's restorative sleep, I hurry down to Glastonbury Abbey's grounds to say hello to Carnaphon. Halfway across the ruins I spy his tall, stately shape, and to little surprise I feel his recognition and reaching out to me in delight. Just like last year, tears are streaming down my face as I hurry forward beneath his canopy and hug his massive trunk. He fiercely hugs me back. Now I'm truly Home.

Without the splendid but *large* duties of last year's Earth-healing "charge," my sense is that I'm here to immerse myself more deeply into Avalon's mysteries, partly for the sake of the evolving Pilgrimage work... and what delight that is... but mostly to hear Spirit's voice and that of Angeline. It is all such an extraordinary blessing.

15th–16th September 2005: Return to Glastonbury! (Silver Journal)

Here again, sitting nestled against the friendly roots of Carnaphon and reconnected with Joseph. Putting down deeper roots and warmed by the sense of welcome I feel everywhere. Beyond the settling in at Jacoby Cottage and pleasant interactions with people there, I am eager to embark on the solitary journey I have been preparing for over these months. This grand and beautiful work offers itself to my embrace which I do with a full heart. I have brought with me the love and good wishes of so many from Mystery School and I draw them into my awareness now. Such loving kindness, such faith that it will be a grand unfolding, and most assuredly a magical one.

"All here seek to know you... you are one of unmistakable eloquence."

The rest of the world seems very far away... I make the "rounds" checking-in to places, the Tor, the library to check e-mails, my favorite cafés...

And then into Chalice Well Garden, the day growing quite cool, but comfortable to sit for a long while at the Well with several others enjoying the shared energy. Walked around the Meadow and was drawn to visit one of the apple trees. There at its base I found a small, silver-metal angel. It feels like a gift and sign of welcome, but its message is that it's time to get down to work. Beginning tomorrow, Mari and I will essentially have the place to ourselves, so the time to begin has arrived. I'm not yet exactly sure of the way in, but the key, without a doubt, is just to begin.

(Entry made at the Blue Note Café, Sunday afternoon, following some time with Carnaphon:)

The path leads on, I must depart/to hidden places of the heart

The silver angel has been joined by a beautiful slender crow feather a-waiting at the foot of the tree where I ate my lunch tucked in the natural area at the back of the Abbey grounds. Amulets and talismans are accumulating in fine fashion!

Four days into our stay, and with Jacoby Cottage soon to be exclusively "ours," I found my way to a quiet place to meditate, and sought both Bar'antha and Mary Magdalene.

18th September 2005: Glastonbury message

Dear Bar'antha... Dear Magdalene,

I am HERE now, fully immersed in this place so rich with nature's beauty and energies, a place so rich in magic and spirit. I have come to your call, brought by my work. I am seeking a way in, a sense of moving forward, some reluctance or disquiet now that I am poised here. I reach out to you. What do I need to do now? What do I need to know? Thank you, thank you, thank you...

Carol,

With this Moon's rising comes much of use, much of outer and inner Light; a deliberate stall until energies aligned, openings felt, but your activities all along the way have met important needs. And that you felt a certain sense of people to meet and open a connection for further kinship—glorious purposes!

Ah, the swallows! They delighted my eyes and ears and were blessed by your presence too. Of course, not for the first time either, something you accept and embrace as a truth. My Spirit's Light has reached certain Ones before. The Flame does not nor will not die. You are going to be breathing newfound energies into it, opening pathways for many others as you travel this sacred journey to your destined reunion.

She awaits you. Her training has given her the necessary imaginings and breadth of faith. Treading carefully this path with a heart full of love—those are guidelines that will prevail for all of this work. No one is more capable than you. Be mindful of its hidden gold. Your generous Angels are arrayed all about you. Call upon them to shine their Light of love, energy, and guidance. Joy of the journey will not diminish and steadily comes forth. There is an honoring of both lives, as they are inextricably linked. The sweet echoes of time and sense flow in an unceasing stream. Use this energy, this rhythm of water to reach back as she reaches forward to you. It is good and fitting work that you both do, Healers of Light.

(She sought me in a time when it was extremely dangerous to do so.)

Thank you for coming, my child.

Live your love, Carol. Live your love.

By the midway point of our stay it had been quite a full set of days. There had been all sorts of wonderful visits to the Tor, to Chalice Well, unhurried time with Carnaphon, quiet meditation in the Magdalene Chapel, and a very special visit upcoming to Stanton Drew's stone circle some fifteen miles or so north of Glastonbury. And though there had been a couple of reasonably productive writing sessions in the Writer's Camp in the company of the church candle I purchased, none felt entirely satisfying. On that Sunday evening I went up to my room and sat on the bed gazing at the ancient rafters with their 450-year-old carpenters' joining marks. I opened my notebook…

25th September: Jacoby Cottage

So here I sit at the window of this amazing room, my knees touching the ancient stonework and the open rafters [of the ancient Slipper Chapel] rising above me holding their secrets. Cars buzz past below going up and down this old, old roadway. Without any doubt, she who I am calling Angeline would have passed this way and perhaps come inside within these walls. I sense I am picking up her story but the "alive" connection I expected is eluding me. Am I using the wrong approach? Am I holding back too much? The strongest sense of *presence* has been when I walked in Christine's backyard and sitting in the Magdalene chapel. But that may not be her but Mary Magdalene's presence. What Angeline and I may have in common is that the Magdalene has called to us both… has (then) called to me before. How odd to view it that way… My visit to the Magdalene Chapel alerted me to a meditation this coming Tuesday evening. This holds great interest for me and perhaps will be a lively opening. Much… so much of this must proceed on faith. A question to ponder: I am aware – somewhat anyway – of Angeline, of who she is. Is she aware of me? What "state" should

I be in to connect with her/myself?

[Moments later, I receive this answer…]

It is a matter, Dear One, of going within sufficiently and with keen faith that the way… though dark in places… pulls you below the distractions arrayed about you in mighty and loud array. A key is to continue past these Earthly "mammons" and remain "on course" long enough to catch the necessary rhythm. Consider the beautiful dance at Mystery School [the Miserlou?] where you simply "stayed with it," relaxing into its beauty and grace and let it carry you at last. Persistence and faith. She will respond, is open to your studied call, hoping for you both to depart the ordinary for the extraordinary. Bear in mind, we are talking two distinct lives as much as you share the life-thread. There are… you are… two separate physical bodies, but your hearts beat in similar rhythms. And you have already guessed your shared love of nature's beauty and the tenderness towards all Earth's creatures. She is more fiery. She knew not a child of her own, something you might share with her.

Ask the Magdalene to help you find a place you might meet. This is very real and here now.

Blessed be your (shared) work.

That was Sunday evening, our second one at Jacoby Cottage. I followed the guidance given me as best I could and went about my "other Glastonbury work" which was getting more things in place for the 2006 Pilgrimage group. I contacted John Green at Avalon Coach, and thanks to his friendly help secured transportation to and from Bristol Airport and also for the day trip to Stonehenge and Glastonbury. And further, he let me in on the fact that as a group leader, I was eligible to request a private entrance hour there for my Pilgrims. How fabulous!

There'd been a couple of wonderful visits with Mano at her home enjoying marvelous conversations over tea. She'd arranged for a friend to take us to the stone circles at Stanton Drew. On Wednesday Carole drove Mari and me there and I spent a mesmerizing hour wandering about the huge pasture with the resident cows placidly looking on, a visit they were used to. *"I spent nearly an hour among the stones awed beyond suitable words. And, like certain labyrinth walks, the full experience will likely unfold in the next little while."* It certainly was not to be the first and last time among the three stone circles there.

Stanton Drew proved to be excellent preparation for the coming evening's nearly overwhelming experience at Chalice Well. At that time there were weekly meditations with the *Blue Bowl* in the Tudor-Pole Room which was on the third floor of Little St. Michael's Retreat House. I'd come to know about this much-revered object through the Glastonbury Tarot card deck that featured the Blue Bowl on one of the cards. It had been found in what was once regarded as a sacred spring near Bride's Mound on the edge of Glastonbury. Its origin has never been entirely determined, but its mystical energy had long been appreciated by those who came into its presence.

When I entered the room that evening, there it lay on a lovely floor altar space. The small bowl's vibrant beauty and almost-glowing presence could be felt as soon as I walked in. Nearly a dozen people from several countries were there as well. When the woman leading the ceremony told us that the bowl would be passed around our circle during the hour, I could scarcely believe my ears.

Our meditation began and the bowl was reverentially passed from one to another. A beautiful dark-skinned woman brought it to me, her lovely eyes connecting deeply with mine. She bent forward with the bowl held in her hands and then there it was, resting warmly in my own cupped hands, a pearly glazing on its surface, the exquisite deep blue flowers seeming to float on the iridescence. It offered me a low humming resonance and I spoke silent words of peace and thanks into its curved bowl. For a long timeless time I held it in my hands, gazing down upon it. Then I stood carefully and offered it to the woman next to me. The shape and feel of it stayed in my hands for the rest of the meditation.

Afterward, we were invited to spend time in the Garden. And so I did, gliding more than walking through the deepening dusk, going first to the Well, thanking the Magdalene for her coming to me in that hour and pledging myself to this unfolding work. A last visit to the Angel Seat, the Lion's Head, King Arthur's Court, and parting hugs to the Guardian yew trees – so wonderful to be essentially alone in these places. Then a good, quiet walk home to Jacoby Cottage, bundled comfortably against the enlivening chill of the Autumn night.

So the final full week of our Jacoby Cottage residence passed. I'd accomplished all I'd wanted and needed to regarding the 2006 Pilgrimage. Mari and I had enjoyed times together "out-and-about" and pleasant hours shared at Jacoby Cottage. On the last Sunday morning, October 2nd, I put in some satisfying time in the Writer's Camp that left me with "a good sense of things opening and a trust developing" between Angeline and me.

Mari and I made our way down to the Blue Note Café for a last lunch on the High Street. The cool and cloudy morning opened to a sunny afternoon so I set off for a walk venturing to the field above Bushey Coombe where a stand of magnificent oaks had long drawn my eye when I was in the Writer's Camp. In my journal that night I wrote, *They were quite easy to get to… three immense and venerable oaks reminding me of Gog and Magog. I could more easily visualize what the lane of [processional] oaks might have been like that reached up the side of the Tor. The view of the Tor was the most stunning of any place I've yet been and so there I stayed, drinking in the view of the Tor and the sweep of the Levels north to Crooked Peak…* I reread what I'd written and then heard a whispered message:

More is coming—More is coming—

Though I'd ended the night's entry with these auspicious words, when I came downstairs early to make my breakfast the next morning, there was little inkling of the phenomenal experience hastening towards me.

I was alone in the kitchen enjoying the deep quiet while I ate and washed up my dishes. I'm not sure what it was that I was considering doing next, but I clearly recall standing beside the kitchen table when a whispered voice spoke insistently in my ear. *"Go and get your journal and come up to the Writer's Camp at once."* The urgency was undeniable and so as fast as my feet could carry me, I dashed up the narrow stairs for my journal.

Hurrying back through the kitchen towards the door, something began to cloud my sight and there was a distinct sensation of something soft and red-tinged beginning to "pour down" gently over my face. I managed to open the back door but when I stepped out into the morning's brightness, the now-moving waves of red were so thick I was worried I might not be able to see the steps leading up to the garden. I grasped the railing, willing myself to stay in this somewhat unnerving experience, and made my way as quickly as possible up through the garden. The flickering red lessened some as I at last reached the Writer's Camp and hurried inside. I fired up my laptop computer willing it to do so speedily, and with the last red tendrils vanishing, let the flow of words rush out through my fingers.

The door between our two lives swung open and a dramatic scene snapped into clear view. Scarcely breathing, I wrote these first two short paragraphs:

The bleeding wouldn't stop. I raised my eyes to Mara's and unspoken words passed between us. With a glance towards the door, she whispered so Nellis wouldn't hear. "It is time."

And yet she made the sign of the cross upon her broad chest. Tear-shaped flecks of blood already made their own design on her tan woolen kirtle...

I stared for a long moment at the words on the screen, took a deep breath, and surrendered to the work. I wrote steadily for a timeless time releasing all judgment and questioning, watching the scene unfold, just staying out of the way as the story tumbled through onto the computer's screen. When at last it ended, I sat back and drew a deep, shaky breath.

Oh yes, and I pressed *Save*.

The impact of this sudden and dramatic entry into Angeline's life and the intensity of the birthing scene made it a challenge to exit the Writer's Camp and return to 21st century Glastonbury. Somehow I managed this though, and ordinary life, as they say, went on through the rest of that day. It was simply a too-amazing experience not to share with Mari that night at supper. And after we cleared the dishes away, we lit candles and I read her the scene that had come through that morning, her eyes widening at several places in the reading. She praised its power and my willingness to *allow* the experience to occur. Having shared so many other wonderful times in the energies of Glastonbury, her warm acceptance of this piece and Angeline's very *being* offered me gratifying affirmation.

The following morning began in less spectacular fashion. I climbed the steps on legs that weren't shaking as they had the previous morning and went up through Michou's beautiful garden for a final writing session in the Writer's Camp. I lit the candle a last time and turned on my laptop. Then I sat silently looking out the window at the early morning, attempting to just be present to everything as much as I possibly could be.

Some minutes later a final piece of writing signaled its arrival. As it had been the day before, I wrote easily and with little pause.

The sun has returned and shines in at the window, casting long shadows along the north side of Chalice Hill's meadows beyond Bushy Coombe. The Earth is still new in this day as am I, departing from the ordinary to this likely limitless adventure. I've answered its call, and I vow to be true to what awaits, to whose voice emerges. Yet I know it will be echoed in my voice, in my life, somehow. Some reluctance lingers, causing me to stand here a-tiptoe at the threshold. But all the signs point in, that whatever bearings I needed to check (and double check) are now sighted and sounded. The flame from the 30-hour church candle is into its fourth hour... and the sweet chickadees by my little house have evidently been attacked by the same hawk just a short time ago. The birthing of this story is underway, and yet I am now so keenly reminded of the cycle of birth-life-death, just as I was that sunny October afternoon a year ago, the hawk swooping in on the birds, snatching one and lifting heavily skyward with its struggling prey, past Gaston and me, its death cries drifting back to us. It shook me to my bones to hear. But the cycle does not stop or cease... it continues. Life perseveres. She has persevered because there have been women like me down through millennia, catching the echoing words and energies and stories and magic. This I know. This work has reached me and entreats my attention. What I possess of talent, time, and energy, I dedicate to this blessed and enlivening work.

The path leads on, I must depart
To hidden places of the heart.
Misty morn conveys its grace
On hearts that dwell in boundless space.

I typed the last stanza of the familiar poem, then sat back and read slowly through what I'd just written, through the thoughts that had come so clearly and easily. I remember that I wept. Then I pressed *Save*, turned off the computer, and blew out the candle.

There was packing to do in preparation for our next day's departure, so I had that to keep myself moving forward through the next several hours. But Avalon's lively Spirits were not quite through with me. That night they brought me a dream.

The Door Dream: 4th October 2005

(Last night in Glastonbury at Jacoby Cottage, the Angel Retreat... deep sleep before early morning waking.)

I am at home, though not in Unadilla Forks.

A delivery truck drives up and two pleasant men come to the door—I am not expecting a delivery and so greet them with a puzzled smile.

"We've brought you your new door!" they tell me enthusiastically.

"New door?" I say, looking even more puzzled. "The one I have is still fine."

They nod, but one of the men says, "Yes, but it's time for its replacement. Just go and check the receipt and you'll see that it's due to be replaced."

They smile happily at me and I believe them.

I turn around to check the receipt, ready to accept the delivery.

When I come fully awake, the images of the dream felt very present and angelic presences in the room seemed quite pleased at presenting me with this going-away present as I was preparing to leave Glastonbury.

It is time to let Angeline tell some of her story, beginning with the first part shared with me that morning in Michou's garden in our Writer's Camp where I crossed the luminous threshold into her life and into my past, on a day not long into the 16th century.

Chapter 6

Angeline's Story
Crossing the Luminous Threshold
Chapter 1

The bleeding wouldn't stop. I raised my eyes to Mara's and unspoken words passed between us. With a glance towards the door, she whispered so Nellis wouldn't hear, "It is time."

And yet she made the sign of the cross upon her broad chest. Tear-shaped flecks of blood already made their own design on her tan woolen kirtle.

I rose to my feet, swaying a moment as lights flashed in my sight, due more to the hours we tended young Hazel, but some I was sure coming through my unspoken prayer-thoughts. Pushing aside the curtain to the great room, I touched Hazel's dear husband gently on his shoulder. He startled from his own weary sleep and lurched up against me. I caught his shoulder to steady him. Something in my face startled him more, and he drew back, wild-eyed. Tears started at the corners of his dark eyes, bleary from grief and exhaustion. "Not gone, is she?"

"No," I said as gently as I could. "But hurry out for more clean straw. Mara and I are doing all we can." I crossed myself, as well I should.

He did the same and nodded, relief returning color to his pale unshaven cheeks and he hurried towards the outer door, hesitating for an instant beside the pathetic little bundle he'd set tenderly on the settle. Then he lifted the latch and went into the night. My own eyes stayed a moment on the bundle that held the girl-baby who had never drawn breath, and I turned away with a silent prayer to Her. We would not lose two lives in one night, I vowed silently.

"Gone now, is he?" Mara asked, the bag of forbidden herbs

already pulled from its secret pocket.

I nodded and sank to my knees at Hazel's shoulder, smoothing back the sweat-soaked hair from her ashen forehead. "She is with you now and always, dear one," I whispered into her ear. I took up the chant softly with Mara as we traced signs of the Mother on the young woman's forehead and chest. Then I held my cupped hands over her empty and tired belly. I closed my aching eyes, rubbed my palms quickly and several times. The heat touched my feet and then rose swiftly upward.

Hazel moaned, her eyes fluttering beneath their pallid lids. Still new to these powers, I suppressed an urge to gasp. Mara sent me a steadying glance and with her old fingers lifted Hazel's head, cradling her like a baby against her bosom, guiding the healing liquid into her mouth.

A sudden scraping sound from the outer room told of Nellis' return. I made a final sweeping pass with my hands from foot to head, raising Hazel's own inner power, calling upon her Helpers who I knew were all about us in a worried circle. One placed a large but gentle hand on my head in unspoken thanks. I nodded to the empty air, saying silently, *Thank you for your help. And thank the Goddess for the time to speak all the words.* The Being drew quietly away. Had I heard the words rightly?

... she will stay with you...

I looked to Mara for affirmation, but she was removing the red-dripping linen that had been packed between Hazel's legs. "She's given us the afterbirth, saints be praised. Now there's a reason for hope."

The curtain stirred and Nellis entered, nearly dropping to his knees at the sight and at the sharp smell of fresh blood. I took the golden straw he clutched and laid a steadying hand on his arm. "We have begged for her life from Holy Mary and Saint Bridget. She is breathing more easily now."

His eyes, so full with fear, tore their gaze from his wife's face. "I... she..." No words found their way from his lips.

"Go rest, Nellis." I steered him gently back towards the doorway. "Say prayers for her and for your little one to go with grace ahead of you to the next world."

We washed Hazel's blanched face with a cool, moistened cloth and her poor tired legs with lavender-scented water. I held the inner-sight of her womb and birth channel shot through and around with the White Light of Healing. Then we dressed her in a clean shift. I felt a new ease in her body and when I looked up at Mara, she nodded *yes*. She sat again on the bedside stool, smoothing out the coverlet, tucking under the stained part.

Outside the day was shyly breaking. Birds stirred beyond the shuttered window readying their voices for morning chorus. A rooster crowed his welcome. Mara and I had been here nearly a full circle of the sun. When I came and stood beside her, she passed a comforting arm around my waist. "We will know soon." She released a great sigh. "But I do think I see the life returning to her face, Bridey be praised. Go and rest there on the window seat, Andalein. I expect Elizabeth will return soon."

I went to the deep window seat, gratefully leaning my head against its wooden frame. Hazel's mother had left with great reluctance at last night's dusk, but duties called her home. She had already seen her daughter through two other sad births, though those babies were small, too early for either one to come into the world. This girl-child Hazel had carried longer under her heart and so we were all hopeful, such loving parents waiting her. But the long labor had brought the sight of the birth cord wrapped about her neck and there was nothing to be done when Mara saw it other than to sever this tie from mother to daughter and hand the unmoving baby to me. I wept silent, hot tears as I washed the tiny body, its warmth remaining for a little, but cooling rapidly. I kissed her two delicately arched brows and folded the cloth over her perfect face.

But more harshness awaited. Hazel had slipped into a deathlike sleep without knowing what had befallen her child.

Someone would need to impart these sad tidings.

I must have dozed when the outer door swung wide and Elizabeth Cooper came hurrying in, her shoulders drooping with the heavy news that Nellis had told her. He came in too, rubbing the sleep from his eyes.

Mara rose stiffly from the bench and took Elizabeth's hands. "The Lord is merciful. She is sleeping comfortably at last. The bleeding has nearly ceased."

A sob caught at Elizabeth's throat. "Oh, Blessed Mary be praised in this sad day that my daughter has not been taken too."

Nellis knelt down by the bed, tears flowing freely down his cheeks. He reached a hand towards Hazel's face, then checked himself and looked to Mara.

"Go ahead, Nellis. When she comes to herself, she will need to be told how the night went. She doesn't yet know. It will be a blow that may undo what Andalein and I have tried to set right. You and Elizabeth are the best ones for these sad words."

Nellis nodded, wiping his face with his sleeve. He was holding Hazel's small hand in his large ones like a most precious jewel. "Aye, then. We will do it as gently as we can. Will she rouse soon?"

"By midday, I suspect," Mara answered. "I did give her some powders in tea that are helping her rest as this was most needed. If you are able to fix a beef broth, it would be the best for her." She sighed and reached for the cloths I held. "This last set of clean linens likely will be enough while the others are washed and dried. Andalein and I will be going now but send for one of us if matters change. I will return on the morrow to check her progress. The heavens smile on Hazel in a fashion, and on you, Nellis. This is a good household you keep under this roof."

"Take my mare for your journey," Elizabeth said, taking Mara's hand. "She brought me here and I'm staying through tomorrow. Nellis can come for her later today. This is wearying work." Nellis nodded too.

Mara pressed her hand. "That it is. Thank you. We'll take turns on her good back. Nellis will find her having a good feed in our barn."

We made our farewells, Nellis embracing each of us in an awkward hug. He pressed two coins wrapped in a bit of blue cloth into Mara's hand. She took out one and put it firmly back in his. Closing the door behind us, I said a silent blessing-prayer with thanks for the Ones who had helped so unstintingly.

The stout gray mare nickered at our approach. I helped Mara up onto her broad back. The gentle creature stood perfectly still, and at my direction turned willingly towards the lane. Above the trees the new day sent streamers of pink and gold high in the turquoise sky. Tired as I was, my heart leapt up with joy. I stroked the mare's shoulder, feeling the muscles move in easy rhythm beneath her warm hide. In short order the woodland trees swallowed the little cottage from our sight. The new day's bird chorus rose all around us.

"A sad, sad business," Mara said, breaking the silence. "The angels must have needed the sweet babe."

I frowned, but not so Mara could see. "Perhaps, but I have to wonder why this little girl was kept from two such loving people. This one would have flourished, not like her other two babes." I kicked at a stone in the path. "If only I'd given her the strengthening herbs earlier, perhaps we would have birthed the little one in time to release the life cord." I glanced up at Mara.

She frowned down at me, not a look she often wore. "Should I have made different choices, perhaps?"

"No. Not that," I said quickly, realizing she thought I questioned her skills. "I'm asking myself if I missed seeing her weakness in good time."

Mara shook her head. "She wore a brave face for long into the night. All seemed well."

"Yes." I recalled how even when the stronger pains gripped her, she had smiled when they subsided, so certain she was of soon holding the baby moving through her birth channel. I sighed deeply and the mare dipped her head to me, fixing me with one kindly brown eye. I stroked the side of her head in thanks.

"The mare knows your thoughts," Mara said quietly, and then laughed her merry low laugh. "Could it be I kept company all night with a hedge witch?"

I looked up, smiling. "Ah, Mara, no wonder others call you a wise woman!" And at that the mare nodded her head up and down, snorting her agreement. Mara and I laughed together, the sound ringing back to us from the glen-sides we were passing through.

Coming to the top of the rise, the trees parted at the edge of fields belonging to Goodman Hadley. The land sloped down a long way to the watery moors with their waving bright-green grasses. We paused, taking in the splendor of the land lying before us in all Her late spring beauty. Perhaps it was because I was tired to the bone, but tears sprang to my eyes. Some eight miles distant, the double line of the Goddess' ancient oaks traced their stately way up the rounded lower slopes of the Tor. In the clear morning light my eyes could see their shadows stretching long into the adjoining meadows.

Mara spoke. "What is it now 'til summer Solstice, nine days?"

I counted on my fingers. "Eight," I said. "I soon need to let Joseph know I am going again to be with my sister for the Fair. Do you think you'll be joining us?"

"Jesus and his Blessed Mother, I hope to do so, but my aching feet may not recover in time." She poked me with the toe of her shoe and I looked up to see her broad smile. "I hope to, my child. And this may be odd to say now at this late time, more than halfway home, but wouldn't you like a turn up here while I walk a little?"

I patted her skirted leg. "No, friend Mara. I am happy to have you ride. It is all downhill from here to your place, and mine not much beyond. I'll part company with you at the bend if you don't mind traveling the last part on your own with Gray Lady here?"

It was soon then that I waved goodbye to Mara and gave the mare a hug before patting her flank to urge her go on without me. The sun's warmth had grown enough that I undid my shawl and tied it around my waist. I stood in the middle of the lane and stretched my arms up to the sky, loosening the tired muscles of my back and shoulders. A light breeze stirred the leaves of Goodman Hadley's apple trees and brought a heady draught of their white and pink blossoms. Closing my eyes, I breathed it in deeply, feasting on such delicate riches. From his barnyard and those of his tenants, roosters crowed and in the distance, Chanticleer, our stalwart cock, raised his voice in answer. In my mind's eye I saw him standing on the roof peak of the chicken croft, his six hens already clucking and scratching about in the vegetable garden.

Goddess hope they hadn't gotten through the willow hedge in my absence and set upon the strawberries in the herb beds. And if they had, Joseph may not have even noticed and chased them out. I roused myself from my sun-filled reverie and set off at a brisk pace towards our homestead.

Chapter 7

All in the loom, and oh! what patterns!
~ Edgar Lee Masters

Returning from Glastonbury always requires a reentry period... sometimes lengthy... to completely reconnect to everyday life once more. This third and longest trip with its otherworldly encounters and experiences made this all the more true. What I was starting to grasp was that these extraordinary Outer Journeys – three times now across the Atlantic Ocean all the way to Southwest England – were being mirrored by a steady deepening of my Inner Journeying.

But now back home in Unadilla Forks, much awaited my attention: precious time with Brianna and Logan, the continuing marriage-counseling sessions, the completion of *Significant Lives*, and the exciting development of the 2006 Glastonbury Pilgrimage.

The Door Dream was often on my mind and dreams continued to supply me with inspiration and support. Barely a week after getting home, the Moon moved through Aries bringing a lunar eclipse. Under this energy came this vivid dream of Gaia.

I am happily mingling with many women, talking, laughing, but not sure why we're together. There are many dark-skinned women and I'm enjoying seeing them. One of them approaches and she is beautiful in stature and of regal if not radiant bearing. Her hair is braided in stunning fashion as well. I also take note of her sweater which is different from any I've ever seen. She is close to me now and smiles warmly, inviting me to speak. I start to compliment her sweater and suddenly see it as part of her skin, not separate from her and then understand that she is a goddess... Gaia! She smiles kindly and nods in affirmation... I know that I am being granted this dream-gift of connecting with her this way and I am so very happy.

Around all this, the outer-world nightmare of the misbegotten war in Iraq grinds along. Just before Samhain... Halloween... I attend a candlelight vigil in nearby Clinton on the beautiful Commons in observance *"of the 2000th American casualty and God/dess knows how many Iraqis dead in this time."* In the chilly dark we sing peace songs and wave our placards bearing messages of peace at passing cars. Many honk in support but a few roll down their windows and shout derisive comments. "You can't win 'em all," someone says, and we nod taking comfort in our solidarity on this late October night.

The months tumble forward through the start of Winter and into 2006. By mid-January the registration for the Pilgrimage is full and amazingly includes a waiting list of two. Details of transportation, housing and meals, and an outline of activities have come together. I am awed by how smoothly the whole process is going. I happily exchange e-mails and phone calls with these first Glastonbury Pilgrims and we already feel the connection of this special journey coming closer. Inevitably there are some abrupt departures from the group in advance of the trip, something I will experience in future Pilgrimages. So the two people on the waiting list... including our "token male," Ken Negus, excitedly find themselves aboard. And for him what will be an especially sweet opportunity to return to England after many years' absence.

Ken and I dutifully continue monthly sessions with our counselor, Cindy, that offer some positive outcomes. The best is that the tension in the house is greatly eased, something we both are grateful for. And we had begun to have a greater respect for each other than had been true in a long time. We explored the ways in which our struggles with parenting our daughter had impacted us, another very helpful benefit of the time and money we were investing in this. I privately had my doubts that it was going to heal the deeper rifts between us, but intended to keep my promise of going through a full year of counseling. Quietly I was giving thought to where I might consider moving to.

I am making notable and satisfying progress on *Significant Lives*, steaming through the fourth rewrite and loving the emerging shape that it's taking. There's no doubt that my second women's fiction offering will be ready to go out in the world by the Fall. It will be late Summer when it all comes together with its new title, *Downstream*. With the intense focus needed for this work, time to develop much more of Angeline's story was a challenge, though it did continue in short bursts, all of which were fascinating.

And another amazing opportunity comes my way when Mystery School friends, Molly Harvey and Louise Griffiths, extend the invitation to be part of their new venture, *Soul School*. The first of three annual gatherings is to take place in Minnesota at a retreat center that has a fabulous-sounding labyrinth. Their vision is for me to lead labyrinth walks to complement the presentations. And my portable Chalice Labyrinth is "invited" too. After weighing various factors and the cost to go, saying "yes" to them feels wonderful. In my heart I knew I was meant to be a part of *Soul School* in this year of so many other "first experiences."

In the early morning hours of April 2nd, a stunning event changed our family dynamics completely. The day before Ken thought he'd pulled a muscle in his chest when he lifted the canoe on and off the truck for his first fishing trip of the season. That evening he sat in his recliner watching television massaging the ache. I felt worried that something more was going on and as we said goodnight I asked him if we shouldn't get him to the ER to have things checked out. He said he'd be fine. I was soon to find that my instinct had been terribly correct.

The nightmare unfolded hours later when I awoke to the sound of Ken retching in the upstairs bathroom and knew he was having a heart attack. When he came down the stairs, it was shocking to see the sallow color of his skin and the terrible pain registering on his face. He vetoed calling the ambulance... a mistake... and said he'd be "more comfortable" if I drove him in to the hospital.

Angels were with us the whole twenty-mile drive as well as when he was treated first in the ER at St. Luke's and then transferred to the Heart Center at St. Elizabeth's across town where he underwent a successful angioplasty procedure to clear his almost completely-blocked artery. By then both our kids and their spouses had arrived after their own hasty drives to Utica and we shared lots of grateful hugs and tears that their dad was still with us.

Five days later he was released from the hospital to begin his convalescence and a new scheme of things around the diabetes condition that had unfortunately also revealed itself. He'd told me in the ICU one afternoon that finding out he was diabetic was harder than having the heart attack.

We had an appointment with Cindy early that next week which of course I called and canceled leaving her a brief message about what had happened. She sent Ken a get-well card with a caring note. We never did return for further sessions. After the many months of the marriage counseling work I just put this all aside, knowing that seeing to his complete recovery outweighed all the rest. And, for now, I dropped any thought of leaving. We never spoke of this, but I knew Ken knew all of this and accepted this new arrangement too. It was an unspoken truce that was to last over a year.

Fortunately this nightmarish event preceded the Pilgrimage with enough time for his medical situation to stabilize and recovery to begin. There was no need to consider calling off the Pilgrimage, nor would he have wanted me to do this.

Beautiful June arrived with the days growing ever longer. And then at last the day arrived to drive down to Newark Liberty

International Airport and meet all ten of my first Glastonbury Pilgrims gathered in the waiting area at our departure gate. Two were already dear friends. Candy, truly a bosom friend since we were little girls, and Elizabeth, through our meeting at the 2001 Glastonbury Writer's Retreat. And there was Ken Negus from the Windsor Writing Retreats. What a delight to meet the rest! I will never forget their shining faces and excited smiles as we greeted each other and then leapt to our feet when our boarding call came.

Every group has received a name sometime during the Pilgrimage, and of course, what better one for the inaugural 2006 Pilgrims than the Trail Blazers?

And so together we boarded our silver-winged plane and flew off into the June dusk towards England and Avalon. A wonderful plus of this flight was that it was directly into Bristol, bypassing the long bus ride from Heathrow. I managed a bit of sleep during the flight, but awoke to see the brilliant light of the rising sun blazing its greeting on the edge of the rounded horizon. And as I'd heard before, the Land once more whispered its "Welcome home..." as we approached the coast of England. Our pilot brought us smoothly in over the beautiful countryside on the outskirts of Bristol and then we touched gently down. Yes, home again.

Coming through Customs, the officer processing our group quickly discovered we were headed for Glastonbury. With tongue-in-cheek, he began to ask each of us the same question. What had we heard of Glastonbury? Did we know exactly what might be in store for us in this most un-ordinary place? There was a wink for me as I came through when he learned that I was leading this group. The last one through was Ken Negus, 78-years-young and on a very long-awaited return to England. He proudly announced to the Customs official that he was our *Token Male*, a designation he happily gave voice to at other moments of the Pilgrimage. I'd like to think that this gentleman went home that day smiling at meeting all of us that morning.

Upon reaching the terminal's lobby, what a welcome sight to find our bus driver, Andrew, waiting with my name written large on a paper he held up. We were to get to know him quite well during our outings aboard our Avalon Coach. Jet-lagged as we were, the hour's drive through the back roads to Glastonbury thrilled us all. And when we came down the Mendip Hills into Wells, he pointed out the Tor in the distance across the Somerset Levels. Lots of "Ohs!" from the group and I felt the same thrill that greeted me five years ago. And how wonderful to share this "first-time" experience with these ten Glastonbury Pilgrims!

Since I could write an entire book on just the pilgrimages themselves, choosing several special moments is all there is space for within this larger tale. Our stay that year was in two adjacent B&Bs, one of course being Jacoby Cottage. The other was just across Bovetown Road, a comfortable more modern place with its own pretty backyard offering a grand view of the Tor.

With all of us safely here and *in residence*, I quickly became awed at watching the ten Pilgrims encountering the "marvels and magicks" of Glastonbury. Things began with the marvelous energies of the Summer Solstice and attending the ceremonies at Chalice Well Garden. There were easily eighty people from all over the world. After the beautiful ceremony at the Holy Well, we went into the Cress Field Meadow where we linked hands in a gigantic circle and joined our voices in an incredible toning to welcome Summer.

A miracle awaited.

Among the ten were four friends who had come together including Hazel and her mother, Linda. It was a lifelong dream of theirs to come to Glastonbury together. Not long after they registered for the trip, a surprising diagnosis came for Linda that she had breast cancer. They'd shared the news privately with me and that the treatment schedule was being structured around the Pilgrimage dates. It was their absolute conviction that the timing of all this was so Linda could come to the Holy Well to receive healing.

The ceremony in the Meadow concluded and people were invited to linger in the Gardens for as long as they liked. I was happily wandering about when I came down the main Garden path to find the four friends sitting together on the Angel Bench with its beautiful leafy canopy and the sweet stone Angel smiling over their shoulders. I was happy to oblige the request to take their picture and took the camera handed over. I sensed the considerable excitement among them as I snapped the photo. "Can you see it?" one of them asked excitedly, huge smiles being exchanged. I looked hard at them and shook my head. "Look through the viewfinder!" As soon as I did I gasped. There to the right was a shadowy figure sitting beside them. Yes, a beautiful Presence, an Angel. As one they beamed and beckoned me closer sharing the story. Hazel and Linda first sat there alone saying healing prayers. A bright light appeared above them and began to shine down until it enveloped Linda. When the other two friends appeared and joined them, they all felt the wonderful Angelic presence. I stood there in the bright June sun, listening and smiling and uplifted. It was glorious.

Our day trip to Stonehenge began with an unexpected visit suggested by our Avalon Coach driver, Andrew, to the magnificent yew tree in the yard of his parish church, St. Andrews, in the perfectly picturesque village of Compton Dundon. He'd heard us talking about trees and thought we'd enjoy meeting this particularly magnificent one thought to be around 1,500 years old. Coming up the walk from the parking area, we all were awed by this impossibly huge Being awaiting us, its deeply fissured trunk needing eight of us to stretch our arms out to encircle it together. It was such a rich and magickal encounter and one that would figure again quite significantly in a future pilgrimage.

Then on to Stonehenge that of course awed everyone as the iconic gray stones came into view. Everyone who's ever come on the Pilgrimage has had a lifelong dream of visiting this place. As we emerged from the entry tunnel and came up the ramp-way, observing the reactions among the Pilgrims moved me so much. With each of these shared experiences I was beginning to appreciate more and more my role in helping create these moments for each person. In subsequent years I would arrange for an hour's "private entrance" among the stones, but no one seemed to feel any less of an impact by being *regular tourists* and staying to the walkway.

Two hours later we were back aboard our Avalon Coach and heading to Avebury, a first-time visit for all of us, including me. I'd been told by others who'd been there that it was even more powerful than Stonehenge, partly because of its huge size... a small village is within its circumference... and partly because you are able to touch and be with all the gigantic, rough-hewn stones of the circles and the outer avenues of the megaliths.

First there was a marvelous lunch to be enjoyed at the picturesque Red Lion Inn that presides over the village of Avebury. Pub food and the experience of ordering it up delighted all of us. Then, with several options of things to see and experience, people went off in various directions with an agreed-upon time to gather and return to the bus. For a time I looked around the village with Candy and Elizabeth. Then I chose to strike out on my own, letting my intuitive sense guide me.

The Avebury Circle is the largest in all of England. There are two types of stones... megaliths... one a rough diamond shape, and others more rectangular. It's thought that the former represent a feminine presence, and the latter a masculine one. As we were to discover each one offers its own unique image and energy. Taking the whole complex in is almost impossible in just one visit.

I must have wandered for the good part of an hour and then, noting the time, realized that I should start back to the village. I had just crossed one of the roads that intersects the Circle and was continuing my process of stopping and lingering at each stone I came to on the path. I was totally absorbed in this and so wasn't aware that I was about to have one of the most powerful experiences of my four visits to England. In a written exchange sometime later with Angeline, this is how I told it:

It was a Summer day… I was with friends visiting the stone circle of Avebury which I'm sure you know. I'd been having a wonderful time being close to the stones, sitting beside a few, taking photos, allowing their energies to meet me. I was walking the paths alone and had crossed the road to walk slowly along the last section before reaching the town's edge. I was stopping at every stone and touching each one, sometimes placing my forehead against them. No other people were in that part of the Circle, so I felt at ease doing this.

Then I saw two people, a man and woman, step onto the path from the village and start in my direction. The woman was dressed in dark clothes and was using some sort of staff. They were still far enough away that I continued communing with the stones. I looked again and saw they were closer.

They were dressed in what looked like costumes to me and were out-of-the-ordinary, even for what we call "New Age" clothing. I remember looking around me to see if anyone else was on the path who might be seeing them too, but no one else was there. The man who I now saw was young, was tall and slim, his pale shirt was loosely cut and with long sleeves. His trousers were a dark color, brown, I think. It was the woman who especially drew my attention. She was certainly an "elder," but guessing her age would have been hard. I remember wondering if she was a priestess and if the young man was her attendant. There was an amulet at her throat and I think she wore some sort of turban. I sensed how very out-of-the-ordinary this encounter already was. Both smiled at me as they drew near and I knew they intended to speak to me.

She came and stood in front of me and looked deeply into my face, her hand held high on the staff. I felt embraced by her presence, and as if she was much larger than she appeared standing before me. "What are the stones saying, my child?" she asked.

I was prepared for an unusual question and said without hesitation,

"They've told me that it is Love that will save the World... that Love is the answer."

She nodded, as if in full agreement. "May I give you a kiss?" she asked. I nodded and bent towards her, again feeling the embrace of her extraordinary presence, seeing her dark eyes and strange beauty very close, feeling more and more certain that this was an otherworldly encounter. She kissed me on the forehead, on my third eye, and then stepped back regarding me with what could only be called Love. I felt deeply blessed and bowed, saying, "Namaste' ." I nodded to the young man, who had remained silent the whole while. He made a little bow and they stepped back onto the path.

We parted from each other and I continued to the last of the stones, finally turning to look and saw them moving slowly along the circle's edge. We were the only people there in all that time. I knew that it was a most special visitation and a privileged encounter.

And like you, I've met her again in dreams and in meditation, and in something called shamanic journeying, so She has come to be a part of my journey... part of our journey...

As these sort of otherworldly encounters continued to occur often when I was off on my own, I somehow managed to return to the 21st century world easily, slipping back into my ordinary self. When I rejoined the Trail Blazers to get back on our bus for the return to Glastonbury, there was plenty of animated sharing about the day's experiences. My profound encounter among the stones I kept to myself.

Trees continued to figure significantly in the Pilgrimage including the ancient yew at St. Andrews and my Copper Beech friend, Carnaphon, in the Abbey grounds who everyone marveled at when I took them to meet him. We spent another morning on a walk up and over the Tor to the two great Oaks, Gog and Magog. These two incredibly ancient Beings that are over 2,000 years old are the only ones remaining of an ancient double row that formed an avenue to the lower terrace of the Tor.

It was my second encounter and I was easily as moved by them again as those Pilgrims who came with me.

With time in Avalon often being decidedly nonlinear, nonetheless the days of this first Pilgrimage drew to an end. As I'd planned earlier in the scheme of things, I was extending my time in Glastonbury for a few days "solo"… a fabulous prospect that, as it came along, I could scarcely believe would happen.

We held a closing ceremony on the last night, sitting together in the solarium of the B&B. Each shared what the pilgrimage had meant, including Linda revealing what had happened at the Chalice Well Garden on the Solstice. The next morning I accompanied the marvelous Trail Blazers to Bristol Airport to see them off. It was quite an emotional leave-taking, this conclusion of our extraordinary adventure shared so intimately in our days together in Avalon. Then I boarded the Avalon Coach one last time for the drive back to Glastonbury with Andrew and we warmly hugged each other goodbye when he dropped me off at the door of Jacoby Cottage. How grateful I was for his lovely presence through that week and for his warm hug goodbye.

On my own at last, I needed first to catch my breath after all the incredible experiences and of serving as the group's guide during the Pilgrimage. As successful and enjoyable as it all had been, it was also tiring. So a good day or two was devoted to rest. And, in typical Glastonbury fashion, I also re-encountered Mano Mannaz and we shared many hours of lively conversation once more. I drifted around with my journals in my backpack, making entries to distill some of my initial thoughts about the Pilgrimage. And though I'd intended connection with Angeline, nothing much came through. But when you're in Avalon there is always plenty going on just beyond one's awareness and I was of course receiving everything I needed to continue our journey together "all in good time."

I set off one morning to honor a commitment made to the group which was to visit a special place we'd not had time to see together: Bride's Mound. This is one of a handful of goddess sites that are lesser known in Avalon, but those who learn of them feel a special draw to seek them out.

I'd managed to find my way there the previous year, undaunted by the trek necessary through Glastonbury's industrial area and past the sewage plant. I'd been given good directions but it nonetheless took some searching to find the deserted-looking dirt road and the field gate leading to the Mound. Though a few years later Bride's Mound was at last to receive loving attention and renewal, in those days it was a brushy, rounded rise next to the town's sewage plant. Most who visit are as struck as I was as to the town's choice to locate that facility there. And while it was not known to many Glastonbury visitors, the worn path through the weeds leading to the small open circle at the top was testament to those who made pilgrimage there. And I a returning Pilgrim.

So on this my second visit, when I at last found my way there bearing the group's gifts, I felt the vibrant welcome of the energies and Spirits of this most sacred place. This year I was carrying several tokens from the Trail Blazers, the most special being a small carved turtle that I'd be placing to honor the memory of Connie's son who'd died only two years before. With no one else anywhere in sight, I set out the things I'd brought in a sacred arrangement, called the Directions, and went into a meditation focusing on beautiful Bridget.

When that was complete, I placed the offerings where I felt they should remain on the Mound, and with everything finished, stood silent, looking around at the wonderful view of Avalon's landscape. It is an especially breathtaking one from Bride's Mound, the hills and sacred landscape of this ancient Isle laid out in lovely array. The course of the River Brue is somewhat hidden, but its quiet presence can be felt flowing nearby at the edge of the farm fields.

A movement in the distance suddenly caught my attention

and my eyes made out a large bird in flight. I gasped to see it was a white swan flying in my direction low over the Levels along the river. Its great wings beat slowly as it flew closer and closer. I was entranced by its steadily nearing presence. Gasping again, I remembered that the swan was Bridget's symbol and so I knew that this was no accidental appearance but *a visitation*. The wonderful Being flew in a graceful arc past me standing there on Bride's Mound, and then off into the distance with the same steady sweep of its huge white wings. When I later related this all to the Trail Blazers it was humbling to share how deeply and magically blessed the prayers and their offerings had been.

In my remaining solo days the need to see to the business end of the Pilgrimage work continued when it became clear that for a 2007 group I would need to find different lodging. People were very helpful with suggestions so that by the time I flew home my inquiries proved fruitful and the structure of the next Pilgrimage was already started. We would be staying at no less a marvelous place than Little St. Michael's Retreat House at Chalice Well Garden!

With this first Pilgrimage now wonderfully complete, early on the last morning I boarded the 376 First bus for Bristol Airport and my return flight to the US. The bus eased around the traffic circle at the edge of Glastonbury and headed out across the Levels towards Wells. I kept the Tor in my sight for as long as I could until it disappeared in the landscape. Tears rose in my throat which I did my best to hold in, but some slipped down my cheeks. My chest ached with this leave-taking. In my heart's ear I heard Joseph's gentle voice telling me to take care, that I was so loved here, and to hurry back. No matter how often I make this leave-taking, it never grows easier.

Back home life was certainly not ordinary, though plenty of pleasant, everyday tasks claimed my time and attention. Ken's convalescence was going well and he felt nearly back to his old self. Justin and Tracy were in the second year of construction of their amazing straw bale house. Ken and I drove down to help out as often as we could. Tracy's parents, Barb and Chuck, along with Ken and I named ourselves "the AARP" crew.

My personal schedule was also delightfully full of creative pursuits that included the very satisfactory completion of the draft of *Downstream*. Now there was the work of final editing and formatting for its hoped-for publication early in the new year. And though modest in numbers, I led a second writer's weekend at The Spiritual Center in Windsor greatly enjoying the five aspiring writers who came together for the experience.

October arrived bringing the Minnesota *Soul School* weekend. With the Chalice Labyrinth stowed aboard, out I flew from Syracuse to Milwaukee, happily bemused by this "next wonder" of the year's larger journey. Lots of *firsts* including renting a car at the airport and driving the hour northwest to the lovely Lake Sylvia Retreat Center to be greeted with whoops of delight by Molly and Louise and several other wonderful Mystery School friends who were taking part.

It was exhilarating to join collaborative forces with them all, facilitating labyrinth walks both on the Center's huge outdoor labyrinth, majestic in the stunning Autumn landscape. And also in its indoor setting, welcoming walkers to the curving path of the more modest-sized but high-vibrational energies of my Chalice Labyrinth.

Under Molly's direction and leadership, it was an exciting and soul-expanding weekend for everyone who had come. Plans were underway for two more sessions of Soul School and I was issued a warm invitation to consider the possibility of taking part again.

Arriving home from Soul School's weekend I write of it in my journal that, *"what emerged most meaningfully was a keen sense of grounded-ness in my work and great confidence in the direction I've chosen, or that has chosen me! Most certainly I've arrived at the threshold of the story I'm next to write..."* And I am also mindful that this is the seventh year since I left classroom teaching. And then of course it's the seventh year since my mother passed on. *"There is then very much a sense of the first phase of this new life's journey coming to its next turning."*

Given the stunning expansiveness of things I'd done and experienced through these ten months of 2006, I found myself more than willing to embrace who and what I was becoming as a writer, a teacher, and a pilgrimage leader. Far different from that of high school teaching, I was becoming comfortable with instructing others in matters of Spirit. *All in the loom, and oh! what patterns!* as that favorite line from Edgar Lee Masters' *Spoon River Anthology* goes.

And though there had been no telling communication with Angeline when I'd been in England with the Trail Blazers, there were still reassuring glimpses of her. So much else going on in my life crowded out focused writing time of this vital story. But when I dared to poke around the edges of this connection, more of her story came through, still solidly in First Person, in her voice. And while it didn't emerge from its source-point in the same unstoppable rush as it had that morning at Jacoby Cottage in Michou's garden, it nonetheless came through easily in these sessions. And no matter when it was I sat at my computer and *received* her story, I always felt total trust in the truth of what wanted to be recorded.

Here she is just returning home after the long night with Mara attending Hazel in her labor and loss.

Crossing the Luminous Threshold
Chapter 1
... continued...

Joseph was bent over the sharpening stone putting a fresh edge on the hay scythe. My husband of now eleven years looked up when he heard my footsteps turn in at the gate. He pushed his straight straw-colored hair back from his eyes. I noted that soon I should cut its length shorter for him. He smiled his greeting, the warmth of it reaching towards me. Whatever else I should think in my heart, I knew my good fortune in this man, so truly gentle. Too many women were bound to husbands of uncaring or even dark hearts. Even on Sabbath days and with their pious faces in place, I could read the misery of their wives as we sat, all of us together in the Lord's house.

Joseph reached for my hand, his smile retreating. "The news must not be good," he said.

"You guess rightly," I said, glad for the comfort of his strong and warm hand. I told him of Hazel's long birth-struggle and its sad ending.

When I'd finished Joseph sighed, his shoulders falling. "How well we know their sadness." He crossed himself, the good Christian that he was. For a moment he placed his hand on my belly. "What life is planted here and then comes to fruit is the Lord's mystery, to be sure." I nodded, swaying with the weariness that would no longer be denied. "Good Heart, you and Mara did all you were able. I have bread warmed by the fire and a cheese round on a plate for you. And there's fresh water in the jug. Go and rest yourself."

I brushed his thick hair with a grateful hand and went towards the cottage.

Entering through the side room that held my herbs and apothecary tools, with a quick hand I checked to see how the lavender was coming that I'd hung two days ago. Its tender fragrance came away with my touch. Puss was curled asleep on the bench beside the pot of rosemary, his favorite place. He raised his old brown head and blinked sleepily at me. "Ah, how are you, my pet?" I crooned, gently caressing his tattered ears. What a scrapper he'd been in his wandering younger days.

Dust motes traced the path of the morning sun coming in at the window. A low flame still danced in the hearth's peat fire, the kettle of wash water steamed on the side hook. The promised plate of bread and cheese made my mouth water and I sat gratefully down on the bench with it. Cool water from the jug was sweet nectar and I closed my eyes with words of thanks for the abundance that was present in our little cottage.

While I ate, I listened to the rhythmic rasp of Joseph at his sharpening chore and felt again his hand laid on my waist. Our years as husband and wife had brought one pregnancy, and that an eight-month baby, a boy who came easily enough but whose life-spark went out before the first sunset of his little life. We mourned him, and though church strictures allowed no naming and no baptism of one so young, we named him David. Sharing this with no one, we buried him at the edge of our small orchard. Joseph tends the place with unceasing devotion, two rosemary plants planted with his own hands mark the little grave.

Since that time, I have not conceived another child. Mara, who tended David's birth, gave the explanation to Joseph that something in the labor had likely damaged my birth organs. The truth of it, kept from him, was that Mara had shared with me the knowledge of herbs that withheld my womb from another child.

Our marriage bed is still a place we enjoy together and sleep content in one another's warm presence, but Joseph's earnest attempts to give us a child are becoming less and less frequent. Devoted as he is to our union, his Christian duty to beget children weighs less on his mind it seems with each passing year. Some might say I should be watchful as perhaps he's dallying in the hedges with younger maids, but I doubt this.

In the first years I took the potion on the days of each moon necessary to use it, I was careful to mix and use the herbs in undisturbed moments. Joseph scarcely questioned what I did with my plants. But then came one day when he happened upon me unexpectedly in the workroom. Half the potion with its odd green color remained in the cup. Startled by his presence, I gasped and choked so that he came into the little room quite concerned for me. Patting me helpfully on my back until I drew easier breath, he asked was I all right, and then peered for a long moment at the half-full mug. I did my best to be at ease lest he have all the more reason to ask what it held.

But then he'd asked, "What have you there, one of your new tea mixtures then?"

"Yes. And this one's not got a good prospect I fear." I raised it to my nose and sniffed it disapprovingly. I gestured towards a pot of comfrey recently boiled to soften the tough roots. "But it may add some vigor to the lavender so I'll put it out there with that liquid when it cools enough."

Content that I was now recovered, he nodded his head at these words and went on through to the main room. From that time on I've exercised greater caution and taken the herbs only when he is far out in the field or gone off to town. Within another year or two, if I can trust the signs of my body, I may well have passed the time of needing the herbs' powers. Beyond easing the vigilance I must still exercise, I look forward to the day I will be welcomed into the Crone's circle. The Wise Women will assure me of the fullness of these years completed.

Some may say I am a sinner both for deceiving my good husband and perhaps even more a sinner for closing my womb to his seed. It was not that I bore memories of a difficult childhood as is true for many. My home was a warm and loving place with parents as gentle as Nellis and Hazel. My father was the miller some twenty distant, and there was little want in our household for my sister and three brothers. Elizabeth and I, the youngest and second youngest, were coddled by the rest. A miller's children, while not the equals of those of a squire's, nonetheless, have privileges many do not.

Darkness entered our lives when our mother, Hannah of the good heart, took ill with the wasting cough and passed to Heaven in my eleventh summer. Elizabeth and I comforted each other and took on her work for our father and brothers.

Joseph, my eldest brother William's age, came to the mill with his father, their farmstead high in the Mendips. One day when taking our father his noon meal, Joseph and I espied each other for the first time. Already a young man, my sense was that to him I must appear a child, though in truth I was a comely and budding maiden of fifteen. Joseph, shy in nature, especially in those years, carried my image in his heart all that summer when he at last declared this to his parents. So on their next visit to the mill, Joseph's father took my father aside and inquired as to my marriage status.

Bless my good father, he approached me gently with this news and asked what I might think of it. As I was his pet and nearest his heart ("So like your sweet mother you are growing to be," he said often...), he in no way wished to rush me into any unhappy alliance, nor trouble his heart by knowing he'd placed me in an unhappy marriage.

St. Michael's Fair was but a few days later and so it was agreed that we two young people would encounter one another there and take some of each other's measure. It was a sun-rich Autumn day and fills me now with pleasant reverie. This, in truth, is due only in part to the pleasant hours with my good Joseph. St. Michael's Fair is held in a field on the western slope of the great Tor and it was the first time I set foot on that blessed island-mount. While sharing our noon meal seated on the grassy ground, a faint trembling beneath me, like a crowd of horses or cattle passing, drew my attention. None were in view. I looked to see if Joseph felt this, but he was joking with a friend who'd stopped to say hello.

Then a gentle voice whispered unknown words near my ear in syllables I did not know. I was directed to look up into the blue September sky. From above on the tall hill, an immense flock of swallows appeared over the Chapel tower and came near, wheeling and diving over the crowded field. Again I looked to see if Joseph saw too, but he still talked with his friend. With my eyes I followed the birds as they made their dancing way lower over the comely and ancient trees filling the vale below us.

Something filled my chest with unnamed longing as they departed and I was glad not to have to speak for long minutes after the birds had gone from sight.

That day, unknown to me then, I took up not one, but two paths for my life. I struggle now with keeping these paths both open and clear and as well on a parallel track. The one was clear to me as the day ended, riding home in the family wagon close beside Joseph. I was content with knowing that in good time he and I would be husband and wife. The other path was long years away, but crossing the causeway north towards the Mendips, the Tor rose in dark and majestic outline against a glowing red and gold sunset sky. Staring at this splendor, I began shivering. To my later amusement, Joseph asked then if I was cold, and not able to tell the truth of it, I demurred, and consented... happily so... to his putting his strong arm around me. Both of us felt in our hearts how this sealed the commitment to our shared future journey.

For nearly two more years no one of us felt compelled to seal this in marriage. But then, sadly, Joseph's father was killed by the bull brought to breed their cows, caught up against the pen's fence and he not able to reach the gate in time. This left only Joseph and his aging mother to do the farm work, so it was deemed only wise to knit up the marriage knot then and there. A happy day it was, that hot July afternoon, especially as a reason to leave the grief of his good father's death behind. There was much dancing and drinking and warm embraces from friends and family; my father was not a little sad that I was leaving his house at last. We wept in each other's arms at the end of the day.

(There are times I still have a deep longing and my woman's heart aches for the happy childhood I passed beneath my parents' roof there next to the tumbling stream driving the mill wheel round and around...)

But that first night together we made our shy first union and shared true delight in what our bodies showed us to do. For many long months and not a few years, this was to hold true.

Chapter 8

The bowl breaks. Everywhere falls to everywhere.
Nothing else to do.
Here's the new rule: break the wineglass
and fall toward the glassblower's breath.
~ Rumi

2007… a "9" year numerically, the number of completion. And so very much is drawing to completion in the early months of the new year.

Almost impossible to navigate is the ending of the lives of both our elderly horses within two weeks of each other. First, Jill, the thoroughbred mare who was our gelding Thunder's companion, and then sweet, gentle Thunder himself on a bright Sunday morning in January. That we had managed to assist three horses comfortably into their elder years, and finally saw to their departures as well as we could, was all a labor of love for many years. A week after saying goodbye to Thunder, these are my journaled thoughts:

So I have thudded to the bottom of something, or perhaps it's more like completed this part of my life, the part shared with horses. In this year of completion, this is one that is terribly bittersweet.

The morning that I looked out to see the snow had covered Thunder's last tracks through the field was tremendously sad. But in every ending no matter how difficult, there is the grace and seed of a new beginning. My inner Voice has been whispering that once the horses were gone, that I would be free to depart this place too.

I follow the online astrology resource, *Celestial Timings*. On the 4th of February the Moon moves into Virgo in the early morning. I find myself very affected by the posting of this day's celestial alignment. Cayelin Castell writes of this configuration, *"This*

Moon is that of Earth's wisdom-keepers who are stewards of the patterns of life and who know how to maintain balance between the world of form and the other worlds. These are the mysteries of the pattern and it is finding our expression within that pattern that draws the forces of creation to us in a way that helps us to fulfill our soul's purpose."

Understanding and accepting the truth of this, it affirms my working to birth the second Glastonbury Pilgrimage set for August. Already three people are registered including my daughter, Sarah. On January 12th, I speak with a lovely woman at English Heritage's Stonehenge bookings and secure a morning's private entrance for August 13th. This amazing expansion of the Pilgrimage offerings is matched by the unforeseen and incredible option of the group spending a few days on the northern coast of Cornwall. Michou had told me about the beautiful town of Tintagel that is right on the ocean and also recommended I get in touch with the couple who run the Bosayne Guest House. From the first warm e-mail exchange with Keith and Julie Walker, it's clear Spirit is orchestrating this fabulous connection and opportunity for the 2007 Pilgrims.

By March there are multiple factors that are positively impacting my life: the afterglow of the successful publishing and launch of *Downstream*, committing to another level of work with Jean Houston and Peggy Rubin in the Advanced Mystery School sessions, and taking a powerful workshop that leads to attunement with the energies of Isis and Sekhmet. As can and does happen on the World Wide Web, I was led to the work of Nancy Fanara, a modern-day priestess of Isis. A conversation with her on the phone made it abundantly clear that I was to travel to Western Massachusetts to experience her extraordinary teaching. Opening to these new ideas vastly expands my cosmic awareness and understanding. Delightedly I devote time to study and develop these new spiritual practices.

And in an oddly-related personal decision, I stop coloring my hair and begin to let its natural silvery-gray emerge. I'm claiming more and more of my *authentic Self*, or as Jean announces to us loudly at Mystery School, "Be fierce with your own Reality!" There is no doubt that I'm working on that.

With the arrival of the Vernal Equinox, as far as my *work in the world* is concerned, I've reached a point of absolute clarity of what I was up to. With total conviction I write in my Spirit Journal, *"I am a way-shower, a gate-keeper, and as Jean Houston would put it, a* provocateur... *my strengths I know of creating safe space, encouraging exploration, and weaving ritual for exploration of the Deep Within."*

Mostly I walk-my-talk, and it is an exhilarating but on occasion a confusing time. I am always grateful for my journals to mull over where I've gotten to and where it is I might be going. My Solar Return offers a significant indicator. This year's journey commencing once more on my April birthday will be over-lit by the symbol Snake-shedding-its-skin. The unspoken truce that's kept peace in the house since Ken's heart attack nearly a year ago is beginning to show signs of wear. The return of this heavy energy drags us both down more and more frequently.

One morning, after a long absence of this sort of communication, a message of guidance comes through from Archangel Michael.

Greetings (from elsewhere)

It is not that you have asked to stay, it is that it is too early to go. The preparations you are making in so many ways, both outwardly and inwardly, will all serve you well. Relinquish judgment of yourself and those most intimately connected. In due course, in this year of completion, all you need will be revealed to step fully and completely into your star work, your star-born work. Serve yourself first, tho' clearly what you are doing now en-lights others — how wonderful!

... And consider the ineffable joys on every side as you honor the journey, not only the path but the pace best chosen. A certain trust* is at play, the "surrender" as mentioned in material you read yesterday

(*trust in what is meant for you). Learning to be engaged and not engulfed by the adventures of your amazing life... Much, so much, is settled into supportive pattern... Jean Houston's words of weaving [at a recent Mystery School weekend], this fractal so wonderfully embedded in your life, the loom of your life so beautifully sturdy and grand.

    – the ocean of the sky and you plying its cloud-currents with your remarkable heart-powered wings

    – the vastness of your most-treasured inner being is what you are now tending as you nurture yourself in the ways you have nurtured others before now.

    All is definitely as it should be with Infinite and much-deserved Praise to you!

The tremendous comfort this message offers helps me move forward knowing that things ultimately will resolve themselves well for the good of us both.

And that day does come. On a Spring morning in May, Ken and I at last sit down together, and with great respect for each other, calmly sort out the inevitable decision of separation and perhaps a future divorce. I am happy and relieved to write of this in my journal: "So there was a truth-seeking/speaking conversation Thursday with Ken. For him some needed clarity of the uttermost truth (mine) that, to his credit, he seemed to accept... most wonderfully, an easy-enough mention of separation and divorce. Neither of us seemed 'knocked-out,' and I told him how I appreciated his honesty. The elephant in this room is to my mind really a sweet creature. From this conversation I sense there's a movement begun towards a fair and hopefully positive conclusion for everyone."

I write on with further thoughts ending this lengthy entry with great optimism: "What's come through today is a happy sense of approaching independence. I've been sensing this more and more as the afternoon has gone on!"

I am so keenly aware of how my present life is filled with

endings, beginnings, and transformation. How to hold all of this... how to continue with grace. The powerful work begun in February with Isis and Sekhmet has become a daily practice as often as I can manage this. Their increasingly vivid presence brings such a sense of empowerment. I am also tuning in to messages of Archangel Michael channeled by a wonderful South African woman, Celia Fenn, who shares them on her web site, *Starchild Global*. As the June Solstice draws near, these words of Michael: *"... the true power of the Divine Feminine in your New Earth energies is to assist you to create an abundant life with deep passion and from an alignment with your inner wisdom as spoken to you by the Voice of your Heart."*

And as the expression goes, *in the fullness of time* it's the August day of our flight to Bristol and ten Glastonbury Pilgrims, including four lovely fellas... Ken Negus is no longer a token male! ... climb aboard the Avalon Coach for the long drive to Tintagel, Cornwall, on the wild northern coast. Our jet-lagged eyes widen as we drive down from the headlands where the sparkling waters of the Atlantic flash a greeting to us. Soon we pull up to the front door of the Bosayne Guest House and are warmly greeted by our marvelous hosts, Keith and Julie Walker. They usher us into the comfortable lounge for hot tea and refreshments and then show us up to our cozy rooms so we can concentrate on getting over jet lag.

A fabulous Cornish breakfast awaits us in the morning served up in the beautiful stone-walled breakfast room. People often tell me it's one of their favorite memories of Tintagel. Smiles all around as we begin to get to know one another, and then off on our first hike along the shore path to Rocky Valley and St. Nectan's Glen. As we set out, Dick Dalton takes me aside to let me know his doctors had advised him against coming when shortly before the trip he'd been diagnosed with a mystifying intestinal blockage. He'd pledged to undergo complete medical testing upon his return, but was determined to come on the Pilgrimage with his wife, Marsha. They both knew the powerful healing possibilities which awaited at Chalice Well, and indeed he felt all the more certain just why he'd answered the call to come to Glastonbury. Dick gave me a bright smile and assured me all would be well. I knew he was right.

It was a most sobering moment for me as the Pilgrimage leader, but then the experience with Linda's medical situation of the previous year helped me to grasp one of the reasons I was offering this opportunity to people.

The northern Cornish coast is spectacularly beautiful with towering headlands topped with emerald green fields. On a sunny day as it was that morning, the waves breaking below on the jagged black cliffs threw up spumes of white spray. Our first destination was my personal pilgrimage for that year, Rocky Valley and the two ancient labyrinth carvings. When I'd first seen these in a photo on the Internet some years before, I was mesmerized. And when things had worked out so easily for our group to spend three days in Tintagel, I knew almost at once why Spirit had orchestrated it so perfectly.

The Shore Path winds down from the headlands into Rocky Valley and then up along its fast-flowing stream to the ruins of the gristmill that stands within a few feet of the natural rock wall holding the carvings. To reach them, one ducks beneath a low stone arch and steps into the small, natural sanctuary formed by the gristmill wall and the rock face. Many people have come to view the two labyrinths carved side by side, one a little higher up than the other, both about two hands-width across. Their age has been said to be impossible to determine, but they were here long before the mill was built. One of the first things that struck me was that in all the years of the mill's use, barely a dozen feet from its outer wall, no one had disturbed them.

Even as I approached the archway, I could feel their welcoming gentle vibration, and when I stepped into the space joining a half-dozen or so others, only whispers disturbed the air of this sacred place. When it was my turn to step close, I found I almost didn't want to touch them, but just gaze at their curving enigmatic designs carved into the rough rock. But for a few moments I held my hand against the cool moist stone and closed my eyes in thanks for this perfect wonder.

Our two full days in Cornwall were rich in pleasures of exploring the quaint village of Tintagel with its own romantic castle ruins, climbing over the rocks to Merlin's Cave reachable only at low tide where legend has it the baby King Arthur was discovered, and admiring the small harbor with its exquisite waterfall tumbling down into the sea.

Our Avalon Coach driver, Keith, came to collect us and it was off through beautiful Devonshire to Glastonbury and Little St. Michael's Retreat House at Chalice Well. Already steeped with Cornwall's special magic, we were prepared to feel the welcome of the vibrant energies of Chalice Well. As guests in the Retreat House, we were able to go into the Garden at any hour of the day. (Each room even had a flashlight to make after-dark visits possible.) And most meaningfully, Dick Dalton would take advantage of the pre-public hours to bathe in the healing pool of King Arthur's court, always a bracing experience to immerse oneself in the 52-degree water. I never have gotten beyond wading myself.

Showing the group around the Garden felt such an incredible honor, acquainting them with all the wonderful trees as we went, and gathering for a few minutes together at the Holy Well. It was beyond delightful to watch everyone take this all in, all of us including me realizing the privilege of staying for several days in this incredible place. Another advantage of being at Little St. Michael's was how close by was the entrance to the pathway to the Tor. There was enough time remaining that day for a first walk up to the Tower, and most of us made the trek to watch the glories of the sunset over the distant Bristol Channel.

Anticipation was already high for our day trip to Stonehenge and Avebury with the promise of the early morning's private entrance at Stonehenge. Privately I wondered what potent encounters might await me this year. The mysterious woman-priestess had come to me more than once in dreams, always a powerful visitation. Somewhere in my reading that year I came across information about the goddess Nemetona, protector of Celtic sacred sites. Was it She who had sought me out that day? Would she be waiting for me again?

With "private entrances" limited to 24 people, the hour's time allows for deep and unhurried interaction with these ancient stone-Beings. Our hour's time among them proved to be nearly beyond description. At one point I sat down next to one of the megaliths, closed my eyes, and placed my hands on the ground. The intent was to do a light meditation. I let my thoughts drift. What I most sensed was the grass and cool earth beneath my hands. Then a subtle vibration began to register itself followed by a faint humming. Could this be? Yes, it was a humming of human voices. As if at a distance below me in the earth, I heard men's voices chanting. At first I was fascinated but then the chant grew quickly louder and with the distinct sense of this "presence" rising upwards through the ground towards me. I jerked my hands away in near fright breaking the "connection." I took a deep breath and none-too-steadily got to my feet, glad for the experience and all in all not much surprised at this encounter among the stones.

Our driver, Keith, knew quite a bit about the ancient sites, and on the way to Avebury brought us to the site of a "wood henge" called the Sanctuary. It is understood to be an important part of Avebury's sacred landscape and its annual rites. Another startling auditory encounter was waiting for me there.

The Sanctuary was constructed from standing timbers arranged in the familiar sacred circle, but of course no traces of the wooden columns remain above ground. Modern "detection techniques" have located traces of the structure hidden beneath the surface and each timber is marked by a numbered stone marker.

Lost in our own thoughts, we walked about the area that's half a football field or so in size. I was slowly tracing the henge's outer circle, occasionally holding my palm towards the ground to pick up any possible energy or vibrations. Coming to one marker that seemed no different than the rest, I stopped, and held out both hands. At once, as if they were magnetized, "something" tugged my hands down towards the ground. A disembodied voice rose up seemingly between my hands repeating one word louder and louder, "Joy! Joy! Joy! Joy!" The last "Joy!" felt like it was tossed high into the air. My hands were released and I stood looking at my palms, incredulous. Fascinated, I cupped them together over the marker and the exact same thing happened once again, the word "Joy!" vibrating up and through my hands.

Some of the others had noticed something odd was happening and came over to investigate. I described what happened and held out my hands once more over the marker. Again the downward tug of the energy and the upward rush of "Joys" though only audible to me. But this time several people standing close also felt the upsurge of the energy from the ground. We looked around at each other, speechless. Bob Burns had a guide to the numbered markers and checked information for the one at our feet. "Oh, wow, Carol, guess what's at this marker." He paused, looking again at the page. "It contains the skeleton of a person who was likely sacrificed when the Sanctuary was built." More stunned silence as we grasped the possible truth. The individual buried beneath our feet, a ritual sacrifice, may well have gone to his or her death gladly... in Joy... and that all of us standing there at the gravesite in the 21st century sunshine had just been given this message.

We trooped back to the bus for the short drive from the Sanctuary to Avebury. As we had done the year before, we headed first for The Red Lion to fortify ourselves with a delicious pub meal for the afternoon's adventures among the stones. I'll tell you, people were really "primed" for more!

Somewhat overwhelmed by the day's two "close encounters," I sought a quiet place to reflect and do some journaling. I found a secluded spot in a grove of trees but had no sooner settled myself and opened my journal when there was a rustle in the bushes and my daughter appeared, brimming with excitement. "Mom, there's a crop circle over there." She pointed past the henge ditch.

"Yeah, right," I said, half-amused at what I was sure was a joke and half-annoyed at being located at all by anyone, even Sarah.

"I'm not kidding! There *is* a crop circle over there, and I've just been in it!" Extraordinary event Number Three of-the-day beckoned. So of course, I got up and followed her. She pointed me up a lane and after a short walk, out in the field of swaying barley, I could see the outlines of massive circles pressed into the grain. No one else was about as I almost tiptoed into the field along the path left by previous visitors to the crop circle. I came to the edge of it and stood spellbound by the wide path of stalks pressed close to the ground looking as if they had been plaited together by an unknowable force. I took a breath and spoke out loud, asking permission from whatever Energies were present to step into the circle. No answer, and feeling the deep silence, I took a careful step onto the flattened barley. I walked about slowly for a few minutes, and then satisfied it was enough, went back to where I'd entered and returned to the tractor lane. Another totally unique Pilgrimage experience registered itself in my heart.

We arrived back at Little St. Michael's weary from the long day but oh-so-replete and filled by all the mystical *magicks* of our experiences.

On the final evening of the Pilgrimage we held a wonderful closing ceremony in the Garden at the Holy Thorn that stands above the Lion's Head fountain. Each of us tied strips of cloth to its branches with a message or prayer request and expressed our thanks for this marvelous shared experience of the 2007 Pilgrimage. We stood in a half circle before the Thorn, the sense of special kinship drawing us close born through our shared and extraordinary adventures.

Once again I accompanied this second amazing group of Glastonbury Pilgrims to Bristol Airport to see them off, reminding Dick to send word of how he made out with the medical tests scheduled for the day after he returned home. Back in Glastonbury for my three solo days, I saw to arrangements for a 2008 group, spent unhurried time with Carnaphon, enjoyed a visit with Mano, and generally reveled in my solitary immersion in Avalon's energies. Checking my e-mail two days later, I found Dick's note with the wonderful and astonishing report that his medical tests revealed all was well and that the blockage was totally gone. His doctors were quite startled, but Dick wasn't at all. Not one bit. And of course, neither was I.

Two years, two pilgrimage groups. Not without a bump or two during our days together, but all in all quite an extraordinary sense of delight and pleasure at making this happen for those nearly two dozen adventurous souls who had answered Avalon's call.

So into the Autumn with the growing anticipation of the upcoming major shift that will see me moving out of my home of thirty-two years for an as-yet unknown place of my own. This was still six months away but quite an immense transition to contemplate and start planning. There's also the continuing work at building Justin and Tracy's home, so there were numerous trips to pitch in. It's taking definite shape with the straw bale walls now up and being plastered. The more this Earth-honoring house takes shape, the more beautiful and amazing it is. And with dates already agreed upon for Chalice Well's 2008 stay, advertising is going out for the third Glastonbury Pilgrimage.

In the whirl of all this, worries and doubts creep in at unguarded moments. The immensity of it looms up suddenly now and then often with the sense of being in a whole new territory of my life. How on earth will I manage all of this? How to keep my balance? Searching for answers and support, I venture inward using a new skill I'm learning... shamanic journeying. A friend I'd made through the Onondaga Lake Peace Festival had introduced me to shamanism in the last year and I'd taken part in a beginning workshop not long after I'd returned from England. Among the intriguing experiences of that first weekend was learning who my power animals and allies were: Horse and Snake. Of course...

9th November: Message of shamanic journey

A time that will return... at time that will return...

A spring much clogged with dark matter that is now being cleared. The waters will run clear again and abundantly from the heart of the Mother. You are aiding this by bringing healers to Glastonbury's deep and sacred Well. Do not cease this work but magnify your efforts. Such communion conducted by you, a great Enchantress. Enhance, enlarge, empower this Earth music. Pour forth your soul's song. Unburden the spring source. Clear the debris, Earth daughter. Your magnificent wings are unfolding from the chrysalis of your earth-born youth. Others are joining you; no need to worry or despair. Embrace the abundance which is your life. Partnered now and always with greatness. Let petty concerns slip away now. The world awaits, needing your larger work in all its mighty beauty and grace.

And my always-helpful Muse reminds me of Rumi's glorious poem that I'd encountered at Mystery School,

The bowl breaks. Everywhere falls to everywhere.
Nothing else to do.
Here's the new rule: break the wineglass

and fall toward the glassblower's breath.

Rumi's powerful message is utterly clear to me, but human that I am, a hesitancy to allow its complete embrace persists. In my journal this entry where I weave through my thoughts like the drunken sailor I often feel myself to be:

20th November: Journal entry

... Perhaps I become confused between my present Earth journey-work, the Pilgrimage, the retreats, and the storytelling. It's been necessary to work on my *own story* and orchestrating the next chapter which now at least has an outline. Simply allowing *all* to unfold with grace is what's required.

My possibly strongest suit in this marvelous crazy-quilt of a life is that I accept the fullness of who I am, saying, "Yes!" enthusiastically to my own evolution. I am most assuredly *following my bliss.* (Continued thanks to Joe Campbell for these empowering words!)

Some truly revelatory dreams these past 2 nights: In one I was journeying by car to some destination and was searching for shortcuts. I tried two, both times driving down a steep hill where I took a turn each time but soon found the paved road changed to a dirt path that unnerved me. One time it quickly became slick with dark mud, a swamp on both sides of the road. I turned the car around fast and drove out and up the hill. I'd seen a couple of people who might have given me directions, but I chose not to ask. My sense as this was happening (or when I came more awake) was that this was a level of my subconscious that I was in, perhaps not to be avoided. I definitely felt uncomfortable there!

But then this speaks to my "reluctance" and foot-dragging around this new work with Angeline. Going into the dark is likely what's required.

I was in hopes that my Guides and other Beings traveling with me were appreciative of my clear-eyed admission of foot-dragging and frequent reluctance. This short message from them on that same potent November day offered considerable comfort as well as encouragement for the forward journey.

And so, our beloved, the wind is at your back.
Your powers as a translator are kindly requested.
Take the long view, for that will reveal
the greatest detail and at the least, show you the entry point.

They knew the *entry point* was not far off... not far off at all. Another message arrives soon that brings further extraordinary insight into this hidden landscape which had been beckoning to me for so long. Although my days spent in 21st century Glastonbury offered compelling experiences and invigorating resources, I was receiving glimpses of how just far back this whole journey stretched. And I was also beginning to understand just how important... how crucial... it was that I should accept this Sight.

I was fast falling toward the glassblower's breath. In its trans-formational fire I would find Angeline waiting for me.

Message, late 2007

Glorious awakening when these matters at last emerge/return to accrue to them your devout focus and fineness of loving attention; to apply all your amazing energy (which, doubt you not, you have). There is a clamor now for this to emerge through your fine-tuned and magnificent Self. Oh, the smiles and happiness to welcome you to this work! A tale you know in your heart, from your heart and soul.

Signal fires flash in the dark as the hill looms high above you. You will go there often and to the hidden glen to sing the forbidden songs. Allies are present but enemies of Earth persist. See her sweet face and know your vital connection and partnership. You certainly can return to the crossroad, but other avenues beckon. Others know of your entry point into this world and await your return. Trust the avenues you have explored.

You are the Voice, some say of She… no, not yet, but soon emerging. Excitement… Pleasure… your marvelous gift to them and the world, to the Great Mother… and you then, now, and always a divine daughter (the cows did love you, Little One).

Venture forth with trust in who we are and in your own adventuresome Being-ness. Never was one better suited to this "task." From here the vista stretches far to the sounding Sea and you will come to know it well, to re-member your place and time and weave these words into y/our story's gift to the planet. ~ Namaste'

Chapter 9

Commit yourself to joy and you will see that it brings you out, takes you to the doorstep of others, calls forth your words, your power, your wisdom.
~ Jan Phillips, New Year's 2008, Museletter

New Year's Day 2008 held a view of a wondrous year ahead filled with exciting and transformative events, all of which I eagerly and joyfully welcomed. No later than the Fall I would be moving from Unadilla Forks, my home of thirty-two years, to a new, still-unknown address. In June I would be making the first of two extraordinary trips to England, taking part once again in a Soul School weekend in Liverpool, Molly's hometown. The prospect of traveling across the ocean with my Chalice Labyrinth for people to enjoy felt unbelievable at times but was so fabulously real. And though registration was off to a slow start, the third Glastonbury Pilgrimage was set for early October.

There was of course *The Book*, this "mildly intimidating but exciting venture!" as I said of it in a January journal-note. Three Mystery School weekends would bring blessed and supportive community for all these undertakings. *"What is very true is that I am in most excellent company, that the year promises many 'brilliant adventures,' and that by its end I will find myself in a pretty interesting place... somewhere downstream!"*

And by this time I am over halfway along in my Solar Year with its over-arching and potent image of Snake-shedding-its-skin.

A most-timely quote in Jan Phillips' always-inspiring *Museletter* for New Year's offered this challenge: *"Commit yourself to joy and you will see that it brings you out, takes you to the doorstep of others, calls forth your words, your power, your wisdom."*

There were days I circled back to the familiar territory of

nervous uncertainty that I was possibly not up to all of this. No doubt there was something of "performance anxiety" going on, something I only *saw* in hindsight. In my journal entry of January 2nd I mused, *"Much of the success of everything I think rests on my allowing the flow to happen—'show up' and get to work while also embracing the joy that comes along... accepting these gifts."*

The Universe took me at my word with a quite amazing and beautiful *delivery*. Two nights later under a starry January sky holding a potent configuration of the Moon, Venus, and the star, Antares, I am visited by a most profound lucid dream and a door swings open. Sadly, not only does the next morning bring a clear memory of this dream, but news of John O'Donohue's unexpected passing during that night. A young man still at fifty-two, this Jesuit priest and mystic had written *Anam Cara*, a book that had long been a guide to my deeper Self and luminous Inner World.

4th January 2008

I am back in England with my group and we are visiting a small town. I walk along a street beside a river and spot a shop with a sign above the door, "The Medusa Café." I'm much intrigued and enter to find a corridor that leads to a turn and a lighted door. Through the window I see an entrancing gift shop and enter. Behind the counter is the owner who smiles in greeting. She is dark-haired and exotic looking. I admire the gorgeous jewelry which I know is worn to honor the Goddess. The woman gestures to the other side of the shop which is the café. She invites me to have a seat and wishes to serve me a special drink that's just been made.

I sit down at a small table and find a young woman sitting there already. She is dark-haired and dressed in clothes I recognize are of a much-earlier time. We smile at each other without speaking. The shopkeeper comes with cups and saucers and a glass tray on which is the most beautiful array of gelatin-like confections that almost glow. I select a gold one in which I see something that looks like a pale ivory blossom.

Gingerly I take a bite and the blossom crunches like a wafer. I suddenly realize I must go... the group is waiting for me. So I spring up from the table with apologies to both women and rush out of the shop.

I hurry along the street and reach the large parking lot. Our bus is on the other side with everyone already on board. I'm starting across to it when I hear someone calling my name and turn to see the young woman rushing towards me. I am astonished that she's now wearing clothes identical to mine, a yellow polo shirt and khaki pants. When she reaches me she grabs my hand, "Please don't go! I've just found you again!" There is both delight and anxiety in her voice. We are standing so close together that I feel our shoulders touching.

It's a confusing but powerful moment. I tilt my head to look into her dark eyes now feeling I do know her but am not sure how that is. "Do I know you? Did we meet each other last year?" We make a mutual promise to see one another again and reluctantly release each other's hand.

When I wake in the morning the dream encounter is vividly present, the sensation of biting into the confection still on my tongue, and even more immediate, the sense of the pressure of her hand holding mine tightly and of our shoulders touching as we stood so closely beside each other.

It is becoming for me more and more a sense of occupying two lives under this roof where I've lived for nearly thirty-two years. In the more ordinary, daily one, I'm an almost-independent woman still on civil and mostly pleasant terms with Ken, doing household chores as the days come and go, sorting through belongings I will take with me to my unknown new address, keeping up connections with family and friends. And then there's the non-ordinary life spent in my workroom at my writing desk, tapping away on the computer keyboard or filling page after page in my journal with thoughts and reflections. And now in that room the keen sense of another's presence, Angeline's, which has never been more real or more palpable. Going in and out of the door to my room is the crossing of this dimensional threshold.

A week after the Dream, I am so pleased to receive a marvelous epiphany and some inspired guidance in how to maneuver in this now startlingly three-dimensional landscape.

Journal thoughts

… after I eat that odd "confection" at the Medusa shop and café, a vivid sense of eating the dried petals of the ivory flower embedded in the gel, like a crunchy wafer. When I left the café to join the group, A. appeared in modern clothes. Perhaps or likely she'd found a way to come across to me in this time. This would mean it isn't a one-way move or action such as me "going there" and returning "here." She equally curious of me and this time has learned a way or discovered a crossing point. So it's not going to be me simply "looking in" on A.'s life and recording what I see, but of her "coming across" carrying her story with her for me to know and learn.

Message

Flame of the heart's passion, Isis-borne magic instilled so deep within; this magnificent celebration of new journey refreshed from reopened channels. Wings lift, spread, lift me into ecstatic joyous flight. The silver earth-cord is the web with which you weave. Clasp hands in the dance with your laughing, smiling partners. Eyes, sweet lips, amorous connections promised, fulfilled. The path is the lighted emblem, the sweet joy of seeking the profound depths within and the joy and triumph of return. Chalice Light, holder of the flame, resident Spirit dwelling therein.

Beyond these ponderings, I'm guided to seek the insights of the perfect resource, a woman who I know in our Mystery School community. Betty Rothenberger is a wonderful Wise Woman in the ancient and powerful meaning of that term. She has great knowledge of dreams, myth, and archetypes. She responds enthusiastically to my request for a phone call with an initial observation via e-mail that: "Carol, this book is dreaming you!" We set a date for a few days away and I am excited by what further information and secrets will be unlocked through this conversation.

We talk for well over an hour and it is just as rich and inspiring a conversation as I expected it would be. Betty has observed my metaphysical journey and evolution of the past four years and welcomes this opportunity to dive deep with me into what's emerging around this storytelling. Betty gave me something I was in great need of... the absolute reassurance that this was wonderful and important work and that I should not doubt any of it... not one single thing.

The many vivid components of the dream signaled how powerful the story was becoming. The shopkeeper is likely a goddess offering her services to Angeline and me as we enter this deep and most magical work, perhaps even receiving her protection. And there's Medusa's great significance representing woman's unlimited powers. This intimidated some people, often and especially men, so that she was made into a fearsome and threatening figure. "Consider how she's over-lighting your work, Carol... yours and Angeline's."

But perhaps the best of all, Betty explains, is that *The Medusa Café* has been offered up as a perfect place for Angeline and me to meet and share our stories. Spirit has indeed had a hand in this! And it should be possible, she tells me, to return there not just during my dream-time. "Seek this through meditation," she advises, "and have your notebook ready to record your conversations with Angeline."

I chose a red notebook that I'd bought in Glastonbury to dedicate to this writing. Following Betty's guidelines, I sat down at my writing table on January 29th and opened the notebook. For this first attempt, I choose not to try out The Medusa Café, perhaps a little skittish of voluntarily reconnecting with its powerful and magical forces. Instead I enter a light meditative state. I'm given the image of a hearth with a fire burning, one that had been in other dream connections with Angeline. I take some centering breaths to ground myself and begin to write.

29th January: Dialogue Journal

Hello Angeline,

I am here beside our own small fire thinking of you and how you spent so much time beside your own hearth. Fire is an element of strong presence for us both. And our own fiery nature is perhaps shown in our impatience which springs forth too often. By its light we can, I hope, drawn by the courage it also brings, be reassured by its heat and illumination. It also brings me the guidance of an Ancient One who is also Eternal and I am now striving to accept her presence/presents more, not only in this work but in this Life.

I am re-membering the dream where we met so vividly. I think you were in the shop first — maybe that's where you saw me. Was it the food I ate that opened my eyes? The texture of the dried blossom is still on my tongue. Soon after you ran to me before I could get on the bus. "Please don't go!" you said, grabbing my hand. "I've just found you again!" We were both wearing yellow shirts, or more accurately you had put one on that was just like mine.

Forgive me for not knowing you at once because I looked at you intently and said, "Do I know you? Did we meet each other last year?" But you were so familiar… I vividly remember your hand holding mine, our shoulders touching, we were standing so close together.

So what I want to do now as I embrace the memory and reality of our dream meeting is to pledge to you my heart-born promise to write this story, yours and mine. Let us both embrace this adventure so that its gifts of Light will spill out for all who are open to them.

There is just a brief pause and I'm given these first words to record, not Angeline's it seems, but of Another whose important connection to our story I feel…

Within the midst of this, a great burst of love, so much engendered and fostered by grace of this **soul progression**—

Then, unmistakably, I hear words that I know are Angeline's and I write them down rapidly.

Who are we to doubt for one moment the truth of this ever-widening awareness? I live in a time where women's ideas are often questioned, even reviled, if Father [?] is who we are speaking of. It is only the Virgin whose presence envelops the Great Church and which so blessedly softens some of those dour men. So come with me, my sweet friend, and we will share more of these days, yours and mine. I do not know what is more useful to you in your story. I will offer what I can. I sense in you a gentleness. Let us consider this like a deep pool that as we gaze upon it we see reflected back our faces and the sky's deep bowl, but as we gaze longer our eyes allow us a vision deeper down.

And then there is the Holy Well, a place we both know. I live not far from there. I tire and ask of you to withdraw for this night. I dream you as a special angel and give you thanks at returning to me. Let us replace our doubts with faith and speak to each other in the Light.

Respecting her words, I put down my pen and reread the entries marveling at what's begun, thrilled with this first lively exchange. It is more than enough for our initial sharing.

The next day I return to what I'm calling the *Dialogue Journal*, awed by what came through the day before and have a brief but even more powerful experience when not only Angeline speaks to me, but another Presence addresses us both:

Carol: We are both bathed in the Light of this land, though mine is more a deep memory for a good part of this life's journey. The spark of it must continue to be fostered, to be fed. Some very eloquent moments have occurred in this present year as you returned yet again.

Angeline: Those who support your quest held the energy and Circle while the Voice uttering, "Joy!" rose from the sacred ground and into your waiting arms.

Another: [Bar'antha?!] Live with her in her story which is also yours.

The Light of the Land is a powerful, grace-filled presence for you both.

This is the true beginning of your companionship —
Your eyes see with hers, her heart is your heart.

Two weeks later I find the courage to visit The Medusa Café for the first time and begin an entry, but before Angeline can respond I am interrupted by some outside interference from the "real world" and so depart the Café before I can listen for her reply. I close the Dialogue Journal and end the session. Though the progress had been halting, it was increasingly comfortable and exciting to be actively engaging with Angeline in her time. When I ended our session that day it was with every intention to return to its pages soon. For reasons beyond what I understood, a lengthy departure to the outer world was beginning. It would be a full year before the next visit to The Medusa Café.

But I had found the crossing place and had ventured however timidly across the threshold. Events in the rest of my life take over my time and energy.

The rest of the Snake's skin loosens and slips free.

Though it was still Winter, my Guides suggested that it was time to figure out my new address. I'd narrowed down areas to Binghamton in New York's Southern Tier. There was the potential for sisterly-support of several women friends who lived there and the pleasant advantage of being closer to my daughter and grandchildren in Ithaca which was not far from there. The last time I'd been a renter was all the way back in college. Would there be any place where I'd feel at home? And how would it be to live in a city area, even a suburb? It was intimidating at first to call prospective landlords, but after a few calls I got the hang of it. The prospect was daunting but I had to admit felt pretty exciting at moments. Things would work themselves out.

When the few places that sounded at all appealing fell through because they were already rented, I grew a bit discouraged. Then one man I spoke with helpfully suggested I try Craigslist. I went online, and after just a brief search on that site, I came to an ad for a small house for rent in the town of Endicott, a Binghamton suburb. I read the details with rapidly growing interest and clicked on the MapQuest link to see that it was on a short street ending at the Susquehanna River and... wonder of wonders... there was a park very nearby!

A sense of rightness began to sink in as I called the number connecting me at once with the young man who would soon become my landlord. I made plans to drive down to see the place the next day which would be March 30th. I hung up the phone feeling like a kid on Christmas Eve.

Energies of my *Greater Story* were being set into motion that would shift into sudden dramatic clarity the next morning. Four years earlier during my first year of Mystery School on the always-incredible Gifting Night, I'd brought my gifting request to Jean Houston for "a place of my own to write and work." It was my first experience of this, and I was properly awed by people telling me what amazing things happened through Jean's formidable powers of manifestation. So when she said in response to my request, "Keep on looking down the River..." I took her at her word. On my drives south along the Unadilla River Valley I had looked... and looked... but nothing substantial had ever come of it. In truth, I'd nearly forgotten all about it. But this was about to change!

This still hadn't crystallized as I set out on the 90-mile drive the next morning, a wonderfully mild and sunny early Spring day. Nearing Endicott, I took the exit off NY 17 and drove across the bridge over the Susquehanna River. I reflected on how I'd followed the Unadilla River downstream and how it was a tributary of this larger river. Leon had told me that when I crossed the bridge I'd see Round Top Hill a little ways further, my destination. And there it was, its rounded tree-topped shape rising from the river's edge.

Suddenly I was electrified with the memory of Jean's prediction years earlier that the place I sought was *waiting down the River*. My hands began to tremble on the steering wheel.

A few minutes later I climbed the steep steps following Leon and saw the brown-shingled, steep-roofed little house waiting for me, tucked cozily against the flank of Round Top Hill. Just as we reached the door, Leon stopped and gestured behind us. "Check out the view of the River from here." I turned and saw the Susquehanna's vast silvery expanse flowing straight towards us. I managed to say something like, "Wow! Beautiful!"

How totally extraordinary... my search was over. I'd found my new home.

A little over two weeks later on my 59th birthday, I claimed this sweet place as mine. With the help of my moving-team, Ken, Justin, and Tracy, we moved my things in. And because it was my birthday, when we finished we drove over to the neighborhood *Friendly's* for celebratory ice cream desserts and I was sung a round of *Happy Birthday* led by Ken. Then we hugged goodbye and got into our respective vehicles. They drove off back towards Binghamton. I caught sight of Ken's truck and Justin and Tracy's station wagon moving away down the street.

I paused at the parking lot's exit with my blinker clicking and thought, "Well, if this is going to be hard, it's right *now*." I pulled out onto the street towards Round Top Hill feeling just wonderful.

Letting myself back into the cottage, I went around the rooms taking photos with my digital camera. Upstairs in the large open room with its slanted ceiling, I snapped a picture from the top of the stairs and crossed to look out the window to the River below. I took a photo of the room from that angle and went back across to the stairs. Something nudged me to check the viewfinder. And there they were. Three energy orbs floating right in the middle of the room that all but winked at me in the viewer. "Oh my!" I gasped, looking up, feeling at once the sense of welcome. Whoever these lovely Beings or Energies were, I was being warmly received.

In those first weeks as I set up housekeeping the little house seemed to wrap itself around me. I thought the name Riverside Cottage suited it well. But not long into the Spring I received its true name... Dragonfly Cottage.

Through the first months of my new independence I led a very happy gypsy life with trips to visit a good friend in NYC, attending a Mystery School reunion in the Catskills, and most magically, flying to Liverpool, England for June's Soul School gathering. I hadn't been able to attend the second one in Ireland, but it felt strongly destined that I be a part of the third and final one, joining forces again with Louise and Molly.

The experience from beginning to end was magickal in more ways than could be counted. There is space for only a little of the story. As was true two years earlier in Minnesota, a fabulous group had chosen to take part in the weekend-long program at Hope University. Many had attended the previous two and were eager to be a part of this concluding gathering.

I was teamed up with a wonderful young woman from Ireland who led us in sacred movement exercises and we incorporated the labyrinth into several of these. Our large meeting room opened onto a courtyard where the most lovely tree stood. During breaks people enjoyed going outside to spend time with its friendly presence and in the balmy June sunshine which blessed the weekend. I'd set up the labyrinth next to the windows so people could enjoy the tree while they walked. It wasn't long before we began to notice how the tree responded to our presence, its leaves trembling visibly when people took note of it, and with no sign of any breeze to have caused this. When we walked into the room both mornings its leaves quivered in friendly greeting. After the first labyrinth walk I was delighted when the tree sent me a message that it was especially pleased to "share my energy" when we were walking the labyrinth.

In other magickal matters, I became very aware of how happy the Chalice Labyrinth was to be a part of Soul School again. Some people in the group had never walked a labyrinth, and as was always true, I was deeply honored to facilitate their first experience. After a walk on Saturday we gathered in a circle to share experiences. One young man spoke with amazement and grateful tears of how his departed father had joined him on the labyrinth and how they had walked it together.

Our Soul School experiences grew richer and more profound as the weekend went along. It was during the last labyrinth walk on Sunday morning when they reached a peak that no one would ever forget. There was a lovely older couple there, close friends of Molly's, who were much enjoying everything. The woman (whose name I wish I remembered) got about with the aid of a walker. She loved learning about the labyrinth and had enjoyed watching the rest of us walking it. After everyone had finished, I'd persuaded her to take a short walk. Two of us helped smooth out the labyrinth's canvas as she slid the walker slowly along.

A contemplative labyrinth walk was to be one of the last things we would do together. The courtyard tree shimmered its welcome as the music began. People quietly formed a line awaiting their turn to enter the path. I took up my post at the entrance, welcoming each one. Several gave me a hug before they set off. And as I regularly do, I circled the perimeter a time or two honoring and amplifying the rising energies. By the time there were only a few people still waiting to walk, I was quite deeply absorbed in the work. I began to make a last circuit to the left around the outer edge when I felt an electricity rise near at hand. I turned and nearly gasped to see the final three people who were entering the Chalice Labyrinth together. It was this beautiful woman with two of her friends. She had her hands on the shoulders of the woman walking ahead of her, the other woman following close behind. The metal walker had been left beside her chair.

I stopped where I was, summoning all my facilitating skills to assist them in whatever way was meant to be, knowing the holiness of what was taking place. The three moved slowly along together, haltingly but powerfully navigating the curves and turns. Around the room everyone offered their own silent witness, all of us mesmerized by what was happening on the labyrinth. It was one of the most incredible sights I'd ever beheld in all of the walks I'd ever facilitated. And perhaps what was most extraordinary was sensing how the Chalice Labyrinth literally raised protective energy around them, steadying and supporting her all along its path to center and return. If there was anything even more wonderful, it was her radiant face and smile to all of us when she and her friends emerged together.

After these marvelous days of Soul School, I could nearly have flown home without benefit of an airplane. And the thought that I'd be returning to England in October with a third pilgrimage group almost felt too good to be true. But before then there was lots to enjoy in my new home in this first Summer beside the beautiful Susquehanna River.

I happily explored the trails along the River and all the many delights awaiting me on Round Top Hill with its several paths and pleasant town park where I often went to write. I much enjoyed observing people walking their dogs, families on picnics, or like me, just enjoying the beautiful surroundings.

Adjusting to my new small town life was proving much easier than I'd ever expected it to be, though a few things were harder to take. From the start I missed terribly the country nights with their dark starry skies and resented the intrusion of streetlights. It was some comfort that the wooded hillside behind the cottage at least shielded me from some of this "light pollution." And then there was the nearly constant hum of traffic on Route 17, barely a half-mile away. But I found that if I woke between 3 and 5AM, it was almost completely quiet with only the insects' chirring holding forth in the Summer night. When I woke into this blessed stillness, I'd hold onto that comforting quiet for a while before falling back to sleep.

By late July the minimal interest in the Pilgrimage scheduled for early October had me pretty discouraged, especially since the other two had gone so well. The busy-ness of this first solo Summer was also making it a challenge to find time for my usual spiritual practices. Needing to sort things out, especially around the Pilgrimage, on the day of the August New Moon, I sought the council of my Guides.

1st August 2008

Dear Guides, Dear Teachers,

What message would you have me know? What further clarity do I need on this path I have chosen, and as I have opened my heart to this way of being...

Dear One, Dear Heart,

So it is not so much answers you seek but reassurance of the soundness of your decisions in this past year, and without any doubt, this has gone exceedingly well even with the labor of grief and perceived anger. No rendering of negative attitude, words, but what was endurable. It is a necessary growth for all and timely (beyond what you indeed know) for your growth, "evolution" as you like to call it. Such a sacred transformation of Essence come to bear on the Truth of what brings you here in this Life. Some will continue their judgmental chatter but your precious cottage holds you safe, shelters you from unwanted contacts. Do not look to take on any further energies of others — you need the openness of your unfettered spirit life to make the crossings that are coming. Be chary of your communication from this New to Full Moon. Rely on the River, the Hill, and the Trees for company and their shy citizenry. Boldness of spirit is what is called for and you possess the knowledge of how to call upon that.

Yes, settle business matters during designated hours, a patrin or two will offer evidence of your whereabouts. Your work now requires a pure vein, a clear flow. So very much is dependent upon this simple truth: that you exercise your power of choosing separateness. You have gained and gleaned much wisdom in this past year. Do not yet rule out time in Glaston—put forth your request. On this turn of the Spiral, you are opening to the full magnificence of your Journey. Trust in the fullness and celebrate its joy. You are buoyed by its flood tide, now and always.

This powerful reassurance and clear advice helped me to continue to look into creative options and weigh my decision about going ahead with the Pilgrimage or not. I contacted the people at Chalice Well to discuss things which led to canceling the group reservation but happily with the agreement that I could come for my own retreat week in October. And I also set new dates for a group to come in 2009, a satisfactory resolution for all concerned. So the way had opened for my first solo trip to Glastonbury, something I'd dreamed about but never thought would happen. My Guides, I knew, were surely smiling.

So just six weeks later, the plane set down smoothly at Bristol Airport in the bright morning sunshine. Somewhat groggy as always from the night flight from Newark, the public transport connections were all familiar ones and soon I was on the First 376 bus speeding across the Somerset countryside. The Tor beckoned as we came down from the Mendips and minutes later I stepped off at the top of the High Street and set off towards Chalice Well wheeling my suitcase. Jet lag didn't dampen how deliciously extraordinary it was to be shown to my room in Little St. Michael's by Jenny, the lovely housekeeper.

Once settled in a bit, I hurried into the Garden to visit all the Tree-Beings and special places, drinking deep of the cold water flowing from the Lion's Head. Up in the Meadow I sat on the swing seat and gazed at the Tor rising steeply above Chalice Well, feeling the welcome it signaled. I was Home once more with eight magical days stretching before me. I knew my time here was a priceless gift and that my goal was to remain open to whatever experiences were coming my way.

Spirit's words echoed, *On this turn of the Spiral, you are opening to the full magnificence of your Journey. Trust in the fullness and celebrate its joy. You are buoyed by its flood tide, now and always.*

The first morning dawned bright but with thick mists cloaking the land. Yes, indeed, the Mists of Avalon! I set off as soon as I could to climb the Tor, the foggy whiteness swirling all about me obscuring all but the path leading upwards. It was early and I doubted there would be many people out yet. The strong but invisible sun warmed me despite the morning's dampness.

Reaching the top, I found the cattle herd lying down all around Michael's Tower and I stepped carefully around these large, gentle creatures to go inside. I looked up into its roofless height to see three white doves sheltering high up against the still-gray sky.

More than once I'd heard described how magic it is to be on the Tor when the mists clear. How marvelous that I was about to experience this! I leaned back against the Tower facing the still unseen sun and waited for its coming. A few others came up the path and quietly joined the vigil. Maybe fifteen minutes passed and then, imperceptibly at first, the thick mists became gauzier, and then glimpses of the Levels started to appear through sudden openings. More of the Tor came into view and wide swaths of bright blue sky appeared above us. Then came a sudden lifting away of the floating mists and in moments it just vanished altogether.

Apart from this disappearing act, I could not believe the intensity of the colors of every part of Glastonbury's landscape spread out before us. I stared and stared, truly dazzled by this bejeweled radiance, the sense of enchantment enveloping me completely. I lingered for a while longer, watching it slowly transform to more ordinary shades and tones of the Somerset

Levels, and then made my way back down to Chalice Well.

What Spirit seemed to have planned were several memorable encounters at Little St. Michael's. Because my group's reservation had been canceled, there was opportunity for other people to come for their own private retreats. I met Stuart when I first arrived, a lovely young man from Scotland who was there for a short stay. No others were about that first night, and so our hours-long conversation over supper was uninterrupted and we shared expansively about our lives and what had drawn us to Glastonbury. It was also the night of the Full Moon. We felt called to go into the Garden and sit beside the Well together for a long quiet time, offering our unspoken prayers and welcoming whatever messages were seeking us in that ancient, sacred Place. It remains one of the most memorable times I've ever spent in Avalon.

Stuart was on his way a day later and we exchanged warm hugs, promising to stay in touch. Others were due to arrive by afternoon. By then I'd started considering that whoever arrived was somehow part of my unofficial 2008 Pilgrimage group. I'd long subscribed to the truth that there are no accidental meetings! Polly arrived, a retreat at Chalice Well a gift to herself for her 60th birthday. She was so grateful that the vacancy had occurred after all, but was sorry for the circumstances. "Not that I'm happy that your group didn't come together for you, Carol," she said, "but I'm really so glad that I could be here for this!" I assured her that it was all exactly as it was meant to be and happy to help celebrate her significant birthday with her.

And there was John, a man who'd come to ponder some major transitions in his life. Our encounter at Chalice Well would spark a lasting friendship, and he was to become key to a truly incredible experience with Angeline when I returned the next Summer.

Rounding out our number was a couple who had interesting ties to Chalice Well, Sandy and Bruce Stuart. Over our meals together in the dining room, they told us some of the history of the formation of the place from the days of Wellesley Tudor Pole, a charismatic figure in Glastonbury, and particularly to Chalice Well. There were also tantalizing hints of the spiritual work they themselves did. In turn they were curious about my background and what had drawn me to Glastonbury both personally and for the pilgrimage work. I was pleased and honored by their interest.

Nearing the last of our days together we were finishing breakfast one morning when Sandy said that they'd like to offer me a channeling session. I was thrilled and we agreed to meet shortly later in the meditation room on the top floor of Little St. Michael's. It had been designed by Wellesley Pole in the 1950s and was a space that hummed with ethereal energies that I'd experienced more than once.

They are waiting for me when I enter the room, and quickly I understand what it is they do together. Bruce channels the Spirits and Beings who wish to come through and Sandy serves as a facilitator of the session. Bruce was sitting quietly, eyes closed, establishing contact with his Spirit-Guide, Master Chew. Once I'm settled comfortably, Sandy tells me with a smile that an unusually large number of Guides have already "formed a queue" to have the chance speak to me. I sit really still looking at her as she says this, and prepare myself to be completely open to what's to come. The power of it is already rising around us.

With a whimsical smile Bruce began to speak in Master Chew's soft, accented voice. We all three slip together into kairos time. Later in the day I find a quiet place to write a long journal entry about the morning's profound experience:

"In addition to the message itself, Sandy and Bruce told me I work with many strong Beings and that I am quite a strong Spirit, that there are not that many at this level. All of this adds significantly to my self-awareness and strengthens my self-identity. I was told that I entered this life at an advanced level of *spirit feeling* and recognized this very early… yes. So to negotiate the 'small discomforts' that life brings, my knowledge of how to 'gather spirit into bundles' helps me to draw on this resource when I need it.

I'm not sure exactly why they chose to offer me this session, but in part it seems my Guides wanted this more direct interaction with me while I'm here on this solo pilgrimage. The sheer number of them was 'what explains it,' Sandy said (and smiled). When Master Chew came in, he said how very crowded it was and that a queue was forming. His gentle humor set the warm and upbeat tone that characterized much of the session. 'I've just gotten out of my bed!' he tells me with a chuckle, yawning.

Once order was established, the one I know as Michael the Archangel spoke first, offering how loved I am by them all and honored for my journey and work. Bruce later described him as of noble bearing... his voice was familiar, deeply resonant with warm overtones. He spoke of my life as always attuned to spirit and rich awareness, and that my insights into this journey were and are to be trusted. And of course to know how *they* all are present to me always.

Then he said, 'Two are come to give you this cloak. Now you will feel it placed around your shoulders. It is made of the finest feathers.' (Oh yes! Oh yes! How I felt its gentle weight so lovingly draped upon me.) 'The feathers are of all the colors. This is how we see you, as a bright rainbow! This cape is to comfort you and also for protection when you need it.'

He then indicated the next Guide approaching... 'One of the Moon,' he told me. I felt her tall and gentle presence standing there before me. She told me her name, Warm Water. By then Sandy prompted me to open my eyes so that I might catch glimpses of the *Over Shadow* on Bruce as he spoke.

Warm Water was majestic in her presence with goddess energy deeply vibrant, her voice wise, loving, and ancient. Her presence enfolded me as she asked, 'What questions do you have for us?' I spoke of the story and the woman of my past life, of this present work Angeline and I were doing together. 'Ah!' said Warm Water. 'We heartily agree to its importance!' She holds up a large crystal which I have some sight of through my half-open eyes. 'Your human journey is like this crystal. It is beautiful but raw and rough to begin. With each life (she makes a downward motion with one hand) a side of the crystal is cleared and polished. Another life (she turns the crystal, sweeps down her hand again) another place is polished.' She studies me for a moment to see if I understand, then continues. 'Your writing comes to you as a... (she pauses, pantomimes a pen moving) takes you into a flow, and there is then a spiritual experience for you – yes!' I agree with her wholeheartedly.

Her departing words are these... 'We see you soon rising as a person who is important to many people in the world.'

Another feminine Guide comes forward. As I write this now, I feel this was and is my dearest Guide Edna-thael for she tells me, 'You may think of me as a Sister-of-the-Heart, for so we are.' It's clear she and I have been together through many lives. She speaks of our being strong women, that 'Men will push in and announce their good intent. But we do not need them! We are strong women who care for each other; who can cry when we need to in each other's arms; and also share each other's joys. We do not need men to complete us in any way.'

Sandy then asks Edna-thael to give me the crystal she's brought to the session. I see the tall womanly figure extend her hand to take the smooth salmon-pink agate from Sandy. Then I open my hand for this gift. She bends down to me. When our hands touch it is quite emotional for both of us and the magic of it glimmers between us for a long moment.

Not long after, Master Chew returns and notes the presence of Wellesley Tudor Pole and Joseph of Arimathea. They both wished to meet me, saying they are honored and wish to affirm my work. And with that Master Chew draws the session to its close."

When the session ended and we three returned to our 21st

century selves, Sandy and Bruce gave me huge hugs sharing heart-to-heart energy that shimmers still as a most brilliant marker on my Path. The only words I can find to say are a simple thank you, but their warm smiles let me know it is enough.

Spirit's gift of this eight-day "solo pilgrimage" had already been filled with wonderful and extraordinary experiences. And whenever I look back on this magical hour with Bruce and Sandy my gratitude for what they offered me that morning knows no bounds.

Chapter 10

That stone path you can see from the road,
its forks lead nowhere you know
but everywhere you've been calling to
from your wild heart.
~ from *The Small Song*, Lauren de Boer

And so for the second time that year... wonders never cease! ... I fly home from England to Dragonfly Cottage waiting for me on Round Top Hill. It does not escape my notice that, like Glastonbury Tor, I now am closely connected to another magical hill. My solo pilgrimage to Chalice Well with all the incredible encounters and profound experiences had been one of both deep healing and an invitation to allow further transformation of who I was in the world.

More and more I understood that I was completing the grounding I sought in my newly-chosen path as a woman on her own, complete in her own company and Self. Somewhere in my metaphysical studies I had come across the true meaning of the word "alone." Its full meaning is "all one" which affirmed what I was both experiencing and feeling in this solitary and richly satisfying new life.

In those first months on Round Top Hill very seldom am I anything other than delighted in the quiet ways I can pursue my days. Even the most mundane things I do puttering around as I fully settle into this magic wee house enchant me.

My deep gratitude for being here in Dragonfly Cottage knows no bounds in its absolute perfect-ness as a refuge, a sacred space, my creative cauldron, my Hill Home. My psychic and spiritual framework feels filled out and increasingly solid. (12th November 2008)

And it is with great pleasure I am witnessing my first Autumn here, filled with the wonderful sense of now being entirely at home perched high above the Susquehanna. In the outside world a marvelous event occurs with the triumphant election of Barack Obama as our 44th President. The day after the election I go out for a walk along the now familiar path by the river. The trees are all nearly bare of their leaves and the water is running high from recent rains. I come to the bend with its beautiful view of the river flowing off into the west. The late afternoon sun dances in the clouds, their colors and shifting shapes offering gorgeous reflections on the swift current. Round Top Hill rises in its quiet brooding presence, Dragonfly Cottage nestled securely on its side.

A vision and message received in yesterday's meditation replays itself: I saw myself holding my ceremonial hawk wing fan, ready for the work. *"Anchor the light in the hidden hill... a doorway emerging."*

A few days later an intriguing lucid dream visits me as the Moon goes through Aries...

"I am 'awakened' by the sound of a door being opened and shut downstairs and I knew someone was trying to attract my attention. Leaving my sleeping self, I came down, and indeed found a door in the kitchen wall that I hadn't seen before. I'm a bit fearful but pull it open and see a stairs leading down and two shadowy Beings at the bottom looking up at me. We stare at each other and I knew they wished me to descend. And while I was somewhat afraid, I leapt down, my cloak billowing out (likely my feather cloak given to me by the Stuarts) and it felt as if I would merge with these Beings. The lucid feel to this continued. After the leap, I felt myself back in bed and then felt someone... a large presence... sit down near to me. I felt myself partly wake up and did very much feel the weight beside me, but I chose to not go further with the experience and the dream ended."

Plans are going forward with advertising for the 2009 Pilgrimage. Further confirmation for pursuing this next Pilgrimage appears when Spirit gives me the theme for the trip. It's to be called *"A*

Journey of Healing and Celebration." I "entertain the possibilities" of new connections made during my solo-stay at Chalice Well and further ponder the meaning of the session with the Stuarts.

I'm in multiple conversations with the seen and unseen worlds as the Wheel of the Year turns towards the Winter Solstice. Increasingly I rely on help with interpretation of all these *phenomena* through practicing shamanic journeying. My power animals Horse and Snake and human-form Guides are pleased to offer insights and advice anytime I venture to this other-dimensional reality. On the morning of the Winter Solstice I record this journey.

21st December 2008

[I spend a brief time in the Upper World where I'm greeted by St. Germain where I asked that he convey my thanks to my Guides for this year's journey.] Then I was "shooed" back to the Middle World and the path at the base of Round Top Hill. Again the village in the woods, a Winter's day. Then a rapid passing of days and seasons, a blur of beautiful scenes, all at the Hill. Asked H. to be present. Greeted by a beautiful woman who took different appearances. *Are you the Spirit of the Land?* **Yes.** Then to an interior of a tent or lodge where we sit on cushions. Spoke first through signing, then She invited me to touch her heart as She did mine. I was shown a tattoo on my shoulder of a nautilus shell. We go to a waterfall, a spring flowing out of the Hill. We hold our hands in the spray together. Each drop held the image of someone. I was being filled with these images (or baptized). At another point I stepped into the River and merged with its flow going to the sea where I stood on the shore. *This beautiful clear healthy River exists now... know this.*

At one point the Spirit of the Land grew into a monolithic goddess as big as the side of the Hill. Was it She who came and sat on the bed in my dream? Such a large, familiar-feeling presence.

And just into the New Year, 2009 which will mark my 60th birthday, another shamanic journey yields these images and messages as I travel with the question of seeking clarity for my work.

Early January 2009

[Lower World] Conscious of the feather cloak as I enter the tunnel beneath the tree. Sun greets me and I start along the well-worn path. Arrive at a rock to sit on and Snake drapes herself over my shoulder, smiling a greeting. Horse appears. "I am seeking ultimate clarity and grounding for this work," I tell him.

We all travel together and come to a beautiful shore. Coming towards us through the woods are several persons carrying torches. Smiling broadly, G. greets me, says the rest are the Ones of the Earth (Round Hill) honoring the work. Bid to walk into the beautiful clear water. G. takes my cloak and I swim out to a small island with G. paddling beside me in a birch canoe. We stand together on the shore looking out across the still waters. *This is a place apart.* Shown a fall of stardust like the dream image of the Star Card. Further along the shore a mountain lion appears, approaches, becomes Sekhmet who rises powerfully before me and holds me in her benevolent gaze, touches my temples, blesses me. A celebration fire is lit on the shore – dancing – succession of images: glimpse the door to The Medusa Café, Angeline's smiling face; flow of dark red... like menses. Told it is the life force I am to share. All is in readiness. They tell me as I leave that I'm to look for a thread to follow at Dragonfly Cottage.

And through non-shamanic channels, my Guides concur when I ask for an audience with them as the New Year slowly gets underway. "What would you have me know?" I ask, my journal open to a fresh page, my pen ready for the response.

January 2009

Joy – we will start with that – deep dancing Joy, for it is from that rich energy that this book and its journey will grow; will grow beautifully and powerfully. Access points are several, most of which you've explored. You have been in need of all the days of rest, bewilderment at times, effort, as you've so bravely faced the hard passages to this quiet shore. Who better than you knows the labyrinth's path to Source at center? Were you not surprised to see how these long curves and turnings brought you at last fully home to your deep essential Self? Your wisdom has revealed that from this rediscovered firm ground, this centering work, the spiral of this rich path now appears in its clarity before you. Be assured that all of its mysteries and magics await you as you resume the journey which first beckoned to you 7 years ago (a wink of time to many of Us!). Your human journey could not be any more beautiful and you have filled many beautiful journals with news of these adventures! There is no need for regret at anything which you might perceive as a hindrance to reaching this day, this moment of our speaking with you. If there's anything you've learned so very well, it's trusting the whole of certain "processes" to flow, for in that is the truest of energies and the full potency of this star-seeded story. You are a magnificent storyteller. You've been told that by many grateful readers! We are pleased for you! These stories have brought much joy, and yes, healing. Given the quiet of the Winter months stretching out before you, you are in the best possible place to unleash the power of this tale. Yes, let the wonderful exuberance you possess serve you as you embrace the story you came to write and know that the story embraces you. Savor the richness of this moment! We are so very jubilant in our Angel Eyes here with you now.

AND SO IT IS. Blessed be this day in its fullness and joy!

And other wonderful energies are arising in the outer world. On the cold and bright 21st of January the jubilant inauguration of

Barack Obama takes place. Well over a million people gather on the Washington Mall. I join my Endicott sister-in-spirit, Renee, one of the 2006 Trail Blazers, to watch the joy-filled morning on television and we revel in the sense of collective celebration rippling out from Washington, DC.

A week later Chinese New Year brings in the Year of the Earth Ox, my sign. A full month now into Winter, and an old-fashioned, very snowy one it's been so far. I've been at Round Top Hill for nearly the full turn of the year's Wheel, each morning opening my eyes to a sensory feast inside and outside of Dragonfly Cottage. I've experienced the landscape, the Hill, and the River in all its seasonal beauties and forms. And after this gradual adjustment to solitary living, I feel myself comfortably settled in within this community so that calling it "home" sounds and feels genuine. Perhaps I will be staying on into a second year and more, I tell myself. And the idea of that suits me really very well.

Registration for the Pilgrimage is slowly growing, with those signed on quite enthusiastic at the prospect of our journey together in June. For the most part, all the details have been seen to, so only my occasional worries about enough people prey on my peace of mind. It's an aspect of offering the pilgrimages that I never learn to handle with complete ease. Still, I've almost completely overcome the nagging concern that this might be another canceled group.

Mystery School is in its final year and financially it's beyond my ability to attend all three weekends. So this supportive community, nearly irreplaceable, becomes more attenuated as I rely on e-mail connections and the taped recordings of the sessions. It's a comfort that among the Pilgrims to Glastonbury this year are two *Mysterians* from the West Coast.

I remain committed to my spiritual practices, knowing that this grounds and centers me. If I allow it and open to the energies, guidance always comes. Back in Unadilla Forks one day, I walk the snowy Morningside Labyrinth wondering about the writing and work with Angeline. A woman *appears* to my Inner Sight dressed in silvery gray and brings this message:

> *You are a Maiden of the Well... You are to ask Angeline to take you to the Holy Well. Go to meet her tomorrow at The Medusa Café. You have shed much of your burden so that your ears and heart are open to receive the story. You are one of those chosen to be my Voice in this Time as you were before. So you remain and are Now. Yours is an ancient voice—the words and songs will return. The Light of this Love is rekindled!*
>
> *Ga dan cha, oh malay meh no mih la way*
> *May it be, may it be. In praise of all we are in Thee!*
> *Blessed be thy Name, oh wondrous One.*
> *In Joy and Wonderment we are ever Thy precious children*
> *serving the Lighted Way and Threefold Path.*

My snug hillside home with its sweeping views of the Susquehanna steadily flowing past this hill is becoming a cauldron of alchemical growth and on multiple levels. Apart from the wonderful Dialogue Journal sessions with Angeline, I am immersing myself in a powerful book, *Sophia: Goddess of Wisdom, Bride of God*, written by a revered Celtic scholar, Caitlin Matthews. It is powerful fuel for the fire of my becoming, and I pore over its pages, underlining and annotating as I go.

As the Winter weeks pass I am often and gently reminded of my Voice and raising it now. The mysteries of Round Top Hill reveal themselves to me more and more.

5th February: Twilight meditation

... this is a signal hill. Messages are sent along it up from the ocean, carried by the beautiful maiden, River Woman. The land sends messages to the ocean. You can and will learn to serve as interpreter, to meet with River Woman... call to her in Dreamtime... follow the path through the cave you see. Others will learn of the path through your teaching. It is of Old yet ever New. Do not doubt your heritage. This

veil is lifting and full sight is returning to you and also to others. Her Voice grows in your heart — a joyful day awaits the full telling of your pen and your heart's desires. Come forth and serve the Light with all the joy you possess. Namaste'

[She appears on the ocean beach where the River flows into the sea. Her canoe is drawn up on the sand. She gestures for me to get in and we return upriver to this place.]

I heed all this and do my best to absorb all these teachings arriving in their several ways. Two nights after this journey, I am awoken from a powerful dream of Sophia, Lady Wisdom, and ringing in my ears is the book's title, *The Land Abides: Crossing the Luminous Threshold.* I reach for the notebook I keep on my night-stand and hurriedly write this down. Coming fully awake, I stare at the words, elated and mesmerized by this powerful *arrival.* My years as a writer have taught me that when the title of something I'm working on "shows up," that the power of the story is now fully available. It is a glorious moment. Glorious!

Time will ultimately bring another evolution of the book's title, but this day is such a wondrous affirmation of the work of all these many years. With increasing frequency I'm receiving potent insights into what it is Angeline and I are up to in our shared journeying.

12th February 2009: Journal notes

I am aware that she lived in a time when the Goddess was being shunted off or worse by the Church, a time when it was perilous or at least unwise to publicly acknowledge Her. Angeline heard the Voice of the Land. And with others, a few at least, they found ways to protect the flame. This hidden flame, safeguarded by so many good, brave souls, is now arising anew. We are in that time that was but a dream to them – I am Angeline's dream. But as Caitlin Matthews notes, it is far from being received warmly in these times – yes, hostility is not unknown. So in working with Angeline on this shared story, we are celebrating our visions of the Goddess and our love of Her. I see the story as, in part at least, an honoring of these spirited and brave foremothers. It also will be my own story of these widening possibilities of knowing our journeys to be nonlinear and rich with multidimensional experiences, a deepening and broadening of consciousness.

11th March 2009 :: Message ::

... You are giving Voice to the Ancient stories and to those who preserved them in secret and at exceeding danger at times. It was not for themselves alone that they took such risks, but in great hope of sending it forward to you. That you were present as the woman, Angeline, is a truth you encountered upon going home for the first visit in this life-journey. You are rediscovering "paths of Spirit" that you trod with loving familiarity "once upon a sacred time"—consider that some of your Guides and Angelic Helpers were with (are with) Angeline too. They are happy to serve as intermediaries in this unfolding process. They have helped you arrive here at the Luminous Threshold. Angeline has been in its proximity longer and in some ways has known of it longer. You have caught glimpses of one another across its glowing portal and have even ventured to step across to speak a time or two with each other. Don't hold back any longer. The time is ripe, as you say here. Your beautiful lives were meant to entwine and the flowers of each life offer their fragrance, beautiful shapes, and vibrant colors to the world. You are, in both your lives, supported by Infinite Grace. Hesitate no longer to share this Gift fully with the world and with each other... for So It Is.

Blessed Be!

With Mystery School coming to its end, the beginnings of new connections and possible new community appear. As Winter gives way to Spring, the Pilgrimage group continues to come together delightfully reaching seven on my April birthday weekend. And an unexpected connection comes about with noted Light-worker, Sheila Applegate, who lives not far from me near Syracuse. As Spirit does so well, a synchronistic connection links us. She works with Mary Magdalene and when she learns about my work in Glastonbury, Spirit takes a hand almost at once.

When we meet in person on a sunny April afternoon, a plan to offer a workshop at Chalice Well emerges. Her more extensive spiritual teaching experiences are key and my enthusiasm provides the fuel. My England friend, John, is invited to join us and things easily fall into place with dizzying speed. He and I had already planned to get together in June after the Pilgrimage, and now we'll also have the chance to work on our August event.

This happy ferment brings me to my 60th birthday and the vibrant conclusion of my Saturn Return year. At times I'm quite giddy with all of it. A few days before my birthday I record these thoughts...

9th April 2009

This year, completed in its fullness in five days more, has taken me completely through the work of healing and transforming so many wounds and disabled parts of myself... my Self... and with both outer and Inner Sight that I am now in and have activated conscious equal partnership with the Divine. And I am keenly aware of my desired goals and dreams AND possess both the knowledge and conviction of how each and all of them will be realized. And to this I say Hallelujah and Blessed Be!!

It's quite the festive time turning 60. For the day itself I make the 12-hour drive to my cousin Mary's home in Detroit. Her brother, Bill, comes from Montana. By interesting coincidence he and I were born the same day. Though I liked to joke that I was slightly younger being born hours after he was near midnight, nearly on April 15th. With the considerable distance separating us and sparse communication, it would be only our second time ever seeing each other, the last time when we were just little kids. It felt perfect to celebrate our Big Day together.

April 14th is every bit as much fun as I expected it to be with quite a lovely gift from my Guides and Angels. The night before I have a Flying Dream and a marvelously lucid one in which I knew my powers without question and flew about huge rooms with great joy. When I wake on my birthday morning in Mary's guest bedroom, I smile at the still very vivid sensations of the dream which linger through the whole day... such a special present transporting me into my 60th year.

With May Day's arrival, Beltane, the final countdown to the June Pilgrimage begins with such palpable excitement, more so than any previous trip. I will be traveling there two days early with one of the group, my childhood friend, Kathie. She is, if anything, more excited than I am about the adventure. And a date is now set for John and I to get together after the Pilgrimage group leaves. The magnitude of experience of that day is yet to be revealed.

And Angeline and I have hopeful plans for our own rendezvous. The Year of the Ox has brought my renewed commitment to return more frequently to The Medusa Café. A distinctive shift is taking place from being the *novelist* to Angeline's story to becoming confidants of one another. Instinctively I trust this evolving and increasingly intimate link knowing that the book will also evolve to encompass this unfolding mystery. With our connection now well established through the pages of the Dialogue Journal, the threshold that links our two lives grows more and more luminous.

Chapter 11

Angeline's Story

Chapter 1, Conclusion

Though the actual writing work is far from steady, my faith in this unfolding narrative grows more certain with each visit to The Medusa Café. It is such a marvel to converse with Angeline! But aside from this dialogue, my novelist instincts had me wanting to explore more of her life story. So making use of the techniques I've relied on before, I slowly am adding more to this expanding computer file. What is different is that Angeline isn't the typical character. There's often a sense of teamwork as she shares more of her life. And when the story does open up to me, the details are as vivid as the morning on the Tor in those first few minutes after the Mists lifted and vanished revealing the otherworldly scene of Glastonbury stretched out below in the luminescent light.

The Wheel of the Year goes round, sometimes when you scarcely notice, and there it is, nearly late Autumn when you swear you just began picking the blackberries ripe and heavy in the hedges. And so my belly swelled with the little boy, David, and his birth night seen through much as was just passed with Hazel and Nellis. That afternoon I'd gone down to the village to buy flour and such, not aware that the little one was so close to wanting to come. I was on my way home, climbing the steep part of the lane not far from Mara's, when a pain gripped me. I cried out and she hurried to me at the sound arriving in time to witness the birth waters running down my trembling legs. She sent her good husband to fetch Joseph and led me into her home.

When the long hours ended and she placed the quiet child to my breast, he took a little of what I had for him, but his tiny fingers clutching my one grew weaker and slipped at last into a tiny curled fist as the last of the sun left the room. Joseph let out a great groan and clutched us both against him. Mara left us alone until our weeping ended, and then came and took our little son. I fell into a fever that kept me in another place for many days, but not before I kissed his little face and watched Joseph walk from the room carrying the little bundle, much as I saw Nellis do in the dark of last night.

They brought me home in their wagon to our house and the loving care of both Joseph and Mother Ann. Mara came every day that first week, staying when my fever-raging was at its worst. But my decision not to tread that path again did not occur for some months more.

Joseph's mother and I grew close in those weeks. She spent long hours beside my bed, giving me the possets and warm drinks I needed made from herbs grown in her own large garden. When at last I knew the world clearly again, I was helped out to a seat under the grape arbor and I watched her as she worked with her plants. So that was how I came to understand the powers and magics of our Mother's weedy treasures given us so freely. I think it possible that had I not had this place to be, with Mother Ann for company and for my teacher in this, I might well have gone on with our son, leaving Joseph to mourn us both.

Once I regained strength and walked on my own again, with Mother Ann to tend to the household duties, I was free to wander the fields. Sunk in grief, dark moods often beset me for much of that summer. The only relief was walking the meadows and sitting at the edge of the woods beneath the friendly trees. As a child I had done such woods-wandering, and once again it gave me sweet comfort to be back again in such green and loving arms.

One quite warm afternoon I sought the shade of an ancient oak of whom I had grown very fond, and lying against his great and sturdy trunk, I fell into a deep sleep. What came to me in a clear dream was a woman who spoke in the sweetest voice and manner. In words like notes the birds sing, she told me something of who I was and that David was to be my only child in life... *in this life.* Even as I wept in my dream, she reached a gentle hand to me and brushed the tears away, her touch as warm as the summer breeze. "Angeline, I will bid you come in good time. For now, rest and be well." With my dreaming eyes, I turned to watch as she moved away into the woods, her long and dark cloak sliding across the grass.

With a gasp I startled fully awake, hearing a soft rustling near at hand. Something moved in the bushes. Then, so quietly she might have been a waking apparition, a roe deer with her fawn stepped into the meadow barely a stone's throw from me. She knew I was there, and a long moment passed as she regarded me with her large eyes, connecting us soul to soul it seemed. She touched the nose of her babe with hers and then she led him along the edge of the meadow until both disappeared from my view.

Enchanted as I was with this apparition, it was then that I tasted on my lips the salt of my tears.

Like precious beads on a thread, I placed this experience safely within along with what had taken place on Michaelmas when Joseph and I were first together. From that day my spirits lifted, and Joseph and Mother Ann were happy I'd at last shaken off my grieving. My full strength returned and I once again could do all that was expected of me in the house and fields. From my days spent with Mother Ann in her garden, I much desired to learn all she could teach about the plants and so we spent happy hours working side by side.

An odd thing began to take place in Mother Ann's garden (that I had begun to think of as somewhat mine too). A planting of Lady's Mantle languished sadly along the wall-side bed. I had been devoting time tenderly caring for it and her neighboring plants. One morning something urged me to dig up and place two of these in different arrangement, one to the west, and one to the east. This I did without gaining permission from Mother Ann, wondering at my boldness.

By then as I was doing more work with the herbs, she spent less time there and more tending household tasks, an unspoken trading of our woman's work. Days of rain followed and kept us both inside. When the sun returned one morning we came together into the garden. Mother Ann gasped, pointing to the Lady's Mantle that now, in some miraculous manner, displayed new and vigorous leaves and surprising size. I stood beside her, nearly as astonished, and shyly pointed out how I'd rearranged the plants on either side.

"And how did you know to do that?" she'd asked, more curious than angry, I thought.

"Something just urged me to do so," was all I could answer, wanting only to be honest.

She said nothing for a moment, me standing meekly as a young girl at her side awaiting a possible scolding for a misdeed. Then she smiled down at the plants at our feet. "Well," she said in a contented voice, "it seems you've made the Lady's Mantle most happy by these new arrangements."

Mara came to visit soon after desiring to know how I was faring and also to acquire some of Mother Ann's herbs as she did from time to time. She announced herself as very pleased at my returning vigor. Mother Ann spoke with pride of my work in the garden and how quickly I was learning herb lore. As she was busying herself making tea and a sweet cake for us to enjoy, Mara and I walked together to the garden to gather the herbs she required.

Mara exclaimed at my handiwork among the beds, seeing for herself what Mother Ann had told her about the Lady's Mantle. We filled her basket with many fragrant flowers, stems and leaves, all the while with her sharing its uses for pregnancy and birthing.

We sat upon the garden bench beneath the grape arbor. It was there that Mara first gently spoke to me of otherworldly things.

She inquired if I had been visited with any strange dreams. With some hesitation I shared the one that came to me under the oak in the upper meadow. As I spoke of what the dream woman said to me, fresh tears rose in my eyes. "Could this be true, Mara, that I am not to have other children?" I did not speak the words I'd heard: "... *in this life.*"

Drying my tears lovingly, she told me she *knew* of my dream. Seeing my wonderment, she spoke of how the Lady visited her with word of me and instructed her to offer friendship and guidance to me in these sacred matters, as I now know them to be.

I still can recall clearly the feel of the hot summer sun on my head and shoulders that had found its way between the arbor's leaves, and the pattern of light and shadow it made on our faces. Seeing that I followed her words and was awakening to their full meaning, she gently explained how it would be that I would not again conceive a child, and that Joseph himself would come to accept that this was so.

"Mother Ann will understand these things truly," Mara told me, and took my hands in hers. And then, in words I will forever hear in my heart, she said, "She who visited you that day has called you to other work in this life. Of that work you need have no fear, and in its doing you will find great joy."

When we returned to the cottage, our conversation returned to more ordinary matters, so much so that I wondered if the conversation in Mother Ann's garden had actually taken place. But when Mara departed and I walked to the gate to say farewell, she touched my forehead gently with the palm of her hand, invoking the blessing I now know so well, and I felt the tingling of its blessing flow through the roots of my hair and warmly down my spine.

Returning to the cottage, I found Mother Ann humming as she tidied the table from our tea.

It has been nearly ten years of learning and deepening my wisdom in these things of spirit. The path that I have followed has not always been clear nor safe. In Mother Ann, though we seldom spoke of these matters, I knew her to be allied with the course newly opened to me that day in her beautiful garden. The months I spent with David growing beneath my heart and his all too brief stay upon this earth brought me the gift of a rich and enduring friendship with my husband's mother. And for several years more we three lived in peaceful harmony. Though she has been gone from this green Earth for many years, I often sense her gentle presence in the garden or in my work space that was once her bed chamber.

Chapter 12

The breeze at dawn has secrets to tell you.
Don't go back to sleep.
You must ask for what you really want.
Don't go back to sleep.
People are going back and forth across the doorsill
where the two worlds touch.
The door is round and open.
Don't go back to sleep.
~ Rumi

Once I'd ventured back across the threshold of The Medusa Café, it hadn't taken long for us, Angeline and me, to grow comfortable with each other and this remarkable connection. With each session it feels more natural to sit at the table by the windows in Dragonfly Cottage with our Dialogue Journal open and act as "Recording Secretary" of our animated conversations. The Dark Lady is always on hand to welcome us and quietly assists the flow of this extraordinary work. And when we're not deep in conversation at the Café, I continue to learn more of Angeline's life and devote time to recording more of this too.

Dialogue Journal: 11th February 2009

[My words are in regular type, Angeline's begin with italics]

... You'll remember this lucid dream and how you ran after me when I abruptly left the café. I promised I would return. Betty Rothenberger has urged me to come back to the café, so I am doing so today. Please come and join me here! The décor is marvelous. Our Hostess won't mind if we sit here together for a long while. She welcomes us both. There are things here which are both old and new, but all are ageless.

Hello Sister, for that is how I sometimes now think of you. The

Angels have sent dreams of our meeting and that we might be as one. This has puzzled me, but again I am told this can be trusted and that all is well. We are in each other's dreams – I know this strongly. My mother, bless her soul, once told me of a strange dream she dreamed of me. It was when I was a little girl, the child myself, in her dream. She called me from my play, and finding no sight of me, called out to the trees in the garden, "Where is my darling girl?" A gusty wind drew her forth and into a forest where an unknown path showed itself to her. She drew her cloak around her and ran along it to where it opened on a lane with a stone wall alongside it. She heard my voice and another speaking in turn. Without sound she crept to the wall and looking over espied me in a garden of bright flowers. I was sitting on a wooden bench and there with me was a tall woman in an odd dress and more strange, a brightness about her person so that my mother thought her an angel. And I at ease and laughing, then looking up to see her, my mother, which frightened the woman who slipped from view. That was how she told the dream to me many years later.

I had not thought of this for a long while. And now, recalling her words, this dream of hers might have been of you. There is also the memory of myself as a little girl – and even a bigger girl of twelve and thirteen, talking to my fairy-friend when I rambled alone in the summer meadows or did the work I was sent to do in the garden. Although there are fairy folk (as Mara has shown me), it is you who have been along the hedges too. My mother would lovingly tease me for these daft tales and so one day told me of the dream which I have shared.

The joint of it is this for me… that we now have come together into this waking dream.

… Yes, my Sister, and we have so much to share both in joy and in truth.

18th February 2009

Hello again, my Sister. It is good to be with you and feel you near. What would you like to know? And I am curious as to how you think of me.

Dear friend, as I was drawn here this day, it was as I was listening to the morning birds, those that call as the sun rises to greet the day. No matter, when it is you are in your time, I am certain you love the birds and their singing too. I feel this strongly in my heart now. I may soon share this with Mara, since we speak of such things as Angels and fairies. I do know some fairy folk and thought you perhaps one of them. But with the dreams visiting, and more and more, you are other than they. Oh, what then shall I call you other than as Sister to me?

In this life I was given the name Carol. I am whispering this in your heart's ear with my heart's voice. Some think of birds singing when they hear this name. And, yes, like you, I do love birds. I live and have lived all my earth-years where there are many birds.

Would I know the place where you dwell? Have those who connect our lives through theirs remained in this country?

I dwell across the wide ocean in a land to the West. Those who connect us in body came here on ships and found a beautiful land offering a good life. Most sadly the gentle people whose homes they found were horribly mistreated in settlement times. I am of an age where this awful business – especially the despoiling of the Earth's treasures – all of this has left wounds of land and peoples. While all from your days to mine bear some measure of blame, it is most often the men who cause the harm. But I came into this life to help bring about the work of healing and restoring the Earth to its full beauty and abundance. Some of this is sad to share with you. But even with the harm done, you would find this place of much beauty and goodness. My Sister, I sense that as we walk more of the path together, you will see and understand this time.

It is something true, my senses tell me. I am sad to hear of the harms done to the peoples of that land. Those of Eire have stories of bountiful, rich lands beyond the shining seas. The farthest land I know of is a place of the hot deserts beside the [Mediterranean] Sea and of the land of Egypt and Palestine. Our Mother's home is there. You know of these places I trust. I tell you this because you know of this land of my birth, and for you I see it as a cradle of the Spirit's journey we share. And I am so very glad to learn that this work of mine goes on in you. It gladdens my heart. It fills me also with a certain joy to know that something of my life goes on past my days. I've always thought this in my heart over and against what the Holy Church teaches to us. And, sister-Spirit Carol, it pleases me to know we share a woman's form in our two lives. I seek to know more of what that is for you in your time. There are certain sufferings of this lifetime for us as women that I pray have passed away. But we have our deep secrets still in our hearts, and mine is a strong one.

It is our bond we share as women, and as women who are healers which has stirred this connection into life. I know you will tell me more of your hardships of women in your time. There remains much suffering for women now, but in many parts of the world women live lives of ease and abundance and have full freedom to *be themselves,* to make decisions about how they will live. I have such a life and I am mindful every day of the blessings I enjoy. This freedom and abundance is what allowed me to travel to Glastonbury nearly eight years ago from this country, America. It was the Summer and that is when I learned of you when we met at the crossroads in my vision. I wonder if you have a memory of this?

Ah! Glaston-town... Glastonbury. Yes, of course, it would be there where we would have clearest sense of each other. Mara would know this at once. I would think that within the denser groves below the Tor-hill a place of the fairy opened for you to see me and I you. Mara and I, and a few other wise ones, make ceremony there in honor of our Mother. These are stories I will share soon. I feel certain the beautiful hill (I call it the Shining Hill), the High Tor, called you on your first journey... it would be the call of your home. I feel this *knowing* strongly about you. Tell me, do you love the land as I do?

Oh yes, Angeline... yes! I love the land fiercely. Yes, the High Tor called me and I came home.

The Voice of the Land is still strong there where you are. Perhaps this is the Voice that has called us together as One.

And the Voice of the new country, your America? Is the Voice there as well?

Yes, oh yes, it is. It is somewhat harder to hear, but I am one who heeds its words and its songs. And it is my joy to offer back my own song and words. Thank you for meeting me here this Winter's day, Angeline. We will share more very soon.

In faith, I too am grateful and depart with love for we two in my heart. As my Grandmum would say, "Go with God." Farewell!

And so may it be. Farewell!

16th March 2009

(We first share details of family and celebrate how we claim each other as sisters. Then we pick up the thread of an earlier conversation when A. asked me, "How fares the Lady?")

It seems to me that you know Her in your life, otherwise I do not think we would now know each other.

Anna, it is quite true that I know Her, but what I wonder is if She appears in the same form to each of us. When some speak of Her now, they mean the Mother of the Christ to whom I know part of the Great Abbey is dedicated. Others speak of the Magdalene, the wife and helpmeet of Jeshua, the Christed One. Can you describe the Lady and who She is to you and the others in your time who honor Her?

I will say to you what had been taught to me and what I know. Some of what I tell you is still unfolding its full truth to me. Both the Holy Mother of Jesus and Mary Magdalene were once in human form and had their earthly lives. Here at the Sacred Well, and yes, at the Mother Church, both are praised and loved, but not all feel kindly towards Magdalene and some to my sorrow revile Her. Mara tells me their closed hearts shut out her Presence which is sad to me. But I have not given you all my answer. As I have learned from the Wise Ones (and some of these are Angels), who it is to whom we address our ceremonies and speak thoughts of our hearts is the Great Mother of All, She who dwells in our hearts as She does in both Marys'. And in each of us some part of Her Spirit does abide. But She is also deeply riven (woven) into the Land and within all who are beings upon it! My words lose some of their meaning, but She is for me the sweetness in my life.

Wonderful words from your heart-source, Anna. A question I have to this is whether the Lady is understood as the Great-Mother-of-All by many people in your time. Or is it that more believe only in one or the other of the Marys?

A question for me to ponder more, dear Sister. Truly, the Holy Mother is one sought by many who travel to Glaston Abbey to beseech Her there.

Could you now, with all this shared, tell me which of these wonderful feminine Beings you inquired about of me?

I would hope that all of them are still amongst you. Perhaps it is the Holy Mother who is still worshiped with Her beautiful Son. But this does not give you an answer to your question. In Her many guises – for that is how Mara speaks of this – the One I most revere is of the Magdalene, She of the wifely-bond to Jeshua. It was of her I spoke, Carol. So now I ask you again this day, how fares the Lady?

Oh, Anna, it gives me tremendous joy to tell you She fares most well, and truly this is a time when She is strengthening Her presence more and more, especially to women, but also to greater numbers of men as well.

Oh, Carol, your words do gladden my heart! I was fearful that I would hear of Her diminishment, or worse, that She had been forgotten! There was a long-ago time when Her Mysteries were eminently present here beneath the High Tor, when priestesses performed them daily at the Well, and the land all about the Shining Isles (as this place was then called) was blessed with the Light of these teachings.

And what of these teachings in your time, Anna? Are they still known?

Some of them, yes. She who is called St. Bridget came to be among us and so helped preserve and save certain energies and sheltered those who pledged themselves to the Lady.

Yes. St. Bridget is known and loved to this day. And you were correct in thinking the Holy Mother is revered. It is a complicated time but one full of promise for Her in all Her guises. It is my sense that because of the Magdalene, we... you and I... have sought one another and it is Her blessings that we are together as we are.

Your words sound so very true in my heart, for there I feel them. We will speak more of all these things, and soon. I bid you now Namaste', Carol, my Sister.

And I the same to you, Anna. Namaste'

30th March 2009

An entry made beside the Susquehanna. We talk of trees and the Tor in Angeline's time.

Greetings, Sister... we meet here again by the River and I ask for the flow of its energies to bless our time together... I pray you are well. The Dark Lady welcomes us and I surrender once more to the truth of our words and the truth of our story.

Greetings, Carol! It is good to be with you here. I am honored and so pleased to be with you once more in this place. Yes, the Dark Lady smiles upon us. I am seeing a tree nearby to you, or so my inner sight shows me. I so love trees! Do you as well?

Oh yes! And since I was the tiniest child. I am fortunate to have always lived near trees and woods. I think of them as such beautiful Beings and as friends.

Ah! You speak for me as well! Not all agree and some tremble at passing through places like this and hurry back to their village homes not willing to linger long in wooded glens. In certain dreams of you, I see you on the slope of a tall hill that is thick with trees. Is this place near to your home? It puts me in mind of the Tor.

Yes, Anna. I live on the side of a hill that people call Round Top. And it is covered nearly entirely with trees. But at its top there is an open meadow where people like to stroll in good weather. It does remind me of the Tor. In your time are there many trees on the Tor?

On its lower slopes, yes. The crown and high meadow has the Brothers' church on it and other buildings for their use. It was not always so and the old stories tell of a large gathering place for the Holy Ones. When people journey to the Great Abbey, the High Tor greets them when they are still many miles away.

In my visions of your home, I believe that you live not too distant from the Tor. Is this so?

My husband and I live not far from the east Roman road and once upon it we are an hour's walk from Glaston. At the top of our far meadow I can catch sight of the High Tor on a clear day.

In a part of your story I have seen and heard, I've witnessed your visit to the Holy Well. It is so very beautiful and lies within a beautiful wood. Many make use of the Well's waters as I understand it. Is this so?

Yes, many love its ruddy waters, though others cannot abide it and choose instead the gushing flow of the White Spring nearby. It is a place of surpassing beauty with its white-coated stream-sides and the encrusted boughs that hang over it. Certain cold winter days there are frozen spears of ice and delicate webs which create a fairy glen. I will tell you that many who travel to the Great Abbey for its wonders take pains to visit the Holy Well and the White Spring. Carol, you've spoken of the Holy Well as present in your time, but now I wonder at your saying nothing until now of the White Spring. I am half-fearful of its destruction.

No, Anna, it is not destroyed but it is sadly much changed and little of its natural beauty remains. I have learned only lately of its former beauty and what must have been wondrous delights such as you tell. Well over a hundred years ago before my time it was decided to channel the waters for the use of the town and so men built a large structure to hold the waters and send it through pipes to the town. Some attempted to stop this destruction but to no avail. Sadder still is that this system was not even used for too long before wells were dug elsewhere to supply Glaston with water. So now a fairly ugly building still stands in that place though the White Spring's waters are sought by many where they flow from a spout there. Good news to add is that a group of people who love the Spring are hoping to remove the building and return some of the natural beauty. I do so hope this will happen. I would like to know more of your stories of the two springs.

I would be pleased to tell more to you. It saddens my heart to hear of the harm done, but how good to learn the Red Spring remains much the same. They are places, both, much visited, though some will not go if dusk is coming or if the day is dark. Most especially this is so if the mists are settled thickly. You likely can imagine that things happen there of phantasmal and ghostly nature, a fright to many. But for children and those who perceive magical energies, it is a place of true fairy delights. I will share more soon.

Anna, I am speaking with you here but also witnessing some of your life's story at other times that I am writing down. Are you aware of this is any way? I have never written in this manner before.

Nor have I had such experiences as these in my life! You are most present to me as I am dreaming, just as is true now. I am not aware of you very often in my waking hours. Perhaps Mara would know of ways to better serve this work you and I do together.

I will leave that to you to decide. I am exceedingly grateful to whatever powers or forces make this possible for us. I think it is now time for me to return to that work, so I depart with deep thanks to you, my Sister-in-Spirit. Namaste'

I wish you well in your waking and dreaming, Carol. Namaste' until next we meet.

Angeline's Story
Chapter 2

The new day has broken warm. Joseph rose as Chanticleer first called and so gently that I knew he hoped not to wake me. When he did not return to our bed, I guessed he'd gone to his workshop to start early on the bowls he was finishing for Thursday's market day.

Fresh strawberries are waiting for our breakfast. The sun's rays slanting through the hedge promise a warm day to come. The bees are already happily at work among the fragrant lavender and I try my best not to disturb them as I pass. I'll wait till dusk to gather its blooms when they are not heavy with morning dew or my humming friends.

Returning to the house, I pass the workshop's closed door and I think to peek in at Joseph to say "Good Morning." Holding the bowl of berries, I tap lightly and lift the latch, but no one is inside. Perhaps in the privy then, but when I passed by the path, the sight of Joseph coming across the meadow told me where it was he'd gone so early.

I hurry into the house to have the table set for him.

"Good morning then, Anna," he said coming in and across the room to where I was setting the plates. "I hope you are well rested."

I nod and smile, taking his hand and holding it against my

chest. "And how is my Joseph this morning? Was it a good hour to walk?"

"The high meadow is always a beautiful place at the sun's rising," he said, pulling me into his arms, the close embrace telling me that he'd stood beside David's little grave to watch the sun come up over the land. He cleared his throat and looked at what I'd laid on the table, the fresh bread, pitcher of cold milk, and the blue bowl with its moist red berries.

"What a feast we have to start our day!" he says, taking his seat and popping a ripe berry into his mouth. "Mmm... wonderful!"

I joined him across the table. "Bless last week's gentle and fine rains for making them so full and sweet this season."

"So you are going to the Well then this morning?"

"Yes, and soon if I can before it becomes too hot, so I will be off after seeing to the hens." I spread honey on my bread, savoring its richness as I took a bite. I watched Joseph enjoying his breakfast, glad to see the shadow gone from his eyes. He met my eyes and we smiled.

"Oh," I added, "and I intend to stop by Mara's to take her the herbs she asked for and perhaps she'll go with me to the Well and back."

Joseph nods. "Then I will not be surprised if it is mid-afternoon before you return," he said with a knowing grin.

"I'm glad for the reason to be out on such a beautiful morning," Mara says, walking at her usual unhurried step beside me. We carry between us a large basket with three stoppered jugs for the Well's red-tinged waters. The road into Glaston is busy with farm wagons and others like us on foot. The green sides of the Tor rise in their fullness from the moorland. At its topmost point small figures of the monks move about Michael's Chapel. My eyes follow the line of the hill down into its shawl of trees where the Well is waiting in its deep-shaded glen.

"Do you think the Brothers will let the Summer Fire be built above the Fair Field again this year?" I ask.

Mara's eyes twinkle. "It depends I think on whether they wish their coffers heaped high as we heard was true last year on Sunday past Solstice."

"I'm to meet Brother Paulus in a few days to go and pick the new mint. Perhaps he'll know what's intended."

Since arriving at the Abbey three years ago Brother Paulus has been the head gardener of the large herb garden on the Abbey's grounds. He and I met by chance one day when I was out gathering willow withes and the seed of our friendship took root on that day.

A pony cart comes up beside us and a woman's voice hails us. "Good Day, Mara! Oh, and it's you, Anna, I wasn't sure who you were," said Hannah Blackman seated next to her husband. Mathias Blackman tipped his straw hat at us and slowed the roan pony so we all walked along together. I reached out to pat the roan's plump side. "Word reached us about Hazel's baby. Such a hard thing for them both, she and Nellis."

While Mara shared the details my gaze wandered the Somerset countryside, fields rich with early summer's green hues, stretched south towards the Polden Hills and north to the long line of the Mendips. We were walking an ancient roadway built by the Romans long ages past, though they weren't the first to fashion walkways across the moorlands. The Wells Road follows some of what is known as the Sweet Track, a causeway so ancient no one knows who its builders were. Sometimes when I am digging marsh plants among the tall sedges, I am sure I feel their ghostly presence.

"When I think of our three young ones birthed so easily, I'm the sadder for families who struggle to have even one living child." Hannah's words jar me back to the present. I look up not meaning to frown but the sun flashes in my eyes. Sudden realization registers on her face and I know she regrets her words. "Well, we must move on now. God be with you both."

Hannah's husband clucks to the pony who picks up his trot once more and we wave farewell to them.

Mara reaches across to pat my arm. "I'm sure you know Hannah's tongue outran her clear memory of you and Joseph."

"She's a good soul," I say. "I was sorry for her discomfort."

Mara nods. "Of course. And then there's more to who you are than most know."

By then we'd reached the first houses at the edge of Glaston and soon turn off onto the path leading into the glen with its shadowed woods and its two ancient springs. Their joined waters flow like some dark ribbon catching diamonds of the sun's beams that fall here and there among the Vale's trees.

It's but a short distance from the roadway to the wellhead. Setting foot on the wide path we're at once in deep shade of the tall hedges and branches of the great and ancient yews planted, some say, by the last of the Druids whose holy place this was. A hush falls too so that the noise of people passing draws off at once. Since learning the Mysteries, it feels to me much like slipping behind an unseen curtain and entering a sacred space, a notion some would roundly condemn. But those of us who know the Well's hidden depths embrace these truths.

We pass by the right-hand path leading to the White Spring's fairy glen set deeply into the Tor's lowest slope. Its gushing waters make a hushed whisper not far off, but it's the Red Spring's wellhead we seek today.

And I can't help but remember finding Brother Paulus here one day when I stopped for a drink, he seeking the same refreshment, a full sack of haws on his back. Entering the clearing quietly, I found him with head bowed and eyes closed. Sensing more than hearing my approach, he looked up with a smile so bright, I felt he was enjoying more than the Well's cool waters.

Today there's no one when we come into the clearing, the nearly midday sun lights up the air in a wide golden column all about the smooth stones in their circle around its top. For a long moment Mara and I stand quietly, watching the dust motes dance and the ferns bowing just so in a gentle stirring of air coming down the slope above the Well.

"Oh, what glory," said Mara, raising her hands to receive the greeting, and I do the same. "And what luck to find no one else here. Let's share a drink and sit on the stones together for a while."

She reaches for the wooden cup left for all who come to the Well and fills it from the steady flow bubbling forth and running off sparkling into the fern-edged run. Then she holds it aloft. "We thank you, Lady of the Well, for your welcome this day and for your abundance that flows to us all." She drinks deeply, rinses the cup, then refills it and hands it to me. I hold it for a moment looking into its mirrored surface. My features waver gently, a white cloud floats in the blue sky above my head. I smile and close my eyes to drink and receive the Water's blessing. Then I too rinse and replace the cup on its ledge.

Mara's eyes are closed and I do the same. For long minutes we sit in silence, the Lady's presence surrounding us, and our thoughts run together asking silent blessing for the stillborn girl-child and for Hazel's recovery. Mara stirs and fills the cup once more. She gestures for me to hold it with her. "We thank you, Great Bridey, for coming to Hazel in her time of need and for helping us to hold the energy needed for the child's birthing. We ask that she be received gently back to the Other World, and that Hazel's journey here be blessed again with full health, and if the Fates allow, a healthy babe to bless their home. And may that which we do in your name be always empowered through your stead." She lifts the cup. "Receive the water's blessing, Angeline."

The cold water splashes on my opened hands. I do the same ritual, pouring water over her out-held hands.

"And so may it be," Mara says.

"And so may it be," I murmur.

Around us a stirring in the trees tells us our prayers have been heard. Our eyes meet, and in the depths of Mara's eyes, not for the first time, I catch a glimpse of her bright spirit. The sound of the Abbey's bell comes through the trees tolling noontime. She sighs, setting the cup firmly back in its place. "The world calls us back, Angeline."

Our three jugs filled, we lift the basket together and take the path back to the roadway.

I shield my eyes to gaze at the sunset's glories, golden-edged cloud castles mount high in the western sky. I am cloaked in veils of lavender-scent, long silver-gray stems thick with purple blossoms are heaped in the gathering basket. A robin lands on the grass nearby and cocks his head conversationally. "Good evening, Bright One," I say, admiring his ruddy breast, and he nods before hopping off along the row of lavender for his own day's last gathering.

I tug loose a few henbane shoots hiding among the low bushes and toss them onto the path. "Kindly grow elsewhere, if you would please," I say, hoping their Over-light helper makes note of my request.

The dusk is deep in my workroom when I come inside so I must peer among the things on the work table to find the hank of string. Sorting the stems more through feel than sight, a small shape runs over my fingers and I start at its tickling passing, but smile at once. "Oh, friend spider, I hope you find your way out to the garden. It's too dark to see where you're hiding yourself but if we meet here on the morrow, I'll help you along."

The door to the main room swings open and Joseph stands silhouetted against the light inside. Though I can't see his face in the shadows, I feel the warmth of his smile reaching to me. "Ho! So it's you and not a thief out here. And it can't be you're talking with Puss as he's in here by the fire." He chuckles at this own humor. "Tell me, would you like the lamp brought out or are you making use of your cat's eyes as you have before?"

Now I laugh. "Cat's eyes indeed, husband mine! I am almost finished with the bundling, but you might leave the door ajar and it will speed my work."

"As I will. Then come and keep me company beside the fire, Mistress of the Green Grove."

"Joseph!" I glance up quickly enough to see his broad grin as he turns away. "Mind that tongue of yours, if you please, and back inside with you at once!" My laugh follows him back to the hearth's bench.

He finds it good sport to tease me for my habits and planterly work. If I'm not "Mistress of the Green Wood," I'm "Fairy Queen," terms that can be tossed about in innocent play. But if too often spoken without care, wagging tongues might cause a stir in places where certain ears might take sour note. Those who practice midwifery like Mara or who cultivate herbs and their healthful properties as do I are well regarded by many as wise women and blessed for their healing work. But others look upon us with narrowed eyes and are quick to criticize if not privately grumble about what it is we do. Joseph is a good-hearted husband, but I dare say some question my meadow rambles in search of the Wild Ones, plants known as helpers to all who seek them. Mother Ann herself urged caution of my woods-ways. "Few will question what you grow in your own garden, but mind where you venture beyond these walls."

The new lavender is all hung in its fragrant row. I make note of the rest that I've readied to take to market early on the morrow. Pleased with its abundance and quality, I step inside the cottage and receive the bright greeting in Joseph's eyes.

"So you will help me pick the berries in the morning for me to take to market with my herbs and all?"

He nods, his yellow hair catching the light. "That I will do gladly."

I settle into the curve of his arm and he draws me close.

Chapter 13

When near the sea,
the water within us sings
like the pure stone tone of
a bell carved from
bone. We are flutes
in the wind's mouth,
unearthed from the
cave of our ancestors' memories,
bone-singers
learning a forgotten
song.
~ *Bone-singers*, Jill Stephanie Morgyn

"You are one of the Old Ones, aren't you?"

At the gentle voice, I looked up from the ancient Yew to see a bespectacled older man smiling at me there in the quiet courtyard of St. Andrew's Church. He sounded confident in addressing me that way as I came slowly around the enormous Yew, my hands caressing its deeply-creviced trunk. I hadn't heard him come up the walk, something I wondered about later.

I considered his sweet smile for a moment and replied with my own, "I do love trees..."

He nodded, "I could see that." His eyes twinkled kindly and with just a hint of mischief. Something in his demeanor and what he'd said made me feel like I was being welcomed back. It was the day after Kathie and I had landed at Bristol Airport and we were out on our solo exploration, heading for Camelot. As we'd approached the little village of Compton Dundon, I suddenly remembered the wonderful Yew beside St. Andrew's, so we'd turned in from the main road and found it easily. Kathie had gone off to wander through the graveyard reading the tombstones while I reconnected with this magnificent and beautiful Tree-being. I'd made its acquaintance on the first group's pilgrimage thanks to our Avalon Coach driver who thought we'd enjoy visiting his parish church... and especially to meet the Yew. This was my third encounter.

Kathie came over and the three of us engaged in a lively and warm conversation. He told us it was a nostalgic visit he was paying to the area where he and his wife had settled after World War II. He shared interesting details about St. Andrew's and urged us to spend time in nearby Somerton which was along our proposed route. We parted company with a promise that we'd head there to take in some of its ancient Roman history, and drove off marveling at the lovely time we'd had talking with him. We never did learn his name.

I told Kathie how he'd appeared seemingly out of nowhere and how it was he addressed me. The more I had been thinking about this, the more magical it began to feel.

"Uh huh," she nodded, paying careful attention to the demands of UK driving. And then, true believer that she is in the Unseen Realms, added thoughtfully, "You know, Carol, I'm thinking he just might not have been human. He might have been something different... maybe even something like, oh, an elf or a Spirit."

I nodded too. It felt quite possible in every way. This unexpected and definitely enchanted encounter, whether elven or human, set the stage perfectly for what was to be an extraordinary ten days together with the rest of the 2009 Pilgrims soon to be joining us.

And to have been welcomed by this man's greeting, "You are one of the Old Ones, aren't you?", was an extraordinary blessing and affirmation of this latest *homecoming*.

And so our group of five women... six, counting me... and two men... our "Token Canucks" as they called themselves... all arrived safely the next day at Little St. Michael's Retreat House:

Kathie, Ruth, Anjeanette, Diane, Erin, Eric, Claude, and me. We'd soon add our Avalon Coach driver, Gary, and my Glaston friend, Mano. The first day ended with a celebration of our youngest pilgrim, Erin's, 21st birthday. The trip was her parents' birthday gift and it must have felt *beyond-amazing* to be sung *Happy Birthday* there in Chalice Well Garden as dusk deepened and the Magic took hold for all of us.

We were sitting in companionable silence at the picnic table feeling the jet lag taking hold, when someone (I can't recall who) announced, "You know, we're a Soul Family!" A happy ripple of agreement flowed around the table, mega-watt smiles beamed at one another. My sense of Pilgrimage-leading leapt to a whole new level. How I slept at all that night for the delight of this truth, I can't imagine now.

Some of this Pilgrimage deserves its own book, but a few more highlights for this one...

The Yews continued a lively communication with us...

Chalice Well was about to celebrate its 50th Anniversary with festivities to begin just after our departure to Cornwall. We enjoyed knowing that our group was helping anchor "good vibes" for the upcoming events. The second morning one of the Trustees came by asking permission for a special visitor to pay a call at Little St. Michael's the next afternoon. He wanted to spend time with one of the more amazing relics kept by Chalice Well.

The visitor would be Alan Meredith, an expert on the Yew, especially the ancient Yews that are considered still youthful at 1,000 years of age. The relic, one I'd heard about, was an extremely old section of a Yew's trunk and root that had been found during an archeological dig in the 1990s in the vicinity of the Holy Well. Carbon dating determined that it was growing beside the Well in the first years of the Millennium, and that at the time it died it was already at least 200 years old. It was Alan who'd come to examine it then, and he wished to come again, 25 years later, to see it once more.

The Trustee hoped this wouldn't disturb us, and I assured him that it wouldn't. Then, with a palpable nudge from my Guides, I asked him if my group could also view the Yew stump for a bit upon Mr. Meredith's departure. He told me, yes, that would be fine, though exactly when the visit would happen the next afternoon wasn't certain. But I already knew that this was all being divinely set up!

This possible "encounter" with the relic had everyone excited, all of us sensing how the dimensions of our Pilgrimage were rapidly expanding. Most of us stayed around Little St. Michael's the next morning, but when no one arrived by noon, Diane and Anjeanette decided to go into Glastonbury for some exploring. The rest of us lingered over lunch. About one o'clock there was a knock on the front door and in came the Trustee with his special guest. He unlocked the storage room door in the kitchen, brought out a canvas bag which held the Yew piece, and disappeared with it into the lounge where Mr. Meredith was waiting.

In the dining room we continued quiet conversation, the anticipation building. Some twenty minutes passed when the Trustee looked in at the door saying now we could come and have a look. I'd expected that he would be there when we viewed the Yew stump, but when the six of us filed into the lounge I was really surprised to find Alan Meredith there too. The Trustee had emphasized he was a private person and I'd thought he'd already slipped out. But no, he stood quietly to one side while we formed a half circle around the stump that was resting on a low table. As we would experience at several points during the Pilgrimage, ordinary time shifted imperceptibly into kairos time.

We stood looking at the Yew stump in silent awe. It was roughly two feet in length and about eighteen inches high, the stump and root sections plain to see. Its rough wood was shades of beautiful reddish brown and it was very much giving off a sense of palpable presence. I asked if we might go closer. The Trustee nodded and each of us took a turn, kneeling down beside the table or bending close to examine the wood's shape and textures. I went forward last, knelt down, and being careful not to touch it, slowly passed my open palm around and over it. The warm electricity it gave off was profound and unforgettable, telling me of its indescribably beautiful and living Presence.

With a deep breath, I rose and stepped back into our respectful half circle. Alan Meredith moved forward at last and stood beside me. For a long moment he gazed steadily at the Yew stump, and then began to speak. One of my Guides whispered in my ear, "Don't worry about remembering everything he's saying. Just let his words go into your heart." I relaxed into myself, breathing into my heart chakra, and felt it open to fully receive what this special man was sharing with us. This account is a faithful reflection of the notes I made later that day and my recollection these several years later.

In a soft voice he first gave us a brief background on the Yew trees, how long-lived they can be, and also spoke of his life's devotion to working with them. Then he paused, and I could sense that this was all going much deeper.

"In ancient Palestine, Yahweh was the name by which God was called. The living Beings who became the Yews resided in the Holy Lands of those long ago times. Within what we call The Garden of Eden lived the Tree of Life, one of these living Beings. Then came the expulsion from The Garden and a time of profound forgetting fell upon the Earth. When Adam fled from the Garden, he took a piece of the World Tree with him. The druids of those days sent out these Great Beings to places of safety including the place called Albion. There and in other places they came to be the Yews that we know now. So much... all *knowing*... was lost fifteen to twenty thousand years ago."

I watched Alan closely as he spoke. He rested his gaze on each of us in turn. When he looked at me, looked deep into my eyes, I saw his beautiful soul and how it reached out to mine. He paused and looked again at the Yew stump, and then spoke with a much different tone. There was no mistaking the sense of his fervent request. Again, he searched our faces.

"This time of profound forgetting must now be reversed if the Earth is to survive. We must listen to the Yews and heed their message and share it with the world. It's up to us." The call he was issuing was unmistakable. There was urgency not just in his voice but also shining from his dark eyes that reached out to touch all of us. "There can be no delay," he said in closing. A resonant silence fell upon the room.

Resting our eyes a last time on the ancient Yew's humble stump, we spoke soft words of thanks to Alan Meredith and quietly went out of the lounge. Back in the dining room, we gathered around the table, looking at each other searchingly but without saying anything. The whole of the Retreat House felt wrapped in a profound silence.

We heard the Trustee shutting and locking the storage room, and then the sound of Little St. Michael's heavy front door closing behind them.

Alan's message traveled with us each hour and each day of the Pilgrimage. We incorporated what we grasped of it into ceremonies we offered at each of the sacred places we visited. We sowed its seeds quietly and carefully in the Garden and cast them into the waters of the Holy Well. Some of this message we all carry still, and it is placed here on these pages now to be heard by all who come to this story.

Mano, who was with us most of the days we were in Glastonbury, was given a name for our Pilgrimage group... we were The Revealers. And to my astonishment, I also received a message for us one morning when I was on the Tor with Erin, Anjeanette, and Diane. I'd taken them to a then little known spot where a huge boulder is nestled into the east side of the hill. It is often called the Women's Rock. I have always had the most wonderful experiences there, all of them filled with deep peace and nourishing Presence.

We'd each brought personal objects for a ceremony and prayer cloths and ribbons to tie on the branches of the low trees growing nearby. As I knew it would be, it was a powerful ritual, and I left the three of them there for their own reflective time, going off a little way to sit on the sunny hillside. I was almost dozing in the warm June sun when the Voice came: *"Get out your pen and journal... we have a Message for you to share with the group..."* I scrambled to reach into my backpack and barely got my journal open to a blank page when the words began to pour through.

Dear Beloveds,

In this time of profound joy and re-membering — and yes, despite the "apparent" darkness and despair (all, ALL illusion)—you have made the heart-choice to come here to the enchanted root of the world, to feel Her heart, to breathe/receive Her breath, to be embraced in Her mighty arms and know you are Home. You have come with your beautiful faces, your beautiful voices, your crystalline energies and heart-borne dreams. Know that all unfolds in perfect beauty, in full and total Joy, in rich and exquisite Harmony and that the gift of your true Selves to Us in these days is received with exultation and the deepest of resonant Joy. Such courage have so many of you to push upon this door, the one in your lives whose threshold you chose to cross to journey here, a labyrinth Path to my Heart where I greet you with all this Love. You go from here in full knowing that you are never, and have never been, and never will be alone. We celebrate with you this joyous work and send through this one Our and My deepest thanks.

It was a glorious nine days together, the last three spent on Cornwall's northern coast in enchanted Tintagel. Kathie had to leave a day early and we reluctantly bid her goodbye. The next morning Gary drove us up from Tintagel, first dropping Ruth and Erin at Bristol Airport for their flights, and then to Temple Meads Rail Station where Gary and I parted company with our two Canucks, Claude and Eric, and Anjeanette and Diane. We all were weeping. I was returning to Glastonbury for my solo week. Somewhere I have the photo Eric took of me looking out the bus window at them, tears streaming down my face. Even Gary was crying.

When we got to the street, Gary looked over at me from behind the bus's steering wheel, wiping his eyes. "Are you all right, love?"

I attempted a smile. "Pretty much."

"Good." He pulled our Avalon Coach into traffic adding with his always-lovely humor, "I'll tell you, I'm glad I've got the driving to do so I can stop myself crying."

Not surprisingly, the next two days I mostly spent missing The Revealers and also attempting to ground something of our incredible pilgrimage. It was a great help to have the day with John approaching. Thoughts of Angeline had been few as there had been little time for this. My "bonus days" in Glastonbury were dedicated to our working together. The plan to possibly find and visit the area where I understood she and Joseph lived was growing stronger.

Angeline's descriptions helped me zero in on Pilton. I received a telling confirmation of this when we passed through there during the group's visit, once with Kathie on our return from Camelot, and then on the day trip to Stonehenge and Avebury. Reaching the edge of the little town, an unknown emotion tugged at me, and I blinked back tears.

June 15th's rendezvous began in the Meadow at Chalice Well Garden where John and I agreed we'd meet, and then it was off to lunch on the High Street. It was an animated conversation as we shared news and discussed the August workshop. John had long known of Angeline and the work she and I did together with the story, so he was very pleased to help out with the plan to hopefully locate her home.

Early that afternoon we got in his car and headed east across the Levels towards Pilton. I have a clear memory of looking through the windshield at the passing landscape scarcely believing in what we were doing. This was my recollection written a few weeks afterward when I'd returned home.

July 2009

I'd passed through Pilton twice in the week, first with Kathie and then on the drive to Stonehenge. The second time through, tears came to my eyes. As John and I drove across the Levels towards Pilton, my heart chakra expanded enormously and a fierce fullness seemed to be engulfing me, not in a fearful way, but an ache of the sweetest anticipation was building. It seemed further than I'd expected, but I think time was slowing, shifting.

I told John I'd "know" the turn to make and as the main road made a sharp right, I said, "Turn here," and we turned left onto a narrow street closely lined with high stone walls and very old houses. We were to keep going and we were soon in the countryside passing between high hedges. There were no houses, just fields.

We came to a pull-off and a short lane to the right leading to two gates and open pastures beyond. "Stop here. This feels 'right.'" He stopped his car and I got out.

A strong, strong pull drew me steadily up the tractor path and to the gate on my right. I came to a halt and felt how the hill and this meadow were reaching out to embrace me with the strongest and sweetest of welcomes.

"You know these fields," a voice whispered. "You are home again..." I gazed and gazed at this beautiful sight, opened to these beautiful Energies, and began to struggle for breath, gasping at the overwhelming Joy of it. I reached out and held onto the gate's top bar [with all my strength].

John came up quietly and stood beside me. What exact words were spoken I don't remember now but I was able to convey that I was home once more. And when the intensity drew heaving sobs from me, he put his hand on my shoulder which I so gladly grasped, thanking him again and again for helping me return. "I am so honored, so deeply honored, to be here with you," he said, offering his strong and steady presence, looking out over the fields with me.

It was a field that looked to be a pasture filled with meadow grasses and wildflowers, especially buttercups holding up their golden yellow and waxy blossoms, nodding in the gentle breeze. There were a few trees along a hedgerow further up the gentle slope, and another field. There were no houses and no animals, just the peace-filled pasture sending me its beautiful welcome, Welcome Home.

I wanted to cry out with joy. Perhaps if I'd been alone I would have. So I could only reach down and touch the ground, feel its solidness holding me, feel its quiet joyfulness seeking its own embrace, recognizing one who lived and died on this land, and who was now returned.

I would have stayed much longer if I'd been free to choose that… would have climbed the gate and walked into the buttercups beckoning and laid myself down on the warm earth of my ancient home, land-of-my-soul, home-land. I silently promised my return. I ran my eyes lovingly over all before me, a soul-embrace.

It was necessary to go, to leave this blessed place. I did not know if my legs could carry me, but when I lifted my hands from the iron gate I was able to stand and to walk slowly down towards John's car.

He gathered me to him in a long, close embrace and I will be forever grateful for that loving gesture. I could scarcely bear any more of the surging emotions. How was I to talk or walk or think normally? John's embrace brought me back through to the June day and this present world, but I was quite sad to get back into the car and allow myself to be driven away, even with the promise to my soul that I will return.

The rest of the day with John was full of its own loveliness with little time to reflect on what had occurred in Pilton. I slept deeply that night and woke to a woman's voice speaking the name "Angeline... Angeline." I sat up, eyes open wide, and heard it distinctly a third time. And so at last I had her name clearly... Angeline!

With the scramble of packing for home and all that this entails, it wasn't until I'd been back home nearly a week that I found time at last to open the Dialogue Journal and learn what Angeline had experienced that day.

28th June 2009

My dear Sister – Angeline – I awoke the morning after my friend, John, brought me to the hillside, and sounding clearly in my hearing was the name "Angeline." Have I the name correctly at last, Dear One?

Yes, Yes! Oh, a thousand times yes, my Sister! You came and then left far too quickly that day, but in all our conversations and our hours together with one another, I both saw and felt you wondrously clearly. Your tears at first confused me but then I swiftly understood they were joyful. And I knew you were not alone, a voice fainter than yours, a man was there with you. I was glad. All this a waking dream that caused me to wake from my sleep with a start and so Joseph stirred too but not awake. I settled myself again to quiet stillness and willed myself at least half-asleep hoping to be with you further. I "saw" the meadows you were gazing upon and even tho' they looked differently from this day, I know you were so wondrously near, just near where the furthest of our meadows fronts the lane. As soon as the day's light showed, I went out to this place, this blessed place to me now, and I stood where I felt you stood and was aware of your presence lingering there. This is so very wonderful, Carol! When I returned to the house Joseph asked if all was well for he could see I had shed tears, but I told him it was my moodiness of near Moon-time and he believed all of this half-truth.

Angeline, I know a possible other truth as I talk with you

today, that this place is the one I came to in another Summer, the first of my journeys to Glaston with a group of writers. In the meditation where I saw you in my inner sight, you came towards me along a country lane near a crossroad. The rightness of this has stayed with me now for some days and so I know it is and must be true. You've told me that you felt my presence when you went to this field corner.

As I did! Oh yes, I knew you were very near!

My dear Sister, Angeline, a time for rejoicing is now. I cannot seem to stay long with these journals as distractions of one sort or another pull me away, but I am wedded to deep joy at this meeting. Not that I've ever doubted we'd lose each other, but this discovery of your beautiful field ensures our devoted connection. Thank you for your patience!

You do not need to ask any forgiveness, Carol. I only feared your leaving at first, once I knew you as Sister and Other Self. But we are never to part again – that is what my heart tells me.

Chapter 14

The path runs true, I must depart
To hidden places of the heart.
No less than this, a pilgrim's prayer
Anoints the one who sojourns there.
~ COB

There's only a little over six weeks until my return to Glastonbury for the workshop with Sheila. Beyond the three successful pilgrimages so far, this opportunity to offer a program at Chalice Well is for me truly *the stuff of dreams.* That this event had all come together so quickly and easily felt reassuring in its *rightness.* This was a comfort when registration numbers remained disturbingly low, but whenever we spoke on the phone Sheila always managed to reassure me we were on the right path.

Though plenty of Summer events with family kept me happily occupied, still Angeline and I managed to find time to *meet* at The Medusa Café. To my immense delight, our connection was growing livelier and livelier.

6th July 2009

Hello this day, my dear Angeline...

Hello, my Heart! A day with summer's Sun?

Yes, and birdsong though I often wish it was not so overladen with the noise of the highway's traffic. We live in a noisy age of which I am little tolerant. I envy you the deep stillness of your fields and woodlands.

I as yet have only quick glimpses of your time, no sound of any sort. Though I am sure I have caught an echo in your voice in my dreams. Yes! When we met at the place you call The Medusa Café, if I have the memory clearly. Yes! We spoke with one another first inside where we sat together at the small table. And then when you suddenly rose and went out telling me you could stay no longer. But I quickly followed calling to you. You heard me, praise Goddess, and I ran as swiftly as I could to stand at your side. Do you remember?

As if it were an hour ago – I remember – you ran over to me and grasped my hand, then stood close beside me, our shoulders touching. You are tall with dark brown hair that comes down to your shoulders. I feel the intensity of your eyes on mine. *(You are nodding now.)*

If I were a writer of stories, I would say that my words spilled from my mouth... they came from my heart when I say, "You can't go... I've just found you!" I hold your hand more tightly. I do not wish for you to go. You have such a beautiful hand with slim fingers tho' I feel how strong they are. I could weep.

I ask a question, puzzled by what is happening. "Did we meet last year?" But I am beginning to know the truth. More is communicated somehow. "You don't seem to know what else to say. Does this sound right to you, Angeline?"

Yes. My words ran out through my heart. Thoughts reached out to you, to your heart.

Somehow my heart heard because I knew I had to come back to this place and see you again.

(Brightening smile... nodding again.)

Oh yes! How my heart leapt for joy when you gave your promise to return. When our dream ended and I awoke, I felt how I had cried tears of joy.

When I awoke, I also felt tears, and I felt how your shoulder and arm touched mine, and how you had taken my hand in yours. It was a beautiful dream and I will be forever grateful. Whatever caused you to run after me I do not know, but I will always think of it as a blessing.

Ah, but it is exactly as I said, dear Sister, when I came into that odd place, like a small tavern, and saw you at the counter (you were looking at the old woman's necklaces there), I felt my destiny somehow was to speak to you. Perhaps she is an angel? I thought. So the old woman brought you to the table where I had sat me down and then she served us cups of tea.

And the confections to eat. I did not know what to make of them. But when I took a bite of the golden one, it was then I began to understand things.

This seems true as I too ate a part of one... perhaps it was something like manna from Heaven as in the Bible story *(laughter!)* but I think me this good woman gave us both biscuits or tarts of some sort with magic worked in, and so our eyes were opened to the truth. What think you of this retelling, Carol?

Oh, I think you are understanding some of the secrets of this dream and our story. I especially agree that the old woman had a hand in this, as we say. And whatever the truth, I am just so happy that it all happened as it did!

Oh, as am I! As you have named it a blessing, it is just that for me, now and always, and in all ways.

7th July 2009
(Partway into our day's conversation.)

Do either of us understand why this has happened that we would meet and know something of one another's lives? But let me return to a thought I seek to share, my Sister. And that is your concern of "looking in" at my life, as if you may be untoward in this. My heart tells me that, in truth, it is *our story* you are witness to, both here as we speak to one another, and also to the rest of my days here in this lifetime. And so it is that this connection has opened a gateway into my story... our story... which is **your** life and which you share with me. So many words but ones I pray do offer what is from my Heart.

Angeline, thank you so very much for sharing these thoughts of your heart. It is such a joy and honor to receive them all. Yes, all is our story and with this full sharing of this day, neither of us need harbor any further doubt. Let there be always be a free and easy flow between us as we explore this wonderful journey together. And perhaps we will then come to know what Force or Divine Spirit sought to encourage this wonderful connection.

I embrace your words with my whole Heart, dear Sister Carol, for it is in my heart where we dwell together. None shall sever this connection nor could they! It is ours to treasure and enjoy always!

I am more and more excited and awed by this expanding dialogue with Angeline. What's more, I've mostly released my doubt about its being true, being *real*. After these sessions where I record our conversations, I make it a practice to let them "sit" for a while before rereading. Every time I return to them I am so in awe of Angeline's palpable presence and separate life in this *other time*, what I understand is the late 15th and early 16th centuries. Her describing the experience of our encounter at The Medusa Café often moves me to tears and touches again the heart-felt sense of joyful reunion.

The Summer weeks pass and I set off for England once again. Registration numbers haven't budged, but I am buoyed by the thought of being near Angeline again and hopefully have the chance to return to the field gate. For reasons that are unclear, communications with John are oddly strained in the last weeks of July. Sheila and I are puzzled but move forward with trust in the outcome.

When we all reach Glastonbury, we rendezvous in front of St. John's Church on the High Street. Mano joins us as well. There's a lovely small labyrinth there and I suggest a walk together. I'd brought my ceremonial hawk wing fan and decide to carry it. Spontaneously we began passing it back and forth as we encounter one another on the curving path creating the most lovely feeling of weaving ourselves and Avalon's energies together. The odd disharmony seemed dispelled, replaced by a sense of an auspicious beginning for our two days of collaboration.

Sheila was holding an evening event at the Daisy Centre and we hoped to entice people to our gathering at Chalice Well. She would be channeling messages from Mary Magdalene and Isis, what she is most known for. Not surprisingly, a large group showed up. The room was so full that Mano and I sat in the corridor. The power of the channeling was enthralling. I was transported by the beautiful message of Love that Sheila brought through from Isis. No matter what the next day would bring, there was no doubt of the divine support we were receiving for the work that had called us to Glastonbury.

But when we reached Chalice Well the next morning, it was clear that something decidedly unwelcoming had been stirred up. John's strange agitation had returned, the room thick with an uncomfortable air. Avalon is a place of powerful energies and when work of Light and Love are intended darker forces may be attracted to contravene. Mano, Sheila, and I spoke quietly together out in the small courtyard contemplating the best action. With little time left before people would begin to arrive, we needed to clear out the negativity as best we could. So in we went, Sheila announcing loudly that we were going to do a "room-blessing." I put on music and we wove its healing energies around the room pushing back against the unfriendly presence.

Within fifteen minutes our small but enthusiastic group had assembled and everyone seemingly very pleased to be there. And though a fierce-some undercurrent of challenging energies still swirled, blessedly no one seemed aware of it. Outside it was a beautiful Summer's day, the golden sunlight already shining in at the windows, its brilliance helping lift the mood as we gathered for the opening circle.

I began with the Call of the Directions to open and dedicate our sacred space. It's something I love doing and do well. Still I was pretty shaky when we turned to the East to begin. But when I lifted the hawk wing fan, I felt a surge of powerful energy enter through the soles of my feet and rise swiftly upward through my core. It was marvelous! With a deep breath, I opened completely to this rising power and let it pour through my words and motions, sweeping around our circle from East to South to West to North. Later Mano said she'd never experienced a more powerful Opening Call.

Though some of the day brought more uncertainties and challenge, Spirit's wonderful presence from those first moments held me and all of us at every turn and buoyed all our efforts.

We planned to use my Chalice Labyrinth for a walking meditation in the afternoon. After lunch we unfolded its 25-foot square which fit snugly and perfectly in the room. Blessedly, a positive energetic shift had been underway bringing a sense of increasing harmony. For his part, John appeared more open and relaxed. He was the last to enter the labyrinth. When the walk was completed, Sheila announced that Isis wished to offer a special clearing and anointing ceremony for anyone who wished to receive it. We each found a place to sit on the labyrinth and entered the meditation. John sat not far away from me, and it was good to feel him more fully present to the afternoon.

As with any powerful experience, words are inadequate to describe what took place during this incredible ceremony. When it was complete, Sheila brought our awareness back to the August afternoon and the meeting room's physical reality.

In the workshop's last half hour people shared thoughts about their day's experiences, everyone saying how grateful they were and glad they'd come. Then it was time for goodbyes. I was staying to close the labyrinth. John was the last to go, and though we said the expected *thank yous* and *it was a good day*, I also sensed a sort of apology from him. *Would I like help folding up the labyrinth?* he asked. I shook my head no, and thanked him saying I wished for quiet time alone.

I stood on the labyrinth conscious of its warm, anchoring Presence and felt him behind me standing in the open door. The silence between us was freighted with emotion. Whatever had happened was finished, and the day was complete. Wonderfully complete, really. Without another word, I felt him go and I was alone in the room. I lay down in the middle of the labyrinth to rest, collapsed really, before starting the work of closing it and folding it back up to put into the carrying bag.

It was then that the Chalice Labyrinth spoke to me saying quietly, "Carol, I have a name... my name is Tula."

I opened my eyes, conscious of its painted pathway beneath me. "Tula," I said softly, "your name is Tula." Tears rose and slid down my face. How could there be any better end to the workshop than this?

I don't know how long I lay there resting, when I heard someone approaching at the upper door from the Garden level. Mike, one of the Chalice Well gardeners, looked in. I sat up. "How did your workshop go today?" he asked, giving me his shy, sweet smile. I came up the steps and we stood talking for a bit. He looked down at Tula, admiring how beautiful she was, listening as I told him a little about her and how I'd made her and how she'd revealed her name to me here in the meeting room. "That's a nice name!" he said, eyes bright with delight. I felt Mike's beautiful energy restoring mine. When he bid me a warm goodbye a few minutes later, I went back down to Tula with tears of gratitude for Mike appearing when he did. Nevermore so than at times like this day had been would a *chance* meeting like this have happened. He'd known somehow I needed him to look in on me just when he did.

So with restored energy, I began the work of straightening and folding the two halves of the labyrinth and within twenty minutes the meeting room was back in its original appearance.

There was one final event, an evening's ceremony in King Arthur's Court to offer healing prayers for Gaia. In addition to Mary Magdalene and Isis, Sheila also worked with the Peacemaker, and knew it would likely be this ceremony when he would come through. With vivid memories of his presence at the

Onondaga Lake Peace Festival, I was looking forward to his joining us here in England, a whole ocean distant from the Lake.

Sheila had changed into her buckskin tunic and by the announced time, there were seven of us... seven women... standing together in a circle beside the healing pool with its quiet, steady flow of the sacred waters passing through it. Since it was an after-visiting hours time, we were the only people in the Garden as the evening's dusk began to settle softly around us. We were all quite tired from the day, but some sense of restorative energy began to arise.

This time Mano gave the opening words. As she spoke, something nudged me to look over my shoulder through the archway behind me. Beyond the brick gateway the two Guardian Yews stood silhouetted against the glowing western horizon. Suddenly a small male figure pranced into view crossing the grass not far from the archway. He paused, one leg raised, and turned his head looking straight in at me. Though backlit by the sunset's light, I glimpsed his bright eyes and a smile that widened when he knew I was seeing him. I had the presence of mind to return his smile. Was this the Green Man? Or maybe Pan? Apparently satisfied, he gave me a jaunty wave and then pranced on out of sight. I turned back to the circle, awed and a little stunned by what had just happened. It had been just a few seconds altogether, but I knew without question that his appearance was deliberate, a blessing from the Divine Masculine, and one meant to coincide with what we women were up to in this enchanted place.

Sheila then welcomed the Peacemaker to our circle and opened to allow him to speak to us through her. She had told me that he especially loved the company of women, and his oversized presence was warm and gentle. He thanked us for our work of this day and said he wished to give each one a healing blessing, one that would help us better do our work in the world. When Sheila came to stand before me, through my half-closed eyes I saw and felt the Peacemaker's tall and powerful form. "My daughter, for long enough you have carried the sorrows of the Land," he told me. Tears welled up at once. "And I speak for the Spirits of the Land who ask that I convey to you their deepest gratitude and thanks." And with that through Sheila's hands he opened my heart to release the sorrow I no longer needed to bear. Hot tears coursed down my face as I experienced this extraordinary blessing. The healing completed, he gently closed my heart and chest, and rested his large hands lightly on my shoulders. "You are to now learn to embody Joy." I bowed to him and Sheila/Peacemaker moved to the next woman and on around our circle. With a final word of thanks, he departed and our ceremony reached its endpoint.

We made our way to the Lion's Head for a restorative and grounding drink of the Red Spring's waters and then on to the Holy Well to end our day with prayers of thanks for all that had been given and received. I was incredibly tired but so light of Spirit. The dusk draped its dusky veils around us as we each found a seat around the Well-head. I went up the short steps to be with the two female Yews who stand sentinel just above the Well. Leaning against one and enjoying her sturdy, peaceful presence, the last and most extraordinary part of this day began.

An unmistakable presence materialized close beside me and in a heartbeat I knew it was Angeline. She leaned close and whispered, "Would you allow me to speak through you?" I didn't hesitate for a moment to wonder how this would happen, I just gave her permission and came back down to the group seated around the Well. I said that one more Being had come who wished to speak to us. As one, their faces lit up and all looked towards me eager to listen. I stood holding a sturdy branch of the shrub beside me, took a centering breath, and let my eyelids partially close. I felt my Self step easily aside and felt Angeline's presence shyly and softly enter. Then my eyes opened and she looked *through them*, however that was possible. She looked around the circle at each woman, and I felt her wonder and joy at seeing them. Then from my slightly remote distance, I heard Angeline's voice.

"In my life which is Carol's past life, I was known by the name of Angeline. Because Carol sought me in her present time – your day – I am able to come and be here with you at the Holy Well, a place I came often in my own time. It was much different then, but of course a most sacred place as it is for all of you now. I and others of my day were Keepers of the Sacred Flame, and our work and ceremonies needing to be done mostly in secret. The times were growing darker and there was often danger in this the things we did. The Work had been passed to us by those who came before and we knew it was our sacred duty to continue in this. We did not know if it would survive the dark times that were growing all around us. But what great joy I know this day, seeing that the ember of the Flame survived and is being brought to life once more through the work you are doing. You are our lineage, our future I give you through my Sister-self, and what thanks can be put into words and spoken here I give you now. I wish you all well with your continued journeys and I depart now giving thanks to Carol for the allowing of my presence."

She took a last look around, my eyelids fluttered down, and I felt her spirit draw gently away. When I opened my eyes, I was once more fully in my body. Sheila beamed a huge smile at me and thanked both of us for the message. The day was complete and all that was left was to gather our things and close the gate of the Chalice Well Garden behind us. With my remaining energy fast fading, I wheeled Tula in her traveling case back to our B&B collapsing onto my bed with total gratitude.

There was a last day with Mano during which we grounded some of the experiences of the week and also celebrated the fabulous parts of it, especially the wonderful company of Isis, Mary Magdalene, Jeshua, and Angeline.

And then the now-familiar bus ride to Bristol, the plane lifting off into the western skies, the long, quiet drive north from Newark. I reached Dragonfly Cottage completely spent. A while before the trip, I'd okayed a visit with a special friend immediately after my return, someone who was quite spiritually attuned. There was no one who could better understand the enormity of the days in Glastonbury. So while any other visitor would have sent me into "the deep end of the pool," Mary Kay helped me paddle to the shallow end where I could put my feet down.

We were sitting together talking, enjoying the view of the River beyond the windows when I saw as well as felt a luminous bubble of pale blue light taking form around us until we were fully enveloped within it. I blinked my eyes to be sure it was there and asked Mary Kay if she could see it. "No," she said, "but I feel it." She was silent for a moment. "It's Mary Magdalene. She's come here to give you a message." She paused, listening, and then smiled at me. "She wants you to know how deeply grateful she and Jeshua are for all that you did in Glastonbury. You're to know that wonderful things were accomplished for many and that you will eventually come to know about all of it. They know how very hard it was but they were with you the entire time. You were never alone. You're to rest now. Just rest. All is well." I felt the loving embrace of these words and the incredible healing that emanated from the pale blue aura encompassing the two of us sitting there. Slowly the luminous pale light began to fade.

"Thank you," I said to her, simply, feeling myself deeply at peace.

Mary Kay smiled her beautiful smile. "Thank *you*! What an honor to have been a part of this."

As the weeks passed the dailiness of my more ordinary life soothed and carried me forward, allowing a "settling out" and releasing of the challenges and impact of those mid-August days. And I did as Magdalene urged me to and rested often.

We were enjoying a lovely and golden Autumn which offered

its own restorative energies. On a mellow October Sunday afternoon, Sheila called offering a phone meditation to reactivate Isis' blessing given to us in Glastonbury. As always, this opportunity was in such exquisite timing. Afterward, feeling wonderfully renewed, I record this pledge in my journal, *"I here now embrace the fierce but friendly flame (re-enchanting the shared journey with you, Angeline) and open to this beautiful and empowering Light in which I live, move, and have my Being."*

Isis responds at once and the words flow from my pen...

Dear One, rejoice in this knowing for in this celebration lies the clarity of truth and from which flows to you unending energy and overflowing of Abundance in all things for body, mind, and spirit. Tho' recent days have brought pain and dis-harmony, much sadness and despair, never was there a doubt that its gifts would so wonderfully outweigh the travails you have now surmounted. I sense your acceptance of this truth at last and so now turn you fully towards the promised Gifts that await, eagerly, to be received by you. Mind the message of the Peacemaker and the healing given in the Garden. In the efforts and learning of this work which is to forgive and embrace your complete whole Self, you have grown so beautifully to recognize your entire Perfect Self, a Daughter of Light, and twinned with your Sister-Self. Hearken to the melody of this ancient song. Allow the dazzlement of this radiant Energy and Illumination to fully enter and embrace your Soul's bright journey. All lies within your heart and All is well, now and always.

You have this now... be at-One-ment...

There was one final piece to be given of those multidimensional events at Chalice Well. It wasn't until mid-November when I once more opened the Dialogue Journal and sought Angeline's company. I simply hadn't felt ready any sooner, but now I was eager to restart our conversation and curious to learn what her experience had been that August day.

For once the enormity of what had happened overwhelmed our first session, and Angeline advised to take the: *"time we need to return to our memories and enter into the space we shared... our Angels will help us..."* As they do. We ask our Guides and Angels for a circle of white Light and I, her faithful scribe, I listen and record her words. Angeline begins to describe her experiences on August 14th at Chalice Well.

I was brought to a room in a large building (in one vision). Long curtains covered one part of the wall. At first the room was empty, the light dim. Voices came and I drew aside, unsure of my place. I moved into a corridor hoping not to be seen. People were now in the room and a few speaking loudly. Then I heard a woman's voice I recognized... it must be you, my Sister! Then you began to sing a beautiful song to music that could only be made by Angels. How I wanted to enter the room and behold you at last, but my legs and feet would not move. People had quieted at the sound of your voice and the music. I could see from where I stood that golden light was filling the room. A voice spoke to me saying that all will be well. Do not fear for her.

I knew I must go but as I began to consider which way a man and woman entered the corridor, her hand clutching his arm. Neither saw me. They whispered together. I saw around them a shadowy presence that made me fearful. The man looked towards me, his eyes showed confusion but then perhaps it was fear. But then I was taken from this vision, leaving you. I prayed that you would know I was near.

[I jump in at this point and without written words convey images to her showing how the day started so chaotically, and then I share this description:]

As the day continued despite the negative energies that first visited, it was a powerful experience. We were honored by the presence and messages of Mary Magdalene and her Twin Flame, Jeshua, who taught us of living fully in the present moment and how to do so by bringing forth the power of Love. Later we walked the sacred path of the labyrinth all of us together... I may have felt your presence then... and found both peace and healing.

By then the restless forces had grown calmer or perhaps had withdrawn.

The Great Isis then desired to give those who wished a powerful blessing of awakening, a sacred connection between our hearts and Higher Selves. And so it was performed. The program then ended, and after all had left, I rested for a while on the labyrinth who had named herself to me as Tula.

I was waiting to be joined by others coming to do the healing ceremony in the Garden. While I was there resting, one of the gardeners, a beautiful young man named Mike, visited the room and admired Tula's design and presence. He was the first to hear her name! His visit restored such warmth to my heart. He seemed then and does now to be an angel.

[Then, again wordlessly, I describe the ceremony in King Arthur's Court with its several wonders and how afterward we went to the Holy Well.]

We spoke to the female Yews who watch over the Well. It was there, Angeline, that you came to me. I knew at once you were beside me and it filled me with joy after this long and daunting but beautiful day that you had come to be with me at the Well. So here in this journal that holds our conversations, I want to express my thanks for coming and joining us in the Garden that evening. When you asked if I would allow you to speak through me, I didn't hesitate for a moment. How it would be, I didn't wonder at since we were all held in total Grace and Love. I have not wondered until this moment what called you to come to be with me, to join with me.

It is our Divine Work, Sister, as one blessed Soul of Light, our shared Lineage, an over-lighting joy that transfigures our earthly work and human labors to serve the cause of Universal Love. My story of that day as it intertwined with yours I've partly told you... that I hid in the corridor observing the things I described. And then that scene closed to me. As we know to be the entry point into each other's lives, it is like the opening and closing of a curtain allowing us to look into our separate journeys. This was how I "returned" to find you coming to the Holy Well. The trees greeted me as they more easily recognize and commune with spirit-beings. The Yew beckoned me to wait beside her as I was trembling with both joy and nervousness. You were so very clear to my eyes, clothed in Light that shaped itself around you, but so wonderfully of flesh and form, so tall and gently regal in your bearing. The Yew-being opened the way between us and I was unafraid to speak with you, trusting what words would come. You are remembering this with joy too, my Sister.

Oh yes, I am, and so very vividly! It was a joyful blessed moment then as it is now recording these words on these pages. Our Guides and Angels bless us. I've hesitated for quite a while to write down what occurred at that moment fearing I would mis-remember some of it, but what I realize now is that it is not the exact words which matter, but more that we honor how we joined together for those minutes at the Well.

Yes, oh yes! It is that! When you spoke to the group saying one more had come who wished to speak to them, it was first their eagerness to hear the message and then you opening to my presence which showed me how to join you completely at that moment. Carol, I felt the warmth of your body and breath, my eyes opened and looked out so clearly through your beautiful eyes at those beautiful women who were there with you. All of you were shining with the Light of your beautiful Selves and the work of the day.

And then, together, we re-membered Angeline's message to us, all seven, which of course includes me, because I listened as closely as did the others seated around the Holy Well, entranced by her voice and her message across the centuries. Her words are already set out on these pages, and now her story of that day is recorded here as well.

And so it is, Blessed Be.

Chapter 15

That stone path you can see from the road
you know, the one that leads to the wooden bridge,
the one crossing the creek
to where there are no wars
and even gypsies stop wandering;
take a left there...
~ from *The Small Song*, Lauren de Boer

With the approach of the Winter Solstice, the soon-to-be second decade of the still-new century was putting out its unique vibrations, some of which were certainly connected to 2012's drawing closer and closer. Word of a 2010 Mystery School reaches me and I knew I was meant to take part. Joined with the release and clearing I've been experiencing in these past months, a surge of fresh energy fuels new work with Angeline. And not surprisingly, she and I are further supported by the friendly influence of the Cosmos. The January 23rd post of The Cosmic Path reinforces it all beautifully: *The Sun checks in with Pluto and Saturn. Your personal evolution is continuing at a noticeable pace. You are already so much clearer and less cluttered than you were even just a few weeks ago before the Holidays. Watch for evidence today of how firm and unshakeable your awareness is of your own power, a reflection of your link to spirit and your true self, and of how naturally you are taking responsibility for yourself.*

Our Dialogue Journal session that morning finds both Angeline and me practically jigging up and down with this lively, renewed energy. Angeline puts it this way:

23rd January 2010

The Lady be praised, Carol! Such a wondrous blessing to find our way to this meeting place once again. The joy in my heart knows no bounds. We have come a fair distance already, do you not agree? Our Angels and Guiding Spirits are happy and eager to bless the rest of our journey we make together. I am ready and eager to continue with you, my Sister... I continue to rejoice at what you once called "our lively connection" and that it is now restored to us! Have you in mind any path for our conversation?

I am unsure this very moment. What I want you to know is my intent to foster the strongest connection possible and continue very focused work for all this Winter Season (as it is for me). It is time our story in all its fullness should be known to all who wish to hear it and to read it!

Oh, that is wonderful! I have wondered what more is to come of this. Carol, I pledge my full energy to this task in whatever manner allows its full flowering. This is so wonderful and joyful. I hope you sense how I am smiling with this great delight and excitement!

Oh, indeed I am smiling with the same joy! And I make my own pledge to work diligently and joyfully together with you as we share all we can of this journey of our two lives. Some of this as you know is written in another place... not our speaking together as we do here... but tales from your life that have appeared to me. At some point soon I will turn my attention to this.

The session continues with my review of earlier entries in the now fifty-plus handwritten pages of our recorded conversations stretching back over more than three years. Our physical presence to each other has never been so palpable, and an hour later the delight in this shared work spills out onto the journal's page...

Oh Angeline! Though I am so well acquainted with what has been shared and written, I see with fresh eyes the wonderful and abundant treasures of this story, our story! It is truly marvelous...

Oh, it is exactly so! I have no better words – just joy surpassing joy that fills me to overflowing looking back through it all with you. I heard your unspoken thoughts... yes, oh yes, how far we've come since espying one another in the lane.

I feel your bright smile, Angeline, and nearly see it at this moment. How wonderful, how extraordinarily wonderful it all is! And so much of wonder and marvel lies ahead.

Truer words could not be spoken than these, my Sister.

In mid-February I set off for a Mystery School gathering at the Garrison Institute perched above the Hudson River in Cold Spring. As always it is a joy- and fun-filled time with old friends and several new ones. All I'd been needing of renewal and resourcing is abundantly present in Jean and Peggy's lectures and exercises, the dancing and singing, and the conversation-feast at each meal. And for those willing to rise early, the delights of Peggy's morning meditations are not to be missed as the perfect way to start the day.

My partner on Saturday morning is Dave Fox, a longtime friend who I treasure. During the meditation he receives two quite wonderful messages for me and Angeline! He's excited to share the image that Spirit sends him of me walking along an English country lane with tall hedgerows on each side. "It's non-ordinary time," he says. "I see that you slip through the hedgerow and this lets you enter another reality or a different time. This is how you and Angeline can meet each other!" His face lights up with his wonderful smile. We continue Peggy's exercise together and another more mysterious and evocative message comes through. "It might be about your work in Glastonbury or maybe it's about the story. I heard the words, 'Carol is connecting with the ignition points of love.'"

So many marvelous gifts to bring back with me from Mystery School. And I am particularly grateful for Dave's messages and enthusiasm during the Saturday meditation. I share the experience with Angeline through our Dialogue Journal. Of the image of my passing through the hedgerow, she says,

Oh, yes! Much as the first time we happened upon each other. And so very much a way of describing how you found your way to the field gate last summer... And is not the title of our story *Crossing the Luminous Threshold*? Ah, such a beautiful and perfect affirmation!

It is that and perfectly so. And it is a special thing that this message was delivered by such a fine and gentle man... I will spend time contemplating the full meaning and possible implications of his other message. An idea that came to me just now has to do with the three places that the Michael and Mary ley lines cross in Glastonbury.

More will come about what this is. The Mystery will be revealed, of this there is no doubt. Our very belief in one another shows how, all unsuspecting though we may be at first, quite extraordinary visions appear and then become manifest in reality.

I am confident in "extraordinary visions" manifesting themselves, an immediate one being a 2010 Pilgrimage group. With the fantastic success of the 2009 Revealers still humming and the avid interest expressed by several of them to return a second time, another successful Pilgrimage felt practically *a given*. The dates are set for June 26th to July 12th. But by mid-March I'm already concerned about the low interest and scramble to widen the advertising.

Shortly after my April birthday it was time to regroup. I call the two Revealers who were definite about going, Diane and Eric, and we put together an itinerary for just the three of us to spend a week in Glastonbury and then three or four days in Cornwall. A silver lining appears at once when our plan to rent a car and do our own driving means that I'll be able to drive myself back to the field gate outside of Pilton. Spirit works in marvelous ways.

It's a relief to abandon the Pilgrimage group effort and I do my best to let it go emotionally. And there's every reason to consider that offering one in 2011 would be a different story.

All these ups and downs take time away from the writing though I sometimes "drop by" the Journal to apologize to Angeline.

15th May 2010

Dear Angeline, hello! Our communication of late has been quick hellos and brief conversations since for some time I've found myself quite caught up with travel, family and friends... busy but mildly frustrating when it comes to this work and play with you! Also a stretch of minor turmoil as the Pilgrimage sorted itself out. This I think you know about, and maybe quite a bit? But what is best – barring any flight delays – I will spend nearly two weeks back in Glastonbury in just over a month's time!

Greetings this day, dearest Sister, and oh my, yes, such marvelous news of which I have had some inkling! And I do apprehend the unmatched joy of our reunion as only this place can offer to us. How greatly this will nourish our work. How the chance to play and dance and sing together will offer such sweet delight... do you not agree??

I could not have expressed it more perfectly... and this fact has me very excited: I can easily envision that a major portion of this story we are together weaving will be completed during our time together.

And if I am understanding things correctly, your visit will take place during the Summer's weather?

Yes! A week after the Summer Solstice with my return to America on the 12th of July.

Ah, lovely. So you will be comfortable being out of doors. I think we can best be close to one another in that realm.

Yes, I feel the same way. I've been having a marvelous time today reading back through the pages of our journal. It is all so wonderful, many times making me smile and even laugh out loud, and sometimes making me weep at its beauty and truth.

Such a rich blessing. A gift from one to another, and beyond us, a gift to those who come to know it, to hear it.

Oh yes, Angeline. And I'll repeat again what I wrote some months ago. You and I "are together weaving such a beautiful tapestry to share with the wider world." I feel this all the more deeply as we journey further and further together.

So with things smoothed out for the coming trip, I have more time to spend with Angeline and make further progress on our writing. For some time we have enjoyed more and more easily *crossing the threshold* between our two time periods. She's even *seen* my laptop computer on which I write and likes to call it "your magic writing machine." I've recently finished reading the most compelling historical novel, *Daughters of the Witching Hill,* by Mary Sharratt. It is based on the famous 1612 witch trials in Lancashire, UK. The main character is based on the oldest of the nine accused, an 80-year-old woman whose life very likely overlapped Angeline's. I can tell such glimpses of 21st century life intrigue and delight her. So on a late May afternoon, I begin our conversation this way:

May 26, 2010

Greetings this warm and sunny afternoon, Angeline. Through our connection here [via the Journal] can you hear the birds singing nearby on my Hill? There's one whose song sounds like a beautiful flute, a wood thrush.

Hello, my Sister. Oh yes! I am hearing some of his song... its beauty sounds in my heart. When I'm walking in the fields and woods, I am ever listening for the birds to sing out their songs to me as I pass by. Oh! I hear another... is that the thrush?

No. I believe that one is a Carolina wren, but he too has something of a flute sound in his singing. We share the world with such wonderful beings. And I am all the more blessed to have this wonderful place, Dragonfly Cottage, in which to reside.

And there's the thrush yet again! It feels delightful to share this enchantment with you, my Sister.

More and more our lives so richly entwine. What was it your friend of the Mystery School "saw" of us? How you in walking along the lane have only to slip through the hedge to step into the other world – mine – but I in turn am able to do the same and be present in your day!

[I smile.] This breath of woods' coolness as the sun slips nearer to the Hill's crest is much welcome refreshment on this unseasonably warm day, though a mosquito has just appeared with its own notions. You are at least safe from his pesky bite! The rumbling of traffic on the highway, now a lawnmower nearby, and just today the neighbor turning on his air conditioner... all these mechanical contraptions do add their noise and distraction. But I am at least well hidden from all eyes in my secret and leafy nook!

And the birds seem not to notice, I have observed. You and I can do the same by their example *(smile).*

Let me return to our discussion of Bess Southerns' story that I've now finished reading. Though I'm aware of this possibly being disturbing to you, Angeline, I did want to at least report I'd completed the book.

In order for many spiritual things to survive, especially of the Great Mother, and of the Genius and Spirits of the Land (fairies, Devas, the folk-of-the-Woods), these needed to vanish, to be "spirited away" for full protection. Mano knows this. And [now] with those dark times well past, you and I share one of the Keys to open the gate to these once-secreted treasures. It is one of the reasons She calls us "Revealers."

I am thinking that even though the fury of the Reformation inundated the Isle of Avalon, thanks to how powerful this sacred landscape is, the pulse remained palpable and "sensible" for those who sought it. The two Springs still flowed; those who stayed connected to the Land – especially herbalists – kept a connection to the Old Ways and their Magicks.

And there were stories—yes, the Energies of the Isle of Glass run very deep. As you are now thinking, Carol, our brethren to the west in Cornwall, to the north in Wales, and most especially across the ocean in Eire, protected and cherished much of this treasure. And some crossed the wide seas to the New World bearing the hidden seeds... and at least one of those seeds bears its fruits in your life! Such a wonderful and blessed Truth!

How lovely are your words, dear Sister. It reminds me yet again of how our lives are woven together across time and space, the tapestry we're creating [and] have created first with our lives and now through this work and play together... it is so beautiful, joyous, and extraordinary! Thank you for today's wonderful sharing, Angeline!

And I in equal measure give my great thanks to you! "See you soon" and as I've heard you say, "sweet dreams."

Dearest Heart, sweet dreams to you.

In present day America, a dark chapter indeed is unfolding in the form of the devastating oil spill in the Gulf of Mexico. Few who read these words will need a reminder of the terrible months of this event and the seemingly endless weeks that crude oil spread and spread its devastating damage to ocean waters and shore-lines all around the Gulf. As our Glastonbury trip draws nearer, I know with increasing certainty that we will offer healing prayer and ceremony at the Chalice Well.

But first there is the simple business of "getting there" via the night flight I always take from Newark to Bristol. And with Diane planning to fly in from Oregon and then on from there together, it all feels perfect. But then last minute disaster when Diane suddenly falls ill and cannot come. So things are turned on their head for the first two days. With Mano's considerable help Eric and I do our best to regroup for the two Earth-healing ceremonies planned for June 26th to coincide with the Capricorn Full Moon and partial eclipse.

With the Gulf Oil Spill still in crisis, many groups around the world are also planning prayer and healing circles for that day. I've shared the time of our evening ceremony with the Mystery School Listserve and some I'm certain will tune in. The Motherhood of Light group plans a conference call to do a meditation at the exact time connecting with us at Chalice Well. Later I will hear from Nancy just how fabulously powerful this was.

There is a sound-healing workshop taking place that day in Chalice Well's meeting room. Eric and I meet the event's leader at breakfast and we invite him and his group to join us that evening. In the afternoon, Mano, Eric, and I do a ceremony in the Garden's meadow that is timed for the eclipse. Under Mano's informed and expert guidance, it was a profound and powerful hour. The plan for the ceremony was to leave it simple and open to Spirit's direction.

We'd also extended an invitation to the staff at Chalice Well and while we weren't sure any would join us, I knew they were pleased that the healing work and ceremony was taking place there on a day of worldwide prayer.

So the three of us set up candles, crystals, and our sacred objects around the Well-head. Just before seven we're joined by a half-dozen people from the workshop. Among them is a young American woman, the co-presenter, who brought along one of her beautiful crystal bowls. Equally marvelous was that her young daughter was there too.

After calling upon the energies of the Sacred Directions to bless our ceremony, we thanked the Lady of the Well for her welcome and witness, and then each called upon our own Guides and Helping Spirits. The candlelit space around us filled with beautiful Presences of all sorts, angelic and magical. Mano led us in a meditation to anchor and amplify our healing prayers. (A few weeks after I return home I receive a message from Spirit explaining that our ceremony and prayers "made use of the Well's vortex energy so all you did was greatly magnified.")

Then we asked everyone present to say anything they wished and several offered such beautiful thoughts and prayers. It was pure enchantment when the young woman played her crystal bowls and sang an exquisitely beautiful song of healing. Then we thanked all the assembled Beings and closed the Circle, leaving the candles glowing while we went down to the meeting room to join the workshop group for the last part of their evening's program. And I was grateful too for how the ceremony offered a welcome touch of healing for Eric and me given the very challenging start to our trip.

After the workshop's own closing ceremony there was time to mingle. The young woman who had played her healing bowls sought out the three of us to share her story. She was an American who lived in Bali pursuing her work as a sound healer. Earlier in the year before the onset of the Gulf Oil Spill crisis, she'd received a vision of Chalice Well and understood she was being summoned to go there and offer her music. When the chance came to co-lead the workshop in Glastonbury, she accepted at once, trusting that the rest of the vision and summons would present itself. Mano, Eric, and I looked at her and each other in total amazement. "And so when I found out this morning that we'd been invited to join your ceremony at the Holy Well tonight, you can imagine how totally thrilled I was!" We smiled and smiled at one another celebrating the wonder of this splendid synchronicity and Spirit's hand in all of it.

The daunting beginning of our England trip was fading away as more remarkable experiences showed up. This included a visit with Mano to a spectacular crop circle which had appeared unusually near to Glastonbury. It is in the wide-open expanses of neighboring Wiltshire where most are found. After bumping along a narrow country lane in our rented car, we reached the edge of a high ridge that gave an incredible view of the splendid formation in the small valley below. Our stunning nearly bird's eye view was mesmerizing of the dozens of small circles joined in a swirling formation. Eric chose to enter the circle while Mano and I were drawn to a cluster of small trees. At once they communicated their desire for us to do an impromptu healing ceremony to further what was done at Chalice Well on the day of the eclipse. We were quite happy to oblige.

In addition to our five days in Glastonbury, Eric and I planned to drive out to Cornwall for three days' stay with the Walkers in Tintagel. After a bit of careful practice, I'd gotten reasonably comfortable with UK driving. I was intent on a solo drive out to Pilton for a visit to the Field and unhurried time with Angeline. I made one attempt but with heavy traffic from crowds leaving the huge Glastonbury Music Festival, it was too much to handle and I reluctantly found a place to turn around and return to town.

More determined than ever, and with lighter traffic at last, I set out late on our last afternoon on the A361, the Old Roman Road, retracing the route John and I had taken the previous Summer. I come to the correct left turn in Pilton, negotiate it safely, and rejoice to find myself on the same quiet lane leading out into the countryside.

Fortunately there's no one behind me, so I drive slowly along and come to the tractor path, familiar and welcoming. Strangely shy, I decide to drive on a bit for a place to turn around and a quarter mile or so further come to the four corners of the tiny hamlet of Perridge Hill. I feel quite compelled to pull the car off the road and get out. No one is about, though there are several houses nearby and I hear voices of people enjoying themselves on this warm Summer evening. There's a strong sense that I know this place well. I look about with loving gaze at the way the roads go off into the distance, and try to see and feel it as it was in that other time.

My confidence restored, I get back in the car and drive slowly back to the Field. I've brought some small things as offerings intending to leave them in a hidden spot. Holding my bag close, I walk up the tractor path and gaze out once more into the Field beyond the farm gate. It is a quieter welcome this time, but there is no mistaking a gentle thrum of gladness from the Land and resident Beings. Memories of my first visit glimmer all around me. I'm so pleased that no one else is in sight, and walk up the gentle slope along the Field's hedgerow to find a good place for my offerings. It looks like a cutting was recently made, so it's easy walking and I keep fingers crossed that I don't intrude on whoever it is that owns the place. It's hard to imagine how I'd explain being there. The hedgerow comes to an end at the top of the rise opening onto another field. I hear children's voices and cautiously step forward just enough to glimpse three children playing near a house at the far end of the field. I'm confident that I'm not seen, and take a long look at what just may be the site of Angeline's... of my... home. It is an indescribable moment.

With immense gratitude, I make my way back along the hedgerow and choose a place near a tall tree. I duck through the bushes to its base and arrange my gifts, a shell, some special stones, a blue jay feather, and two small Herkimer diamonds. All is quiet and peaceful here. After this simple ceremony, I walk a bit further out into the Field and sit down in the grass. The evening sky takes on sunset hues of red and gold. I do my best to simply be fully present in this humble, sacred place. Day's light is beginning to fade, and so with much reluctance I rise and walk down to the car. With each step I am deeply mindful of my feet upon this blessed land and impress as much of its feel into my heart. I'm also mindful of Dave's vision of Angeline and me "slipping through a hedgerow" to meet each other. Perfect. The long minutes at the crossroads and nearly an hour spent in the Field offered us this luminous portal on this beauty-filled evening in early Summer.

A last challenge when I can't find how to turn on the car's headlights. I say a prayer for safety and drive back towards Pilton and on to Glastonbury in the steadily deepening dusk.

Our days in Cornwall offer powerful experiences and considerable joy of just being on the ocean coast and in the Atlantic's powerful, mystical presence. We spend a day traveling down to Penzance following the Walkers' directions and recommendations of places to visit. Eric and I make a good driving team as he's at ease on the high speed roads and I'm adept at navigating the narrow country lanes. A visit to the Merry Maidens Circle was our last stop, and with some persistence we found it at last just outside of Penzance. It is a bit of a rarity in that not a single stone of this ancient circle has been damaged or moved since its builders erected it in that very long ago time. I think of Angeline's telling me that early peoples of this part of the British Isles protected the treasures of the Land when the need to hide them away came.

A few people were there when we arrived and we exchanged hellos. They spoke of how special the place was and wished us our own good visit. We were pleased that we'd have the Circle to ourselves at least for a while. We'd brought some of the water blessed during the Water Healing ceremony at Chalice Well, and planned to offer it here. We'd agreed that we would each "do our own thing" and so first I walked at a distance from the stones all around their perimeter. I could see that Eric was already deeply involved across the Circle as I came close to the place where I felt I would begin the ceremony.

I greeted the stone I'd been drawn to and sat down beside it for a light meditation. How welcomed I felt! Moments after this acknowledgement, I felt a distinct stirring and my Inner Sight gave me the vision of a huge masculine Being rising beside the stone beaming a mega-watt smile right at me. Despite his towering presence, I knew he was a gentle-giant-of-a-Spirit and I was thrilled with his appearance to me.

He was clearly glad that he hadn't frightened me, and in a pleasant, rumbly voice said, "Welcome to our Circle! Thank you for coming with your ceremonial things. Let me show you the best way to do this!" I rose and stood beside him *listening* as he instructed me how to bless each stone with the crystals and water, and also told me what words to say in blessing. He accompanied me to each wonderful stone all the way around the circle, nineteen in all and each one so very alive as I anointed it with the blessed water and spoke my prayer. When we came back to our starting point, my gentle Guide and I stood regarding each other. I thanked him for not only his guidance but for choosing to appear to me. He gave me thanks for himself and the Stones, then made a bow. His dark, sparkly eyes held such a loving look as he quietly withdrew and we parted company.

Eric had completed what he wished to do and just as we'd finished a car drove into the parking area with new visitors. Spirit seems to always arrange for whatever uninterrupted time is needed to do ceremonial work! What a wonderful conversation we have on our drive back to Tintagel comparing our experiences with the very lively Merry Maidens.

Considering the difficult start to our trip, it had expanded into a wonderful adventure, and it was an emotional goodbye when we hugged each other and Eric drove off in our rented car towards Bristol Airport. Following my usual pattern even though it wasn't a usual pilgrimage year, I stayed on another five days. As always there were several more amazing encounters with intriguing people that only can manifest in Glastonbury. And, perhaps not surprisingly despite the year's challenges, I even look in at the Daisy Centre which Mano had suggested might be a good place "for next year's Pilgrimage group." It does indeed look inviting when I visit and meet the owner, Daisy Foss. There's no doubting the sense of kindred spirit I feel as we talk. Oh yes, I do feel a stirring for 2011!

By the time I was on the plane home rising into the West Country sky, the familiar wrench of leaving brings tears as Somerset and England slip from sight behind me.

The "decompression" time needed upon reentering ordinary life post-Avalon is no shorter or less intense than any other return. I push along as best I can lovingly held in the nest of Dragonfly Cottage and Round Top Hill.

A month after my return, Spirit offers me a grace-filled message of my 2010 adventures thus far, beginning with lines from a poem I love, Lauren de Boer's *The Small Song*...

Bridget's fire... Venus' day-shine [the Morning Star appeared that morning] *waiting with her light. "That stone path you can see from the road: its forks lead nowhere you know, but everywhere you've been calling to from your wild heart"... your beautiful, light-filled, untamed heart. In these times of tumult, your life serves as a beacon for many. You allow your roots to sink deep in your daily Going... your conscious pathway upon Mother Earth... a communion with her Great Being,* a joy-laced dance in each day's journey. When these filaments of Light and Love are sent down into Her Body, it is nourishment for you both, a blessed symbiotic alchemy weaving and re-weaving the web of Life:*

Color, Light, Sound, Fragrance, Touch—sensory filaments—quantum energies attuning you (each One) to the mighty and joyous Dance.

And then as sometimes happens, there's a slight pause and Spirit offers two additional notes... "*If we're not supposed to dance, why all this Music?*" Every time I reread this journal entry, I smile at this.

And the last is the footnote I'd been directed to add from the message: "**walking a labyrinth helps people to remember this truth—*"

My ever-lengthening, ever-deepening journey of Spirit is one in which Joy is figuring larger and larger all the while. And when indicators and clues of my purpose and work-in-the-world come along, how I treasure these affirmations.

Chapter 16

*My days, my time, was one of going down into the Dark. Yours, as
I am coming to understand, is a time when the Light is returning,
the Darkness penetrated and illumined by its growing radiance.*
~ Angeline

A very welcome reunion with my friends at Mystery School the
last weekend in August brought a re-centering of my psychic
energies as well as considerable support for launching a 2011
pilgrimage. I'd already sent off a serious inquiry to Daisy Foss in
Glastonbury for an early Spring stay at the Daisy Centre. My
report to Dave on happenings in England was met with his usual
delight and enthusiasm. He was considerably pleased at how his
insights in April had come to manifestation.

Recharged, with fresh focus, and returning to writing work
with Angeline, the energies of mid-September's Virgo New Moon
brought a number of inspiring visions and expansive insights for
where things were going.

Two vivid dreams come early one morning in October. The
first suggests that maybe I'll return to some sort of teaching. In
the dream I'm living in an apartment building and people are
leaving encouraging notes on my door and saying they're
awaiting me down the hall. I know I'm very ready for this "class"
and I go about my apartment happily gathering up things I've
gotten prepared, "ready to proceed."

The second dream intriguingly echoes the Door Dream that I'd
had in Glastonbury five years earlier. I'm in a new home and
things are in a state of disarray. I'm on the phone when there's a
knock on the door. I hurry to open it and see a UPS man returning
to his truck. Several boxes are on the porch. I call out and he
comes back holding a small package. He hands it to me with a
paper to sign explaining, "This had to be personally delivered…

it's a 'hot root.'" I invite him in to show how I'm fixing up my new home. He nods and smiles. "It's going to be comfy and welcoming when it's done!" Just like in the Door Dream, I didn't remember *ordering* the "hot root," but I'm very pleased to receive it.

As a gardener, I know that a "hot root" is a live plant that needs extra care in handling so that the new plant will begin to grow and thrive. But what I take to heart is its lovely metaphoric meaning of fragile but potent development of new possibilities given proper care and attention. Is it possible that these dreams signal that I'll be heading elsewhere before too much longer? This is my second Summer here at Dragonfly Cottage and I am deeply content. And though nearly everything about this special place has come to feel like home, now and then it does occur to me that at some point I'll want a more permanent address.

These messages are expanded the next day through a shamanic journey. The journey's intent is for guidance in returning to the work with Angeline, as so often I regret neglecting it for other things taking precedence in the *outer* world. It begins with a visit to my Native American friend and ally of the Lower World. He first administers healing and strengthening therapy. Of what Angeline and I are doing together he comments, "Oh yes, lots of distractions keep you from the heart of this work. It is something *(your work)* that certain Energies would prefer not to be completed."

I then travel to the Upper World and am met by Archangel Gabriel. His guidance is wonderfully clear: "Yes, the two of you are always connected, inseparable. Only illusion tells you differently. The brightness of Summer brought you great challenges balanced with many magnificent gifts. You are now ready to put each one to use in opening to the intimate, beautiful, and powerful energies of your stories. Dream-work can and should be employed. Return now [from this Journey] refreshed and renewed. I am abundantly present in all ways! Let the immense

218

scale of this work not put you off."

Further powerful clearing-work is evidently called for by Spirit. A few days later I'm prompted to take another shamanic journey in which Angeline and I are brought together. We stand facing each other in a circle formed of our Guides and Helpers. A fine gold mesh we're both wearing is ceremonially removed and given to the flames of a fire. It quickly becomes ash and with thanks we release it to the wind. Certain limiting and binding energies of our shared lives are thereby transmuted and we are assured, *"You are no longer bound by these."* I then travel to Carnaphon for a few precious minutes together. Then I'm summoned to Chalice Well where I pass through a dimensional veil to Angeline's time. We meet on the bank of the White Spring's stream. She takes my hand and leads me to a small stone circle where Mara and others are gathered. As we appear, Mara sees me for the first time. "Welcome, Bright One!" she says. Others catch a glimpse of my feather cloak. Mara draws down protection on us and we all pass through another veil to a beautiful stone building, a chapel of ancient days where Magdalene came to teach. She awaits us on the nearby sandy shore. There's only time for her warm greeting before my journey's Call Back, and I am vividly aware of her piercing but loving gaze.

This is the first experience of being so intimately a part of Angeline's spiritual life. Soon afterward we have a chance to share our thoughts in the Dialogue Journal. I begin:

As to this shared work of weaving our story, what I glimpsed thru the shamanic journey last Friday of your women's circles, this tells me that we are soon to share much deeper experiences of your times.

I feel so too, Carol, and it makes me shiver with both delight and maybe a certain nervousness. I would not call it fear. The clearing ritual we were guided through allows some welcome Energies. The path before us is open and wonderfully clear!

And it is beckoning to us as never before, my Sister. We are soon to begin this new stage of our journey together.

Such joy and delight in this, dear Sister. When next we meet here, we shall link our Spirit-selves and set off along this track. We are powerful healers who work with the Light. I, perhaps, more certain of these powers than you, dear Sister. My days, my time, was one of going down into the Dark. Yours, as I am coming to understand, is a time when the Light is returning, the Darkness penetrated and illumined by its growing radiance. Yet we both know joy and great happiness of home and friends and celebrations marking the passage of the seasons. And for both of us the never-ceasing pleasures of our Mother's creations. It was scarcely ever without risk that our circle could join together, but our wooded glen was always arrayed in such dear beauty and attended by marvelous Beings be they fairy folk, tree or rock people (as I've heard you call them), or angelic presences. What a blessing this was for us all.

So much is stirring as the Autumn Equinox approaches. The *Hot Root* is awakening as Archangel Gabriel foretold and encouraged. An unexpected opportunity arises to join with others for Earth-healing work. A women's gathering is being organized in response to a psychic summons received by my friend and Isis priestess, Nancy Fanara. She is contacted by an etheric group of Native American Elders who wish us to travel to a sacred site north of Boston known as Mystery Hill or more popularly as America's Stonehenge. We're to offer healing ceremony in concert with the Beings who reside there. All indications are that it will be a powerful day.

So on a decidedly chilly late-September Sunday, seven of us drive into the parking area of Mystery Hill. A dear Mystery School friend, Cheryl, is with me and I'm thrilled by her avid desire to join in. I know we will draw deep inspiration from our many shared experiences of that wonderful community.

The cool, cloudy day has kept people away so the place is

largely deserted as we set off along the path into the woodland dotted with brooding, angular stone formations. We know that we'll be drawn to the place where we're to do our ceremony and also that wonders most surely await.

They certainly do.

On a rise near the western edge of the Hill, we find a clearing edged by several massive monoliths, some looking as if they possibly were shaped and others naturally formed. We set up a center altar and smaller ones at each of the Four Directions. Each of us finds the place on the circle's perimeter that feels right and we begin.

I go to each woman with a small bowl of Chalice Well water for a self-blessing, and with the help of our Helpers and Guides, we anchor ourselves deeply for the coming work. Cheryl starts by playing her singing bowl and we begin to raise the energy, signaling to the Beings of this place our presence and intent.

Nancy leads us in the ceremony that she's received and we all soon feel the presence of not only the Elders and Grandmother Spider, but the Tree and Rock people, and most marvelously, the Deva of Mystery Hill. We understand that our overall task is opening and re-attuning the ancient energies of this place of sacred power. We will also be anchoring the "new golden energies and crystalline sapphire Light to help mend the Net of Light."

We focus first on raising and releasing all negativity that has rooted itself in Mystery Hill. Much of this we suspect is from the centuries following the start of European settlement. At the height of this work we hear a wind coming through the woods. It sweeps through the clearing with a suddenness and force that amazes us, and then all is still. Wide-eyed, we smile and nod at each other.

Now to the incredibly dazzling part of welcoming and grounding the Light and reactivating the Earth-power centered here. Around us we can feel the joy and gratitude of the unseen

221

Ones of this sacred place. A special piece of our ceremony we know is happening simultaneously in Glastonbury where Mano Mannaz is offering her own ceremony in the grounds of the Abbey, connecting these energies with us.

A few weeks afterward I am given a message to share with the group about our work at Mystery Hill: *You are a community of strong-hearted women who worked so smoothly together and in complete trust to do such deep work and with considerable joy. You established a network of power lines through your crystals charged at the ceremony and taken to each of your homes. Grounding this energy into your land, you can send and receive energies through the altar site of your healing circle. In essence you are carrying the awakened pulse of this Earth-temple out across the land, helping to re-weave the vital Web.*

And I knew that Angeline had taken part that day. She spoke of this later on through the pages of our Dialogue Journal. The evening before the Mystery Hill ceremony Cheryl and I had driven to the ocean near her home. The weather was still very mild ahead of the next day's chill. We walked down to the water's edge, delighting in the soft, Autumn night and the gentle *swoosh* of the waves washing up on the beach and falling back. The just-risen Aries Full Moon cast its silvery path to us across the restless, mesmerizing ocean swells. Then I felt Angeline's approach and knew she'd come to stand beside me. Surrendering to this magic, we put our arms around each other and gazed out together onto the moonlit ocean, embraced by the sweet mysteries of this night. And as on that other day in Chalice Well's Garden, for several enchanted minutes, we were one.

A month later I am richly blessed to have a second, much longer chance to be beside the ocean with another powerful group of women. On a wonderfully warm October day, I make the four-hour drive to Ocean Grove, New Jersey to take part in Sacred Theater led by the inimitable Peggy Rubin. I know I'm in for a marvelous four days.

The company is extraordinary! I know many of the women from Mystery School and delight in meeting those who are new to me. Peggy leads us in wonderful exercises around the theme of Sophia's Transformative Cauldron. And we have unhurried time each day to make the short walk to the beach and be with Great Mother Ocean. Just as the weekends of Mystery School, I am giddily transported at these riches of experience and learning.

Peggy invites each of us for a one-on-one counseling session with her. I have known this warm, wise, and deeply compassionate woman for six years now. We sit down together the second morning and she takes my hands in hers, regarding me with such a loving gaze. I share some of the highlights of the past year's journey and she's quiet for a little, considering what I've said. Praising the progress I've made in my personal life and the ongoing Earth-healing work, she surprises me with the advice to seek a much slower pace to recuperate from all that's gone on. Of the wonderful Beings I've worked with she says, "Ask them to slow the pace. I've seen this before. When they find a 'live one' like you, so ready and willing, they aren't always aware that you can overdo and exhaust yourself." She smiles, seeing my surprised reaction and pats my hand, a mom giving loving advice to a daughter. "Find and secure your grounding, Carol. Go slowly, and sing... more!" She studies me thoughtfully for several moments and adds, "Be with the night and the dazzling darkness."

Encountering Angels unaware is something I've long embraced as a truth, and have likely had more than one experience of this. Very early one morning I go over to the beach for a walk before breakfast. It's foggy and a bit chilly, so few people are out. It's exhilarating to be alone beside the ocean. I'm immersed in my thoughts when I see a jogger and his dog approaching and can't help feeling annoyed that I'm about to be interrupted. The two draw near. The man is middle-aged, his glasses beaded with water drops from the fog. His dog is trotting ahead, tongue lolling, the picture of doggy delight. It would be rude not to say anything, so I smile at them. "Not a bad day to be out here really!" I gesture around at the mostly empty beach. The man slows his pace and gives me the brightest smile that lights up his face. "No, it's not. It's a nice morning," he says with enthusiasm. For a moment it's like he will linger, but then he starts off after the dog. Again that mega-watt grin. "Have a great day!" he tells me with the same earnestness. "You too," I say. "Both of you!" I watch them moving away down the beach, glad after all for this visitation. Then to my surprise, he calls back over his shoulder, raising his voice so I can hear, "Have a *great* day!" I wave, watching them go, my heart warmed by this sweet encounter, touched in a way I can't quite grasp.

For our morning exercise, Peggy asks us to think of someone who is important to us but with whom we are no longer in touch. We're to write a letter describing something we're grateful for about them. Immediately I think of my father whose passing happened in October of 1964 when I was a high school junior. I open my journal and find that the words come easily.

19th October 2010

Dear Dad,

It may be that this is the October day you left us in that golden autumn of 1964. I am not that good at remembering the exact date, but I know that is okay. Thank the stars and all that is holy that I know you and Mom are together and have been for 11 years. Thank you for every now and then letting me know that you are with me & with Keith & Cliff too. So much of what I love in life, that I love in my waking journey, is because of what you taught me in the 16 years we had each other to say good morning to and to hug each other goodnight. I am the world's luckiest daughter. I love you, Dad.

I breathe out shakily as I finish the writing, glad to have embraced this emotional work. Peggy looked around waiting for everyone to finish. Then she smiled with special warmth and said, "Now let this person write back to you." I caught my breath as did a few others. I had not anticipated this. Looking down at what I'd written, I take a deep breath, and then close my eyes to move to a place where Dad would find the entry point to respond. And something else registers... my encounter with the man and his dog that morning. I feel my father's warm and loving presence and let my pen receive his words.

Dear wonderful Carol, my beautiful daughter,

The day you came to your mother and me was easily one of the happiest days of my life. There was nothing more I wanted or needed, I remember thinking, especially the day we got to bring you home from the hospital—but we did need to wait for Cliff to come and join us, didn't we?

I am so glad that I was with you all when we first visited the sea..........

Perhaps he had more to say to me, but I was choking back tears by then, not only from his words but with the clear image of the man who'd spoken with me by the water. I grasped it now so clearly, why it was I was so touched by the encounter. His face and that so-familiar bright smile were so very much like my father's. And my father would have done the same... stopped to wish a stranger a cheery good morning and wish them a great day. He always found joy in each day. The greater truth stunned me even more, that it may just possibly have been my Dad reaching across to me there on that foggy beach, coming to say hello and *I love you,* and now speaking to me through this letter. It was all so enormous that I got up and went out on the porch to better gather my emotions and thoughts. The certainty of what had actually happened – of what was happening – got stronger and stronger.

In a short while Peggy and two other friends came out and sat with me, wanting to be sure I was all right. "Do you want to tell us what happened?" Peggy asked gently. I did my best to speak without sobbing while they held my hands and stroked my arm, the grounding and support I so needed. They were quite moved by the story and encouraged me to share it with the rest if I was up to it. I wasn't sure I could, but I wanted to try.

So I came back inside and took my seat in the circle, and read the two letters and told of the encounter on the beach. Many shed tears and expressed gratitude for my sharing all of it. Across the room from me, Patti, one of our Sacred Theater hosts, leaned forward, her eyes very bright. "Oh, Carol," she began, awe in her voice, "now I know who it was that came to me in my meditation this morning. It was a man who I didn't know. But he told me that he was here to connect with someone in our group." She paused, tears in her eyes. "Carol, I'm sure it was your Dad." I nodded, knowing this was true. We all felt the truth of this and what joy it was for me.

Abundantly refueled and filled by all my experiences in Ocean Grove, I return home to Dragonfly Cottage where I take Peggy's advice to heart about resting deeply. The days are growing shorter and colder with November's arrival, so it's a good time for going inward. For several weeks I mostly keep to myself and concentrate on being still. Through shamanic journeying comes confirmation that the time at Sacred Theater was a deep and wonderful healing of my Sacred Masculine, and that time I'm devoting to rest and quiet will indeed "secure your grounding" as Peggy had urged.

I learn Angeline is quite aware of what's going on with me, though the conversation that reveals this doesn't happen until nearly three months later. And as has held true for quite a long while, I left the Dialogue Journal untouched until that conversation. So devoted to my intention to deeply rest, I don't even nag myself much for letting this go too. But given that linear time is an illusion, "jumping" to this conversation is perfectly in order, so once more I'll let Angeline share her thoughts.

1st January 2011

Hello Angeline! I have returned once again to this joyful... joy-filled… conversation. Three months have passed since speaking with you here, but we've been together on many other occasions through quite wonderful connections. With that said, please know how good it feels to return to this always-special connection.

Hello, dear Carol, my beautiful Sister. The Goddess be praised for her welcome once again and for holding us in this wondrous place. You and I are dancing once more to and fro, my life to yours and yours to mine. Such a dance we do together!

You describe it wonderfully, my Sister. I have missed this Dance, but most likely you and I have been taken up by "other dancing" in our separate Journeys.

It is just so, Carol. My days are full with my work and life with our home, Joseph's and mine. I pray you are well, dear Sister. The Light I see around you is marvelous Bright this day!

Yes, I do feel this and am very well indeed! Soon after our last conversation here as I told you I would be doing, I journeyed to the gathering in Ocean Grove. Such a fantastic event of sharing, celebrating, and new growth of my Self. My wonderful teacher there, Peggy Rubin, took me aside one morning and offered extraordinary counsel.

And as you felt and are now remembering, Carol, I was nearby this and several other times. What a splendid time for us both! Please forgive what may seem rudeness, but dear Peggy's words to you to seek long and deep rest were much welcome to my ears. Now you will know that I have been quite aware of these months of your much-needed withdrawal. You are so wise to have followed this counsel! Seeing how bright is your Light this day, the needed effects of your retreat near-blind me with lovely brilliance!

The everyday world lives by linear time, so even though I honor the need to not overdo for a while, I pursue some work for the 2011 Pilgrimage. It's starting to come together easily. Once again

Spirit brings me the theme of this year's adventure, "Dancing with Gaia: A Woman's Mystical Journey." And gratifyingly, five women already are expressing enthusiasm for the trip.

My shamanic practice has never been so powerful or wonderful. On a mid-November morning, I travel to the Upper World seeking insights for the Pilgrimage. My journal notes are these.

16th November 2010

Great Owl carries me there. I am greeted by a beautiful Fairy Woman who knows me. We walk through an enchanted landscape to a sunlit courtyard with a fountain. Invited to sit down beside it, Isis appears. "Welcome, daughter." I speak of the Pilgrimage and those who will come. "Yes, it is to be for women exclusively. Each will be making a journey of the soul. You will do what you do best: hold the energy for the deep and joyous work each one comes to do for herself. All is in Divine Order and wonderfully so. One who knows and loves the place is here now to speak to you." She welcomes Mary Magdalene and then withdraws.

We sit together and look out at the summer-land.

[I know that we've come to Avalon... the "Summer-lands," an ancient name for Somerset.]

"I was so deeply at peace here among these good people. I taught both men and women who welcomed my story and that of my Beloved. These truths and teachings were passed on in their full glory and power for many generations. Such powerful truths can never be completely extinguished tho' some worried that this would be so. There is such deep protection here for the Light of this Learning, tho' darkness seemingly prevailed for long, desperate centuries. You will know the whole story of your days as Angeline and she of your time—of your shared and beautiful Lives. There are others... some are still haunted by disturbing dreams, but they will and are awakening. You are blessed with Great Light both then and now. Seek further revelations to help unfold the fullness of this story. Soon all will be revealed. Have no doubt. The joy

of this is beyond anything you have yet known."

I reread these notes many times over the next few weeks, deeply touched by the messages of both the Fairy Woman and Mary Magdalene. Any lingering doubt about undertaking a 2011 Pilgrimage vanishes. Soon the arrangements with the Daisy Centre are finalized for my group's stay there next September. It all feels fabulous!

We enter December, the last month of 2010. 2012 is just over the horizon, twelve months off. The pace of things is soon to quicken exponentially and I will come to be very grateful for the rest and renewal I sought in this Autumn. There will be precious little downtime in the months ahead.

Chapter 17

Indeed, I know the Holy Thorn well, such a dear presence above St. Bridget's holy isle.

Many who came on pilgrimage to Glastonbury sought the way to its sacred place and there thanked St. Joseph for his long and perilous voyage to reach these shores.

~ Angeline

On December 8th of 2010, I'm back in Unadilla Forks staying for the night. As has been true for some time, Ken and I pass the evening companionably. I have an odd headache, something not usual for me. It's low in the back of my head and even aspirin doesn't help much. I go to bed hoping a night's sleep will cure it.

But it's a restless night full of dreams. In one, I come out of a woods into a clearing and find an odd wooden building, a tall tower perhaps three stories high. Curious and without much hesitation I cross the porch and enter to find others there already. There's some sort of gathering, a workshop, I think, and we all go up to the top floor. The workshop is underway when I begin to get an uneasy feeling that something bad is about to happen. The building begins to sway and I jump to my feet seeing that it's already starting to topple. I yell at everyone to get out of the building fast. Somehow we all manage to make it down the stairs and outside just as it crashes to the ground. I stand with the others looking at the wreckage, shaken, but unharmed.

I startle awake, still feeling the horrible sway of the building, the panic of escaping, and the sad destruction of the odd wooden tower. Somehow I manage to fall back to sleep but when I wake in the morning it's with the dream's still vivid, unsettling memory.

I join Ken in the kitchen and open my laptop to check e-mails while I eat my breakfast. Outside the December morning, the 9th, is bright and sunny. *Yahoo Mail* appears and at the very top is an e-mail from Mano. Even as it opens I feel her stunned grief pouring out, delivering the news with such force that I can't breathe. It is unbelievable. She reports that someone has attacked the Holy Thorn with a chainsaw and its severed limbs are lying in pieces around its trunk that somehow miraculously survived the attempt to pull the whole of it down. She had been one of the first people to come having seen its altered shape from her apartment window. Nearly every morning she would look out at Wearyall Hill across town, the Holy Thorn raising its small canopy on the slope. As soon as she'd seen its horribly mutilated form, she rushed there. Her e-mail is full of her anguish.

With fingers that shake so badly that typing is difficult, I write a short reply letting her know the news has reached me and sending every bit of comfort I can to her and those gathering. I describe what happened to Ken who shakes his head in disbelief at people's behavior. He has never been to Glastonbury but he knows what the Holy Thorn means to people. It was meant to be a mortal blow to this beloved tree and the keening grief of people all around the world when they hear the news begins to come in waves to Wearyall Hill.

There is no way to make sense of it, but once my thoughts stop swirling, the dream's meaning snaps into clear focus. More incredibly, I believe there was a message in the odd headache of the evening before. The tall, column-like wooden building was a dream image of the Holy Thorn. The swaying and horrible fall was the Thorn's being severed and dismembered, the work of the people who literally attacked it and were bent on cutting it down. The strange pain at the base of my skull was an etheric echo of the Thorn's pain as its limbs were severed.

Before I got up from the breakfast table, I wrote an e-mail to the Mystery School community knowing the connection many had to Glastonbury and the Holy Thorn. Many replied that day and the next few days with their own incredulous disbelief, mourning this terrible loss, and sending prayers for any possible recovery of this beautiful Being.

These messages joined what rapidly became countless other prayers to the Thorn and the Glastonbury community who so loved it. The news flooded out around the world even making headlines in US newspapers, radio, and television. Amidst all the sharings in the coming weeks, I learned that many others had also had premonitions and nightmares. The Holy Thorn called out to many of us and somehow we must have helped soften the blows as we bore witness, often unwittingly, of the senseless attack and its fall.

More news stories continued coming out: images of the branches being carried reverently away down the hill and of plans hurriedly being put in place to try and salvage viable branches to start new thorns; moving videos of people who came by the dozens and dozens to weep and lovingly touch the tall stump, its shorn limb stubs swathed in protective salve. And there were many ceremonies of healing and thanks to this beautiful One.

Within a very short time, the dark and horrible energy of the attack soon was blessedly and powerfully transformed by the waves of love and healing prayers that poured in from all corners of the Earth. The Holy Thorn had become a bright beacon of hope and an even greater presence than before the pre-dawn attack on December 9th.

No one was ever arrested for this terrible act though a full-scale investigation was launched at once. To speculate on why anyone would do such a thing gains little, though history records one other such wanton attack by the total destruction of an earlier Holy Thorn that stood there when in the 1600s Cromwell zealots hacked that one down and obliterated it. After that venomous era passed, a new one was eventually planted with its latest successor in 1951.

It was not until April that I shared this story with Angeline due to my erratic work with the writing and also my reluctance to share this sadness. One morning we have a conversation about the September Pilgrimage and a ceremony Mano had done for the trip's success. The time had come to tell her. I began by describing Mano's work:

The place she chose [for the ceremony] was at the Copper Beech in the Abbey grounds... such a wonderful joy flowed into my heart in those minutes!

Yes, such beautiful abundance! We have such staunch allies in our tree friends. They pass forward hidden messages and honorable thoughts... I do know the place where your Copper Beech friend now stands – I will try to comment more on this in some future time. There is a sweet story there, but for this moment let it be said how attuned both you and I are to the trees in our lives and wanderings, a kindred tie I treasure, Sister!

And I as well, Angeline. I look forward to hearing more about this particular spot in the Abbey's ground. [I pause and take a deep breath.] Let me put this question to you. What did you know of the Holy Thorn that stood on Wearyall Hill?

Oh yes! Indeed, I know it well... such a dear presence above St. Bridget's holy isle. Many who came on pilgrimage to Glastonbury sought the way to its sacred place and there thanked St. Joseph for his long and perilous voyage to reach these shores (for they were truly shores in that distant time). It is a place where some, most usually women and girls, entertain visions of Mary – a few know her to be our blessed Magdalene. It [the Thorn] is a very ancient one and much weathered by its time on Wearyall. I am sure, Carol, that you must know this place too if you have asked me this question. But what is the odd image that I see through your vision?

[Wordlessly, I convey the story of how the Holy Thorn was vandalized on December 9th and how it has received a tremendous outpouring of Love. And that so wonderfully new growth appeared on the surviving stump on Spring Equinox last month. I feel how this news shocks and saddens Angeline.]

It is a great sadness to hear this, dearest Sister. But there is no surprise in what you tell of how savagely the Thorn was attacked. Mara and others I know tell tales of how the Holy Groves were similarly cut down and so I grasp the sadness and that of all others who wept on that dark day.

Whenever thoughts of this sad matter cross my mind, I often remember that October afternoon when I made my way up to the Thorn through the wild winds to offer the last prayers of the healing journey I'd been on all that day in Avalon. And how I clung to the railing while the Thorn's branches bent in the gale and how it offered sacred witness to the holy words I shared for the final time there beside it. I'd be seeing it in September in its shorn state and wondered how I'd manage when the time comes.

And so 2011 arrives. Twelve months to go until 2012. Trees and Nature-beings figure evermore prominently in dreams and meditations. I settle into a shamanic meditation on January 11th, a portal day: 1/11/2011. With my Guides I travel to a seashore where a celebration is held *"... to show me the vastness of my work opening now. And the theme running through is that it is abundant in Joy and Delight. A Raven figure appears who tells of the state of the world's peoples, of those in particular who might learn of me tho' not all are ready."* The scene shifts and I travel to Angeline's home where she gladly receives me. She shows me a place where she leaves offerings to *The Good Folk.* Bridget joins us and reminds us we are to call on her as we continue our shared story. In the midst of this session, I recall my tree-dream of the previous night. I receive the beautiful insight *"... how we are tree-Beings with roots, trunks, and branches serving as Light (energy) connections between Earth and the Net of Light. We are re-weaving the damaged places in the Net."*

Opportunities to do this work of re-weaving and healing show up in rapid fashion. Out of the blue – or so it always seems – I'm connected with an amazing group of people when I'm invited to join something called the Earth Response Team. This is the work of a California woman, Christan Hummel, who works with Earth elementals, and in particular, Devic Beings. The opportunity to be a part of this comes through Nancy who wrote to Christan about the work we did at Mystery Hill. Christan was mightily impressed and invited us to join her current class at a deep discount. Three of us, Nancy, Kirsten, and me, take her up on her offer. The three-week training will focus on "weather technologies" for healing of the planet. Our time together revolves around weekly sessions held over the phone.

The first ERT call is powerful and spirit-expanding. Nancy phones the next day to say that in a conversation after the class, she and Kirsten sense I am a powerful teacher. It's been mentioned before, but I know this latest nudge is not to be ignored. It does give more fuel for a new undertaking that I've been contemplating for a while at Spirit's suggestion. I'm to try my hand at writing an online blog... the time seems to have arrived. So I set to work on gathering ideas, choosing the right Internet platform, and working on the first piece.

All of this is taking place in the swirl of shock and sorrow around the tragic shooting in Tucson, Arizona on January 8th when a young man attempts to kill Congresswoman Gabby Gifford. As most reading this will remember, she miraculously survives but six people attending her rally are killed. The death of nine-year-old Christina-Taylor Green is the hardest one for most people to handle. President Obama leads the nation in a powerful memorial service which I listen to on the radio. In his 33-minute address, a grace-filled and healing speech, he urges us to seize hope and "turn our actions now to creating a nation as good as the one Christina imagines it to be." In my journal I write my prayer that "this speech and this night will surely mark the start of the shift so long sought and hoped for."

It is the signal to offer my voice more loudly. So on January 13th, I click the "publish" tab and *Notes of an Earth Pilgrim* is launched into cyberspace.

After what have been months of contemplation in starting this blog, I'm borrowing opening words from a man whose life journey has inspired me ever since his book, Anam Cara, *dropped into my hands long ago in a Barnes & Noble aisle. Some will know the name without my writing it... John O'Donohue. This is how he begins his book: "It is strange to be here.*

The Mystery never leaves you alone."

Perhaps because of my Celtic roots, these words hold particular power. I certainly know that as long as I can remember, the powerful Mystery that O'Donohue names has intrigued and enchanted me, and with whatever Grace my life is blessed, may it always be so. Maybe, if not likely, my being Aries-born predisposes me to the delicious enjoyment of exploring this Mystery, to being drawn to embracing adventures that present themselves to me along the way... and by this decade of my life, my sixth, there have been a goodly number! And at the top of the second page of Anam Cara, *this: "Humans are new here. Above us, the galaxies dance out toward infinity. Under our feet is the ancient earth. We are beautifully molded from clay. Yet the smallest stone is millions of years older than us. In your thoughts, the silent universe seeks echo."*

A most memorable moment in my young life was the first Moon-landing. The truly breathtaking photos of Earth taken by the astronauts showed us our beautiful Home, deep blue of the Oceans, white masses of clouds, red-brown of the continents, this "Big Blue Marble" floating against the backdrop of the black and starry heavens, carrying us along in its timeless journey around the Sun. And I a present passenger upon its exquisite, glimmering surface.

Through much of the journey of my life I have kept records of my days in many a diary and journal. Arriving at this time and place where marvels of technology allow such things, I've been nudged to share some of my musings and observations with the "wider World"... with you. Perhaps you'll care to respond with your own comments and notes of your own Earth pilgrimage and I encourage you if that comes to mind.

We are all sharing a marvelous journey here on this beautiful Earth. I'll admit to a bit of trepidation as I click the right buttons to "publish," but all journeys and adventures begin with a first step. So now, on the count of 3, I'm pushing off from Shore... 3... 2... 1... !!!

It garners warm support at once. Nancy writes, *Wonderful to see your bardic spirit in this lovely blog. Congratulations and may it bring many blessings to all.* Rose Husted, my drumming group leader, leaves this comment: *You are a talented writer. I know this because I read your book,* Downstream. *Your blog looks very inviting. Thanks for sharing your gifts.* And my three-time Glastonbury-sister Mari writes, *So exciting to be all aboard another magical mysterious journey with you. WriteON!*

Bardic spirit... sharing my gifts. I am humbly reminded that it's sometimes necessary to let others in and listen to their messages to understand more of my true Self.

The work with the Earth Response Team continues to be potent. Our group includes Ian from Wales, Stephanie in New Zealand, and Sherridan in Australia. My Guides bring through helpful information to support and expand what we're doing. In a Lower World journey Horse introduces a new ally, Crow. Crow speaks to me of matters related to such things as groups, institutions, and forces such as HAARP that are *"flailing about causing apparent harm though not all of it is intended but is 'an unfortunate by-product,' they would say. You with so many others are to focus your Light and Love forces on them. This is a force of golden radiance to heal and whole. Always work from your heart space. It is a power greater exponentially than all these apparently negative ones. As you strengthen this Net of Light and Earth-matrix grid, it is absolutely inevitable that you all will be successful. Allow this message to empower you and source yourself in Joy always!"*

One night Christan leads us in an incredibly powerful meditation bringing us etherically to Uluru in the heart of Australia. She had received a message from an etheric group of Aboriginal Elders to invite us to come there. We began with a fabulous Tree meditation during which I spend time with Carnaphon, and then we descend to a cavern beneath this ancient Earth edifice. My journal reflection is this:

During our soul-stirring time together within the Earth there, I came face to face with Gaia. She was ageless, dressed in a simple brown-gold garment and cloak, of human stature, and gentle and completely welcoming though I sensed a certain weariness. "Our connection is an ancient one, beautiful Earth-Woman. You have honored and enjoyed this bond in nearly all of your many, your myriad, lives here. The warrior-leader that you are is elegantly paired with your soul-connected twin. I will call her Angeline. The treasures you share will be many, my Daughter. The landscape of your travels is vast."

And indeed, Angeline appears and we are together in this wondrous place of Light. The work of our ERT group was exponentially strengthened through a purification by fire leading to an image of us joined together in a circle which becomes a huge, gleaming, light-filled Chalice.

Amidst the swirl of heartbreaking events in the wider world, this time together with Christan and the ERT group is immensely grounding and reaffirming of a better world slowly emerging.

Mid-February and Valentine's Day bring more wonderful encounters and messages. Dragonfly Cottage provides such a wonderful container for the work. The Winter sun pours in through the windows from the sun's rise over the Susquehanna well into late afternoon. Two prisms hanging in the south window strew rainbows lavishly into the room. Though not the best-insulated place, my faux-Franklin stove-heater combined with the fiery and luminous work with Angeline keeps me snug.

Archangel Gabriel and Mary Magdalene have teamed up to aid our work. Frequently I'd puzzled and even anguished over what exactly was the proper form of Angeline's and my story which I was striving to write. One morning they tell me: *"Allow the story to take more of its own shape. Be less anxious in how it is now emerging. All of the beautiful goddesses thru Doreen Virtue's Angel*

Cards that turned up for you this morning trumpet this message of abundance in the flow of this work! And as we encouraged you to do at the end of our visit this morning, jump into these beautiful Light-filled waters and play! Who better than your dolphin friends to companion you in this journey?? Consider what you already know so well, that what lies at the heart of this story is Love. Your twinned lives form a wondrous chalice overflowing now with the radiant energies of this shared journey. Its source is your hearts and there is simply no end and no limit to any of it. And as you both know so very well (but we say it here for Carol to record), we, Gabrielle and Mary of Magdala, are abundantly present to aid you in the en-joy-ment and right-completion of this work. Thank you for calling on us!" And then Mary asks me to draw a smiley face on the page! And I do just that.

I mention this Journey to Angeline in our journal conversation later that day. She replies with such delight,

Dearest Sister, Carol... in hearing all of this and in reading the words of your Journal pages, I can scarce contain my desire to gambol around my work space like one of the young lambs in their meadow. And yes!, you truly must write over the words of blessed Gabrielle and Mary onto these pages. Bring these splendid energies in! Please weave this Light in and through our sharings.

I feel the warmth of her smile and happy presence looking over my shoulder as I do the copying into the journal. Finished with this I add:

And this followed by several more de-Light-ful entries that capture more "magicks, mysteries, and marvels" that speak eloquently of the abundance of this shared journey. As an expression of these days goes, this is all "pretty nifty"!

It is all so beautiful and in my eyes, magnificent – the unfolding of a rare and precious flower whose blooming I scarce dared hope for and now I bear witness to, and do so side by side with you! Such long, barren times came between our two lives, dear Sister. Only echoes in these dim corridors that I have glimpsed in my dreams, scarcely audible to any who found their way within. But then the day arrived when you dared to set your foot on the path to the crossroads!

Such rejoicing there *was* that day among our Helpers and for each of us as well, Angeline, even if it was much longer until we both came to fully comprehend its significance and meaning. When I return to Glastonbury later this year, it will be ten years since our encounter that day... oh my! Yes, it is time for the full flowering of this extraordinary friendship of ours. No longer faint echoes but happy exclamations and songs of Joy! ... And to this end do I pledge the work of my heart, leaving you now with deep thanks and much love, dearest Angeline, beloved Sister. Namaste'

With my gratitude to you in equal measure, dearest, Carol. Such joy there will be when next we meet! Adieu and Namaste'

With March's arrival, I'm mindful of the final weeks of my Solar Year, one in which Venus has been the Ruler. Up early the first day of March, I'm treated to the sight of bright Venus on the horizon sparkling near the waning Moon's crescent and am prompted to listen again to my Solar Return done by my longtime astrologer-extraordinaire, Sr. Paula Mathew. I record these thoughts in my journal:

It has been a profound unfolding of just about everything she spoke of... With Venus, I've been in the quadrant of Snake Shedding its Skin (8th House), and that I would be seeking balance in my emotional life (7th House). Yes! There have been incredible clearings and re-balancings of connections to men—certainly with Ken in moving out of the shadow of the two years of transition and both of us reaching pretty good grounding in our respective lives, and finding we're at least content and often even pleased, if not happy, with just about all of it... Along this vein too was the marvelous experience at Sacred Theatre of reconnecting with Dad, so yes, this alone would fill out this part of my Solar Return.

And so much that I heard again is about this being a year of "marketing myself" and becoming visible. And that "when I apply my initiative, there will be a steady, systematic advancement of my work and goals." Sunday's Unity talk and the greatly-engaging preparation for it is a marvelous exemplar. Not that it's much of a stretch to be enthusiastic about Glastonbury!

Chapter 18

I've listened with rapt delight to my new Solar Return. My year's Ruler is the Beloved bringing "lots of Shakti" and helping to activate all sorts of things! Foreign travel is fully supported this year—as long as I "tend to details diligently"... ah!
~ Journal Entry, 5th April 2011

Sr. Paula's reading for my new year resonated deeply and delightfully and the calendar date of my birthday, the 14th, was still days away. The same journal entry in which I pondered her various messages also captured what was truly fabulous family news:

Surprisingly lengthy pause between entries but not for unpleasant reasons. At the moment a wet snow is falling, but ever so slowly Spring is coming on. By far the biggest, most wonderful news is that Tracy and Justin are pregnant!! They shared the news with Ken and me on Saturday before the rest of the house-warming party arrived. Grandbaby #3 (wow!) is due in mid-November—plenty of time for me to get to England and back. There will be lots of musings on this splendid new part of their and our lives.

So this already incredible year, 2011, takes on an even more lovely and amazing significance for me. I've been delighted from the first day of grand-motherhood to now 11-year-old Brianna, and 7-year-old Logan. It is a completely magical role which I have happily inhabited for eleven years. Now I'll be helping my firstborn, our son, to welcome his own little one to the world and all that this means. And the news gets even more amazing when they share that the due date is 11/11/11. Wonders never cease!

Other promising and exciting portents of my Solar Return are these: *There's also potent support for Earth-healing work and at profound levels since there is an activation of my power as a Healer. I already sense the vibrant connection with another huge gift of this new chart, and that is Paula's enthusiastic statement that it's a year that is "very good for a writer!"*

While I take heart from Sr. Paula's words about positive prospects for writing and especially am pleased with the posts I'm composing for *Notes of an Earth Pilgrim*, the often slow and halting progress on *Luminous Threshold* still brings frequent angst. After all, it's been ten years since Angeline and I encountered one another. A whole decade! And I've been resident at Dragonfly Cottage now for three years with every expectation when I arrived that I'd be galloping along with the book and seeing it to its completion.

With the gaps between sessions, there are times I reread entries in the Dialogue Journal which has just reached one hundred pages. These review sessions serve the purpose of reminding me where we left off. But increasingly often, looking back through the entries I am completely awed by past events and the growing dimensions of this incredible journey Angeline and I are sharing.

During one such morning's musings I'm also nudged to study the intriguing map of Glastonbury which shows the ley lines and energy centers, the amazing work of Palden Jenkins. And then in lovely synchronicity, my eyes rest on one of my quartz points, the Tangerine Quartz. It had come to be with me when I began studies with Nancy and started practicing the Isis Seichim attunement.

I hold the small point in my hand and close my eyes. Within moments it communicates quite a special message: *"Own we must our solitary journeys—but that an illusion as all our hearts are one, whether awakened or closed up in tight bud. Find you the flame hidden in the ember of this seeming insubstantial Fire. Faith, old and renewed, blows life anew into its Heart and from its rapidly (yes) growing Light, the newborn Phoenix arises claiming the upward-spiraling journey once more."*

I swiftly record this resonant message in my journal and am in awe at these amazing, ecstatic images. It is a particularly powerful message for us. Angeline and I are both quite struck by it and share this conversation a few days later…

Such beautiful presence and energies from our time together on Friday, Angeline – you and I returning to our separate lives for a while, but with ever keener awareness of our parallel journeys. But, as on Friday, such a palpable resonance humming between us today!

Ah, yes, dearest Sister, like a nourishing soup that needs a day or two before its full flavor can be most savory! And I too taken by delighted surprise at the message of the Tangerine Quartz. More and more magick comes to us the further we journey together.

It is a cauldron of possibilities and transformation, I do believe – and the events and "unfoldings" of these times in which I… Carol… live have called us to the work of *allowing* its total and all-encompassing alchemy… More time in this next week to be in deeper connection with our work, especially nice in the timing of my birthday's arrival and the exciting details of my new Solar Return! We are sailing into such exciting and promising waters…

Yes! I feel myself attuned quite wonderfully to these messages… Thinking of our journey together as a voyage, it has never been quite so wondrous! And I am seeing something more clearly, and perhaps for the first time grasping its true dimensions. Here it is: though it is in our opening our lives in trust to each other, and though I know I am assisting you by revealing, *sharing,* my life to you, it is you who are charged with the work of fashioning all of these "bits and bobs" into written pages that others then can look upon to gain a full and fair understanding of our story. And all that I need do is go about this life of mine and then engage my Soul's voice (for that truly is what I see it to be) to you. Carol, your work is *much* harder than mine could ever be! My admiration for all you are doing knows no bounds, dear Sister. Pray do not ever be discouraged.

Angeline, I am most grateful for your words and their heartening effect! I am on some days more frustrated than I am discouraged. Much of that is due to what feels like "slow progress." But with the messages of my Solar Return comes the marvelous affirmation that all is in Perfect Timing. What energies and experiences that are promised in this year ahead will witness the full revealing and manifestation of our interwoven lives... and what of *all this* is meant to touch others' lives. [I pause and reread what I've just written.] There is something so stunning and extraordinary in recording these thoughts.

And so very beautiful in their powerful truths... so very beautiful! The Goddess, Brigid, is smiling to us!

An opportunity to see what my Solar Return meant about the greater activation of my work as an Earth-healer is just around the corner. I'm set to travel to Nashville to join my Mystery School roommate and dear friend, Dawn, for a week's visit culminating in a gathering she's calling, *Marry the Earth*. I'm going to offer a part of the ceremony connecting us with the element of water and of course bringing in Glastonbury's sacred energies.

But before this I'm part of two closer-to-home gatherings, first traveling with a busload of local people to an anti-fracking rally at the State Capitol in Albany. We gather with hundreds of others listening to inspiring speakers, and raising our voices lustily intending to be heard by the legislators and the governor. My hand-lettered sign says, *"Clean Air & Water for my Grandchildren and the Next 7 Generations,"* and I've attached a photo of Brianna and Logan in the corner. It's an excellent day of raising Fractivist-energy together.

I should have taken more heed of Sr. Paula's advice about "tending to details diligently" when traveling. I set out on the first leg of my journey to Nashville driving to my cousin's home in Cleveland where I'd spend the night and then take the bus from there the next morning. An hour along I discover that I'd left behind the folder with both the MapQuest printout to her home along with the bus tickets. My hosts were actually not at home, but assured me others had stayed there "solo" as I was about to do. I was anticipating that the trickiest part would be letting myself in without setting off the burglar alarm and thereby summoning the police!

Bless cell phones, since a couple calls to Anne and husband, Jim, gave me all the details I needed. That, and a good memory of the map guided me successfully into their Cleveland neighborhood late that afternoon after rush hour. And then success in opening the door to their comfortable condo without raising a ruckus. That was an especially good moment!

Their neighbors were expecting me and were most helpful in helping to print off a fresh set of tickets. And then as planned, early the next morning they drove me to the bus station, a kindness I so appreciated. So a bit past 8AM our group of us eighteen or so travelers were heading South into Spring leaving the chilly Northeast behind. Among my fellow passengers was a polite-spoken young man who I'd talked to in line before boarding, an Afghan vet who was on his way to a new life.

Dusk is deepening when I step off the bus in Nashville and hear Dawn's excited voice in the crowd, "Carol!" A strong hug and then into her car. On the way to her home we stop to see the famous Parthenon in its lighted splendor. It's like gazing through a portal into another world, maybe a parallel reality. We'll be returning here the next day for a mesmerizing start to our adventures.

We're joined by Dawn's friend, Marion, a sister-spirit and passionate Earth-lover. She will be doing the Earth-element part of the Sunday gathering. Dawn and I had earlier observed that this time together had a distinctive "Mystery School" sense about it. Apart from Dawn's original vision of the *Marrying the Earth* ceremony, there were definitely other things already calling to us.

Our very first morning in true Mystery School fashion, *chronos time* shifted to *kairos*. We began by visiting the Parthenon and spending time with Athena replicated in the full and glorious dimensions of her original counterpart in Greece. We left with her blessings for the work of the days ahead. All three of us felt Gaia also joining us to direct our steps and activities. And very soon too the increasingly strong presence of lively Elemental Beings of Nashville's ancient landscape who desired to connect with us in the various places we were guided to visit.

Dawn's knowledge of Nashville's deep history gave us insights into its having been a sacred place of the Native Americans. And there were intriguing hints of perhaps an even more ancient lineage. In particular she had been investigating Bicentennial Park in the center of the city and its mile-long layout below the Capitol's buildings on their stately hilltop. We focused quite a bit of our attention there.

As is true of any urban landscape, the long years of *occupation* and urbanization had heavily damaged both the land and its hidden, metaphysical history. We understood our role of that day's work was one of re-cognition, offering gratitude, and manifesting healing as best we were able.

Following Dawn's intuitive sense of places we were to go to, further subtle beckonings began to come to us individually and also as simultaneous awarenesses. Well versed as we all were in ceremonial practice, once guided to those wounded places, we made our offerings of love and gratitude and most especially of healing.

This day of sacred Earth-healing work richly deserves a longer writing, and perhaps someday I'll see that it's done. But one incident deserves to be included. We moved slowly along through Bicentennial Park pausing at the places we sensed sought our presence and ministering at each one as we felt inspired to do. Reaching the western end we stood on the sidewalk while Dawn pointed out some of the historical events connected with the spot. I suddenly felt a strong "tug" from something across the busy street. We crossed together and I followed the energy-thread into a small, empty parking lot that was decidedly the worse for wear. There on the edge stood a huge boulder. It was clearly beckoning to us. We each chose a place beside it and rested our hands on its craggy surface, at once feeling a low vibration, almost an audible hum. Silently we tuned in to this ancient Rock Being sending it love and healing. I was reminded of the ancient megalith of Mystery Hill. After several minutes we felt a *clearing* and a deep gratitude for our having responded to its call. We bid it farewell and headed back to Dawn's car, musing on this especially magickal-ending of our day.

At week's end we drove to Dawn and partner Jerry's beautiful country home high in the hills an hour outside of Nashville. Close to twenty-five people had responded to say they were coming to take part in the *Marry the Earth* celebration. Buoyed by the rich and heart-expanding experiences of the previous several days in Nashville, Dawn, Marion, and I... Jerry too... were very excited about hosting this gathering.

Their land was already so deeply blessed by their loving and attentive presence. It was a great joy to spend time with the Nature Beings of the land, the stones, flowers, and especially the magnificent trees.

Afternoon of the next day was special in every way Dawn envisioned it to be. It was unseasonably cool for early May in Tennessee, but the warmth we shared through the Earth-element work and mutual recognition of the Earth-lover in all of us more than made up for this. By the time Dawn and Jerry led us in the ceremony of Marrying the Earth, all felt Gaia's loving presence with us. Each one in turn spoke their vow to Her and then proceeded along the ceremonial path back to the house. Dusk settled in and we celebrated this extraordinary day with food and fellowship.

As the Summer of 2011 approached, life brought continued

demands of time and energy, physical and psychic. While I'd love to just continue hiding away at Dragonfly Cottage with Angeline and our writing, some invitations to be elsewhere just can't be turned down.

When time does come to reconnect with Angeline, it is always a rich experience. This never changes, a constancy that comforts me. A shamanic journey in early June reveals more of our mystical connections.

... a Middle World journey over the waves to Glaston: A whirlwind visit to the Trees of Chalice Well, then to the Abbey and Carnaphon. Then time jump to be with Angeline. Before we could connect, saw a tallow candle flickering in a dark space. A cavern behind the White Springs—others there... two lovers who parted quickly and hurried away. A voice says, "There are more tunnels thru here." // Now I'm in a woods amidst huge trees... A.'s voice, "I am a woods-wanderer seeking wild plants for my work." Shown how she and others knew of the ley lines and their capacities. Glimpses of "undercover" gatherings of wise women. Oh! A. tells me that on rare occasion in days of thick mists she might encounter one of the Old Ones as their worlds touched and overlapped. More to explore here in re-weaving the web. Then it is that we become very present to each other so that we reach out and clasp our hands together in great, great joy, and we share such beautiful words.

Call Back and reluctantly we let go!

In a Dialogue Journal session a few days later, we share observations about our Spirit Helpers and, most wonderfully, about those she calls *the Old Ones*.

... you have experienced this for yourself, Carol, when you have been here on this land... the woodlands and the meadows, the high places, and of course the wells and the springs. In all of these places dwell Beings of the Other World. Some are fairies, some are most ancient Spirits of Holy Nature to the Old Ones (those who I spoke of before), goddesses and gods as you might name them. And most especially, the spirits of the trees and

plants, the stones, and the Voice of the Land which has spoken to me or so I feel she has. I have forgotten the Angels! I do not mean just those that the Church names, but those who come to us in dreams and unheralded to our presence (as I have found true!). Do I stray from what you are asking?

No... it is a vast topic. Who are the particular Beings most meaningful to you? And I would also add that, like you, I am especially close to the nature spirits!

The Lady of the Holy Well, She-of-the-White Spring (these are two, not one), and the Great Goddess of the Ancient Grove known as Nemetona. These three are of particular importance. And I would also name both Bridget (most call her St. Bridget, others Bride), and our Mother Mary of the Great Church. There is of course the blessed and wondrous Mary Magdalene. All of these, and St. Michael too, enter into the story you are recording on your computer writing-machine. Glastonbury has seen many saints both earthly and some more exalted. It can be quite the tangle [smile]... But none of us are alone! I never want for pleasant company when I am off alone to the meadows and the trees.

[*We continue to "discuss" the topic directly with one another in our unspoken thoughts, as happens on occasion, returning to the Dialogue Journal to capture some of the conversation...*]

We both seem to agree that those patrons of our shared lives and play-full work are Archangel Gabrielle, beautiful Bridget, and the Goddess Nemetona. They are over-lighting our story-weaving and its ultimate birth to the wider world. What do you think of this, my beautiful Sister?

In as strong a voice as I can raise to you, I feel the absolute truth of those Ones you have named. We are so mightily blessed by their presence *to* and *with* us. And we both know there are many more besides these three. It is a marvelous company! And we are at this moment *remembering* your greeting by the Spirit of the Land – what you call the Deva – when you arrived at the field gate. Let us both call upon her each time we come together to do this blessed work!

What a lovely ritual to add to our future sessions! And so it shall be!

And not long after this conversation, no better example of these loving Beings present to us than a beautiful time we share together through a Middle World journey:

Astride Pegasus to A.'s time directly to Glaston's streets on Market Day, and right to A.'s booth! I startle her and she gives me a huge smile. Sr. Susan arrives "on cue" and perceives my Spirit-form, very pleased at this. She takes me into the Abbey to the Mary Chapel. We enter through huge carved doors to the stunning interior... deep reds, blues, golds, bronzes... luxuriant in every possible detail. "We spare no expense for Our Heavenly Mother," Sr. S. says silently, eyes a-twinkle. A glimpse into the Cloister with its emerald green lawns and plantings, a splashing fountain in the center.

As Angeline and I prepare to depart for her home, a warm encounter with Br. Paulus (who is unaware of me). He gives A. his blessing for a safe journey.

Only a glimpse of the house and Joseph. A. tells him she's off to the high field to gather a certain plant before the evening dew descends, so off we go together "arm in arm." What an incredible view of the Summer's land at sunset! We tend to the hidden place where I left crystals last Summer. A Deva's appearance coincides with appearance of shadowy figures that may be the Old Ones. Flash of a night scene of a ritual fire set within a small stone circle. A. and I pledge our unceasing devotion to the Deva and love of the Land, and also to one another.

As I finished writing these journey notes, I receive this additional message: *"Rejoice now and always. There is no end of this Light and Love."*

July bustles in with plenty of demands on time and energy including welcoming my new housemate, Angus, Justin and

Tracy's cat who had worn out his welcome at their place with his singular black-cat personality. It's a mostly-smooth adjustment and I'm happy to have this particular feline with me under the roof of Dragonfly Cottage. Just maybe I've acquired a special Muse to help with the writing... a thought that makes me smile.

The number of people for September's pilgrimage spirals up and down generating predictable angst for me. Ah, familiar territory. I'm no better this time at handling this distraction to my creative life. On the morning of July 5th my peace of mind is quite well restored when I receive this wonderful message from Mary Magdalene.

Dear One, beautiful Daughter,

It is I, the Magdalene, seeking you in this moment, respectfully requesting this ecstatic connection with you, beautiful way-shower to the portal called by the name Avalon. Fear not for any part of this year's gathering as all is very well in its full and complete unfolding, most especially for your own ecstatic journey that is already blessed with exquisite treasure, some known and so very much that will be revealed. Do not let un-grounded anxieties—all of them needless—dim the Light and vibration of the summons you have so eloquently and artfully crafted.

Let all know that I am beckoning and am awaiting all of you with much Love and Light. It is time to come home. Let the Light that dwells within you be fed with Avalon's ecstatic energies, those of our beautiful Gaia's loving heart, that of our mighty protector, Archangel Michael, and the divine Joy of the Great Deva of Glastonbury. Yes, beautiful Bridget and wondrous Epona join me in this welcome. Our mighty patron, Archangel Michael, joins his presence with ours to amplify the crystal radiance of the Tor's magnificent beacon.

My and our profound gratitude to you, Carol. And to all your splendid company who give such loving support in both your powerful identities. We celebrate both!

And now, Namaste'

And so as the group's final number settles at five... I come to call them *The Fantastic Five!* ... I send Magdalene's message of welcome to them. The special bond that connects all in the group begins to strengthen, as it always does in the weeks leading to departure. After these now six years of offering the Avalon Pilgrimage, this delightful reoccurrence warms my heart and lifts my spirits.

I release any further doubt that it will be anything but a marvelous pilgrimage-journey together in September. Home to Avalon, home to my dear Sister, Angeline.

Chapter 19

What should I be
but just what I am?
~ Edna St. Vincent Millay

August brings some blessed days of slower pace with time to soak up some of the sunny Summer weather. All is in readiness for the September 15th departure for Glastonbury and I luxuriate in these days of ease. My across-the-yard neighbors, my landlord and family, take a short trip bringing even greater peace and quiet for a few days. It's marvelous to have the whole place to myself.

One of those extra-quiet mornings I was looking through the box of my journals and discovered one I'd been looking for, for quite a while. It held entries from the mid-90s all the way through 2004. It was the absolute perfect day to sit with it looking back through the nearly ten years of entries. When I "emerged" hours later I was somewhat drained from this all re-membering, but with a gratifyingly fresh focus of how this decade so thoroughly shaped my present life. Spirit's hand in this "reconnoitering" would become clearer in the not-too-distant future.

A family camping trip to the St. Lawrence River had been in the works for late August. It nearly didn't happen when Hurricane Irene thundered up the East Coast bringing severe flooding and wind damage, especially to the Schoharie and Hudson Valleys of New York and to Vermont. After only a one-day delay, we all made it to the campground and had a lovely three days together. "Lots of fishing, swimming, campfires, s'mores and sparklers, and Great horned owls calling," I write in my journal. Another sweet gathering takes place on Labor Day Weekend with a family baby shower for Tracy and Justin. It is a delight to watch the two of them opening gifts, many handmade, for their baby whose arrival is only six weeks or so away. Lots of oohing and ahhing!

With little respite, the Northeast is again bracing for another hurricane. Hurricane Lee is set to come through barely a week after Irene. Flooding is certain with waterways still running high and the land already saturated. It is small comfort when Lee is downgraded to a Tropical Storm as we await its arrival late on Wednesday, September 7th. In the Binghamton area we are put on notice that evacuations may be necessary for all of us along the Susquehanna River.

The rain sets in by late afternoon, at once falling in silvery-gray curtains that are seemingly relentless. Somehow I fall asleep despite the din of the heavy rain, a sound unlike any other storm I'd ever experienced.

Just before 3AM I bolt awake to the sound of a tree crashing down somewhere above on the hill. And at the same time I hear an eerie disembodied voice being broadcast from emergency vehicles on the streets below, calling for all to evacuate the neighborhood. Firemen are going door-to-door with the same message. Minutes later my landlord calls my cell phone to tell me this and offer suggestions of where to go. It is a most surreal fifteen minutes of hastily gathering a few things I think I might need, filling up the cat's food and water dishes, and then squishing my way down the steps to the car. I know with us so high up on Round Top Hill our homes are safe, but the concern is that the power will soon go out and remain out for an indefinite time.

Driving out of the neighborhood in the deluge, I stop to speak to a fireman. He tells me of the two nearest shelters and warns that the Vestal bridge may already be closed. The river is already well above flood stage. Endicott's Main Street is deserted but oddly Dunkin' Donuts is open and I stop to buy coffee not sure when it might be that I'll have another cup of good coffee. Two people are working and say they're staying open as long as they have power or until they too are forced to evacuate. We part company wishing one another, "Good luck and stay safe."

I drive on through heavy sheets of rain, the streets mostly empty, traffic and streetlights out in many places. Crossing the larger Route 26 bridge I can't see the Susquehanna down below in the dark but can feel its swift-flowing presence as I drive cautiously across towards the evacuation center. When I reach Binghamton University's Events Center I follow buses that are bringing in hundreds of people from downtown apartment buildings. I join them and people like myself who've driven there in their own cars. I manage to find a parking place at the edge of one of the already-full lots, gather up my gear hoping to keep it somewhat dry, and head to the brightly-lit Center. There's such a long line to check in that I decide to go back out to the car until it's light. One thing's for certain, it will be a lot more private than going inside.

How strange this all is... how incredibly strange. So I bed down as comfortably as I can in my small gold Hyundai affectionately known as Finch, and somehow manage to fall asleep to the rain's incessant drumming.

Bright morning sun greets my eyes when I wake, and though I know exactly where I am, it is another surreal moment. I unfold myself from my sleeping position and once again cross the jammed parking lot to the Center. Inside there are several thousand other evacuees and I stand for several minutes looking down over the rows of cots and somewhat disheveled heaps of backpacks and personal belongings. We are definitely "all in this together."

"Evacuee"... what an odd name to subscribe to myself. So at last I check in and am given a paper bracelet. Breakfast is already being served by Red Cross volunteers and I am mightily impressed with how efficiently this all is being managed.

Gratefully I take my plate of scrambled eggs and toast and go back outside to sit in the already warm sunshine. Others are doing the same, everyone sharing stories of the night and how we got to the evacuation center. The day is clearly going to be a beautiful early Autumn day, that fact as strangely unreal as the night we all have just lived through together. Stories circulate about how bad the damage is so far and there's much speculation about when the River will crest and just what that likely-staggering level might be.

For a couple of hours I wander about exchanging information with fellow storm-refugees. Near midday someone tells me that the Route 26 bridge is open to traffic. I decide to try and go home to check on Angus. By then my landlord has been in touch by cell phone to ask how I am. It's so comforting to hear his familiar voice and know that they are also all okay. He tells me they're planning to go back to their house too.

I set off cautiously and on the way there see several abandoned cars in a shopping mall parking lot with water to their roofs. It's a sobering sight. I cross the incredibly swollen Susquehanna River roaring through the landscape and knowing it has yet to reach its expected crest. Tree branches litter the streets in Endicott but there are no downed lines or other dangers. I reach our neighborhood, turn into Davis Ave, and pull into my parking spot.

When I open the door of Dragonfly Cottage I find the lights and water on and Angus-cat quite happy to see me. Leon and his family arrive soon. No one appears to tell us we can't stay, and with the power remaining on at least on our street, we count ourselves lucky and settle back in. Power is out nearly every-where else and we never do learn how our part of town managed differently.

That night the almost-Full Moon sails magnificently through a clear and starry sky. I stand for a long while at the bedroom window looking out, the moonlit landscape dark nearly as far as I could see. A few cars' lights appear briefly like fireflies across the river on Route 26 above Vestal. Otherwise there are no street-lights, no house or building lights near or far, the incessant hum of traffic on 17 eerily absent.

A sound like no other fills the air… a loud rushing like a train coming rises from below me as the River's unfathomable torrent of water sweeps through the bank-side trees swaying in the silvery moonlight. It's already a dozen feet or more above flood stage and still rising. It would crest the next day a little past 2PM at thirty-six feet, eighteen feet above flood.

I stand in the moonlight transfixed by this view and the river's powerful, mesmerizing presence filling the August night. I say prayers for us all.

The damage to homes and property is beyond the telling, but it is a great comfort that no lives are lost in our part of the Southern Tier. The lower-lying streets of our neighborhood are flooded with water levels filling basements and rising into first floors. When the waters receded allowing people to return, vast heaps of water-damaged furniture, appliances, and anything touched by the water began to rise along the streets. The sight of these towering piles leaves me speechless as I drive a zigzag route to one of the two area grocery stores that had managed to escape the waters. Everywhere people reach out to help each other, all of us determined to begin the work to repair and rebuild.

The night before I leave for England, I post this note on Facebook along with a photo of Chalice Well: *A still nearly-full Harvest Moon is rising over the waters of the Susquehanna that is blessedly now at "normal flood." The power was just restored to the streets below me, at least that much of help to those whose homes were damaged by the high waters. I'll be posting a last set of photos that I took over the weekend before I set off tomorrow for this year's Glastonbury Pilgrimage. Next Tuesday five enthusiastic adventurers will join me for this year's "magical mystery tour." Visits here on Facebook will be rare for the next several weeks. Until I return to Dragonfly Cottage on October 11th, I wish you all well in these last days of Summer and many blessings for the start of Autumn. Take good care, everyone! ~Carol*

And so, ten years and a bit more after my first journey there, I board a plane for the night flight to England. I arrive at Bristol Airport to the welcome of Mano and her friend, Alan, who drive up to meet me. How wonderful to be greeted by their smiles and warm hugs and then a comfortable car ride to Glastonbury instead of aboard the local bus. She has offered her place before the Pilgrimage group comes, and I'll have it all to myself while she's away for the weekend. What fabulous luxury to thoroughly rest up from the flight in her comfortable apartment and get over the jet lag.

As with the 2009 group, Mano would be an intimate part of this Pilgrimage. We planned to begin the first day with a walk to Wearyall Hill to visit the Holy Thorn and offer it a healing ceremony. From her apartment window I could see its shorn trunk standing in faithful vigil above Glastonbury. Knowing how emotional it would be to encounter it in this state, I wanted to spend some time there on my own before the group came.

So with that purpose in mind, late the first morning I set off towards Wearyall Hill. As wonderful as it was to be walking along the familiar streets and past such well-loved places, my heart felt somehow unprepared for what was awaiting me. I made my way up Fisher Hill and then turned up the Old Roman Way. Houses hide the Thorn until you reach the field at the top of the street and go in through the gate.

When at last it came into view, I stopped and took in its angular, almost skeletal form above me on the hill. The sight pierced my heart.

I was very glad that no one else was there. No one was coming up the street behind me so I knew I'd be alone there. On somewhat unsteady legs I took the well-worn path through the pasture grass, my eyes fixed on the Thorn. Images I'd seen online played in my mind of people grieving beside it that first morning, and of its severed limbs and branches being carried reverently away down this very path.

When I drew to within perhaps thirty feet, I sensed a loving welcome from this beautiful Being and began to weep, hurrying forward then to reach through the railing and lay my shaking hands on its trunk. I felt the little tree receive all of this, but very soon came a clear and amazing message.

"It's all right… it's all right," the Holy Thorn told me. *"All is really very well. You do not need to weep, though I thank you for your tears. The grieving is done and complete. Remember how I became an even brighter Beacon through receiving all of the Love sent here from people all around the Earth. This loving Energy is here gathered and it is this I share with you and all who come to visit me. Again, I say, do not weep, for all is well."*

Its gentle presence and strength conveyed to me, I sat down beside it, deeply consoled and heartened. I took in some slow breaths and looked around once more at Avalon's incredible landscape that soon would be welcoming the 2011 Fantastic Five. I'd just experienced the first Wonder of this year's Pilgrimage. All was indeed very well.

On Tuesday morning everyone arrived on the same flight into Bristol. As they emerged from the "Arrivals" door at the airport, what fun to greet them and welcome them to England! Our minivan transport was waiting to carry us to Glastonbury. Soon we were driving down from the Mendip Hills and exclaiming at the first glimpses of the Tor rising above the Somerset Levels, flashing its Welcome.

So after the first night's sleep and a wonderful breakfast in the Daisy Centre's solarium, we began our pilgrimage adventure on a bright and sparkling Autumn morning. Mano led us through the same streets I'd walked two days earlier and we soon came to stand in a reverent circle around the Holy Thorn. We were joined by another special Avalon citizen, a young man named Tor Webster, and the American woman he was guiding that day. Mano and Tor, who knew each other well, led us in an impromptu healing ritual for the Thorn.

The Pilgrimage's seven days were each full with notable experiences of places we visited in and around Glastonbury: Chalice Well where we joined with so many others to celebrate the Autumn Equinox, the Magdalene Chapel, Glastonbury Abbey, walking the labyrinth at St. John's, exploring nearby Wells with its Cathedral and Market, the always-awesome visit to Stonehenge and Avebury, and a day trip by public bus to Bath and its famous Roman ruins. In the evenings we donned our PJs and gathered in my room to share thoughts of the day's adventures and discuss what was coming next, an "Avalon-dorm party" of the most magical sort.

Time always goes both slow and fast, the magic-elasticity of the Avalon Pilgrimage. But ultimately the end-point arrives. I saw off the last two Pilgrims on the two o'clock bus to Bristol, a misty-eyed parting as always. There is no adequate way to describe the deep and special bond that develops among us over the days and experiences shared in this extraordinary place. Just about everything had gone exceptionally smoothly and wonderfully. And for me the keen sense of celebrating the tenth year of my own personal pilgrimage made it all the more special.

Now there were the five days of my extended pilgrimage to enjoy. It began with a three-day trip to Liverpool to visit Molly Harvey. I travel there by train, a new experience, and one that's great fun. With our mutual experiences of Mystery School, and of Soul School in Minnesota and Liverpool, we talked nearly nonstop of these shared times and our separate journeys of Spirit.

Being around Molly with her always-engaging Irish energies often promotes otherworldly contacts. So it was no surprise when I turned off the lamp on the first night that for a while sparkling lights winked and danced around the bed. The house fairies had come to bid me greeting. "Oh, yes," Molly said the next morning, her eyes twinkling, "there's often a fairy-party to be enjoyed in that bedroom! I trust you told them when you needed your sleep." I had, indeed.

I returned to Glastonbury for my last two days, delighted to be spending them with Mano. My Spirit-Guides kept urging me to have a Vortex Healing from Daisy Foss. I seldom spent money on that sort of thing when it came to myself, but their insistence won me over. It was certainly a powerful session that afternoon in her healing room with a profound sense of clearing and release of "old stuff," as she put it. Some was certainly from the rocky years with Ken towards the end of our marriage. She told me that relationships run in seven-year cycles. So that meant our separation begun in 2008 was halfway along. A delightful bonus was her describing a "luminescent pearl" at my heart center and also seeing Angeline standing on my left side during the session. Thanking her for her profound and skilled work, I left the Daisy Centre tucking these images into my heart.

It was a rainy, wild morning for my return flight, the wind blowing a gale. Our pilot said with confidence that we'd be up and over the weather in minutes, not to worry. We rumbled down the runway straight into the wind and with hardly much of a bump, just as he'd said, we were soon above the clouds and flying smoothly across the English Channel in the morning's brilliant sky to the Charles De Gaulle Airport where I'd catch the connecting flight back to Newark.

A few hours later we were out over the Atlantic and then cruising down over the Canadian Maritimes and New England towards New Jersey on a clear Autumn afternoon. My thoughts were filled with the great satisfaction of how well the 2011 Pilgrimage had gone, really even beyond expectations.

But perhaps this particular work-in-the-world... offering the Pilgrimages... had reached its end. How true it was that as fabulous as these pilgrimages most always were, it was also very often a labor of love. As a final group, I couldn't do better than these Fantastic Five. My "bonus time" had been wonderful too, even if there hadn't been much spent with Angeline. But well I knew that every bit of my time in Avalon was marvelous fuel for our work together once I got home.

While I was gone the cleanup work had come a long way to our flood-ravaged community but a daunting amount of the recovery effort remained. A heartbreaking number of homes and businesses were determined to be uninhabitable not only in our area but everywhere that had felt the impact of Hurricanes Irene and Lee.

That first night back in Dragonfly Cottage, I lay listening to the traffic hum on 17 across the River and for once welcomed its sound rather than finding it annoying. When we were in England our group had performed a special ceremony at Bride's Mound for the healing of the land and for all living beings affected by those devastating days of rain and flood. Strangely enough and oddly appropriate, the morning we chose to do this was the only chill and rainy one of the entire Pilgrimage.

Less than two months of 2011 remained. 2012's intriguing mysteries were quickly making their way towards us. But before that, and most exciting of all, we'd soon be meeting our new grandchild with his or her intriguing due date of 11/11/11. All was marvelous and bright. What more could I ask for?

Babies have their own ideas of when they make their entrance, so on November 12th, the second night of November's Full Moon, Ken and I drove the two hours to Albany to be there to greet our third grandchild. Our daughter-in-law, Tracy, was well along with her labor and we drove as quickly as we could through the moonlit landscape hoping to be there in time. Besides the euphoric anticipation, this happy event was a most welcome respite for me.

The weeks between my returning to Dragonfly Cottage on October 11th and that night had been fraught with emotional chaos that I in no way saw coming. Bless my Guides' advance knowledge of it all and especially for "signing me up" for the healing and clearing session with Daisy.

I'd been back home only three days and was just beginning to ground the energy of the trip and the Pilgrimage when Ken called and announced he wished the divorce process to begin. He was entitled to make the request, but the timing could not have been more horrible. Though I'm always blissed-out when I get back from England, I'm physically spent. And my psychic and emotional reserves are always low too. So I entered the incredibly dark passage that would be the *processing work* of the soon-to-be divorce with an alarming deficit.

For long days and several weeks I went back and forth on a spectrum of "somewhat unsettled" at one end and "shattering despair" on the other. It astonished me how many tears a human could shed. I lost nearly fifteen pounds since eating became some weird option and sleep was hard to find on too many nights. I was at first startled and then increasingly worried when I found myself unable to journal about what I was going through. Never before had I been unable to take refuge in my journals.

I averaged one night of sleep out of three with two mostly sleepless nights following. My companion on those nights was Angus who seemed to know how much I needed his purring companionship, curled close beside me. When I woke weeping as I often did, he'd start purring, never once leaving my side.

At moments I'd think how odd this all was since I'd truly believed that I'd come to terms with everything emotionally and otherwise during these nearly four years of the separation. No one had told me this is a stage most people divorcing go through. Oh no, I wasn't exempt, nor would I choose to be. I recognized the shamanic journey it was and felt fortunate to have the skills needed to navigate this daunting, uncharted terrain.

Long ago I'd come to understand that even the darkest of times bring their gifts, hidden though they often are at first. A close circle of friends was on speed-dial for many hours of comforting conversation. All assured me I could call at any hour of the day or night. A time or two I think one or another of them felt she ought to jump in her car and drive to Endicott. But I had the paths on Round Top Hill and those by the River to wander along, and all this was enough. So between Angus and these four, it was exactly the support group I needed.

I emerged at last, at first definitely worse for the wear... but the sun was shining.

Some months later I was telling a good friend about this passage. Our grandchild's arrival aside, I laughingly called November of 2011 my Month of Murk. How perfectly this summed it up and made me smile at the same time. That and fondness for the truth, *What doesn't kill you, makes you stronger.*

Aven Kestrel Manning took her time those two days following 11/11/11. Our speedy travel that moonlit night wasn't necessary after all. She joined us finally in the early evening of November 13th to her parents' relief, especially Tracy's. "You have a little granddaughter!" their smiling obstetrician told us assembled grandparents, and as one we leapt up from our seats with shouts of joy and fist-pumped the air. When she got back to Tracy and Justin in the birthing room she told them, "I've announced the good news to lots of relatives, but your parents are the happiest ones ever!" It's a story that never gets old in the telling.

Endings and beginnings. And what a magick and marvelous *Beginning* we shared that November evening, Ken and I, helping to welcome sweet Aven Kestrel to the world.

So a slimmer me set off in earnest into the final month of 2011. I had great fun buying new pants a whole size smaller than my usual one, dubbing them my Divorce Pants. No better example of *Snake shedding its Skin*, and oh! had I shed some, body-wise, emotion-wise, Spirit-wise. All... I knew absolutely... was in preparation for 2012, the Year of the Snake.

There were lovely places still to go before the end of that particular December, and some intriguing new people would be crossing my path...

But that's a story for another day.

Chapter 20

Dear One,
The sacred seed is restored,
its encoded message unfurling to tender but sturdy growth.
~ Meditation message, 19th March 2012

(An Epilogue, if you will...)

It was nearly 2012's Vernal Equinox before Life granted an opportunity to open the Dialogue Journal and seek Angeline once more. As always, I was apologetic for the lengthy absence, and as always she told me all was just fine.

19th March 2012: Return & again Returning

Hello my dearest Sister, Angeline... coming home to our shared conversation here this day before the Spring Equinox of 2012, the three Spring days of equal day and night. This day I have reacquainted myself with so many marvelous moments of our journey together which once again was set aside for a long while. But at long last I see and feel that this is the final disruption of our story-weaving efforts! And in this day's review I've been prompted to invoke the Spirit of the Land to bless and over-light that which we do together here. I call out to you now to join me once more in our sacred and truly joyful work... hello again, Angeline!

Oh dear Sister, dearest Carol! The passing time of which you speak truly is not of any great significance to my own days. So I gently remind you once again that all is well with us. My heart is joyful and that is all! Yes, we are reunited in this wondrous journey... what an incredible number of this year of your life, 2012, though I do remember how startling it was to first learn of the years in which your, our, days are now lived. You know I am smiling now, Carol!

Yes, I glimpse your amused smile, Angeline! At moments this number seems odd even to me… but what is especially wondrous at this time of our now-long connection ("long" in the years of this life as "me" at least!) is that never before have we had all the factors necessary for the perfect outcome of this writing – of our book – to be fully and delightfully completed. Some of this may well come to be revealed to you, and I hope that most, if not all, will be. Some three years ago you said to me, *"We are the bright mirrors of one another's lives."* It now feels so very true that in this year, 2012, we are moving into the fullness of those words, dear Sister.

I pause in my "note-taking" as I finish this sentence and then… so typically… something calls me away to the Outer World. A week goes by – the first full week of Spring 2012. Three months of 2012 have passed. The days are bringing more and more light and the sense of promising *possibilities* and new beginnings steadily nearing.

On the morning of March 28th, I do a meditation and am given this message to record in our Dialogue Journal. It is intended for both of us.

Dear One,

The sacred seed is restored, its encoded message unfurling to tender but sturdy growth, its secret chamber revealed and now no longer needed. The Tree of Life sends down its root to the Mother's waiting crystalline embrace. You who have found your way to the wondrous ancient Garden (and who are, indeed, Gardeners there), you who have served as Guardians, the time of rejoicing is at hand! Push open the Gates and beckon to others to enter and re-member their Sacred Selves, the imprint of their forgotten heritage, the stirring of the ancient Dance…

I feel Angeline approach and look over my shoulder, considering this message with me. Her now long-familiar and sturdy presence touches my heart. In the humming, companionable silence, together we ponder the words. And then I write this to her...

I am sure there is more to come – yes – You and I are now working in the growing light of this year's seasonal Wheel as this story of ours becomes fully manifested.

Oh yes! I knew it from that day when you brought Tula to the meeting room at Chalice Well. Yes, my Sister, we are both Guardians and Gardeners of Sacred Spirit. Our separate and shared Earth journeys stand testament to this Greater Story.

So many now are heeding the signs. So many now are re-membering their Voice with its beautiful Song. As Rumi urges us, we will not go back to sleep... especially you and me!

Sitting there at my writing table in the sun-filled living room of Dragonfly Cottage, I glimpse Angeline's bright smile and her nodding in happy agreement. I smile back at her. Then she says,

We are Way-showers, dear Sister... especially you!

The Small Song

That stone path you can see from the road,
you know, the one that leads to the wooden bridge,
the one crossing the creek
to where there are no more wars
and even gypsies stop wandering;
take a left there
and go until you come to a straw hut
that breathes steadily in the yellow dusk.
It will whisper a small song
that might carry into the next valley;
it might be your older name, the one mountains know.
To enter the hut is to hold your face
next to the warm Earth, to remember
your flesh in a thousand ways.
Inside are the quiet places even the wind can't find.
That stone path you can see from the road,
its forks lead nowhere you know
but everywhere you've been calling to
from your wild heart.
It forks until there are no forks
where your footfalls become as natural as rain,
in a country where fear has no name.
Lauren de Boer

BOOKS

O-BOOKS

SPIRITUALITY

O is a symbol of the world, of oneness and unity; this eye represents knowledge and insight. We publish titles on general spirituality and living a spiritual life. We aim to inform and help you on your own journey in this life.

If you have enjoyed this book, why not tell other readers by posting a review on your preferred book site? Recent bestsellers from O-Books are:

Heart of Tantric Sex
Diana Richardson
Revealing Eastern secrets of deep love and intimacy to Western couples.
Paperback: 978-1-90381-637-0 ebook: 978-1-84694-637-0

Crystal Prescriptions
The A-Z guide to over 1,200 symptoms and their healing crystals
Judy Hall
The first in the popular series of five books, this handy little guide is packed as tight as a pill-bottle with crystal remedies for ailments.
Paperback: 978-1-90504-740-6 ebook: 978-1-84694-629-5

Take Me To Truth
Undoing the Ego
Nouk Sanchez, Tomas Vieira
The best-selling step-by-step book on shedding the Ego, using
the teachings of *A Course In Miracles*.
Paperback: 978-1-84694-050-7 ebook: 978-1-84694-654-7

The 7 Myths about Love...Actually!
The journey from your HEAD to the HEART of your SOUL
Mike George
Smashes all the myths about LOVE.
Paperback: 978-1-84694-288-4 ebook: 978-1-84694-682-0

The Holy Spirit's Interpretation of the New Testament
A course in Understanding and Acceptance
Regina Dawn Akers
Following on from the strength of *A Course In Miracles*, NTI
teaches us how to experience the love and oneness of God.
Paperback: 978-1-84694-085-9 ebook: 978-1-78099-083-5

The Message of A Course In Miracles
A translation of the text in plain language
Elizabeth A. Cronkhite
A translation of *A Course in Miracles* into plain, everyday
language for anyone seeking inner peace. The companion
volume, *Practicing a Course In Miracles*, offers practical lessons
and mentoring.
Paperback: 978-1-84694-319-5 ebook: 978-1-84694-642-4

Rising in Love
My Wild and Crazy Ride to Here and Now, with Amma, the
Hugging Saint
Ram Das Batchelder
Rising in Love conveys an author's extraordinary journey of

spiritual awakening with the Guru, Amma.
Paperback: 978-1-78279-687-9 ebook: 978-1-78279-686-2

Thinker's Guide to God
Peter Vardy
An introduction to key issues in the philosophy of religion.
Paperback: 978-1-90381-622-6

Your Simple Path
Find happiness in every step
Ian Tucker
A guide to helping us reconnect with what is really important in
our lives.
Paperback: 978-1-78279-349-6 ebook: 978-1-78279-348-9

365 Days of Wisdom
Daily Messages To Inspire You Through The Year
Dadi Janki
Daily messages which cool the mind, warm the heart and guide
you along your journey.
Paperback: 978-1-84694-863-3 ebook: 978-1-84694-864-0

Body of Wisdom
Women's Spiritual Power and How it Serves
Hilary Hart
Bringing together the dreams and experiences of women across
the world with today's most visionary spiritual teachers.
Paperback: 978-1-78099-696-7 ebook: 978-1-78099-695-0

Dying to Be Free
From Enforced Secrecy to Near Death to True Transformation
Hannah Robinson
After an unexpected accident and near-death experience,
Hannah Robinson found herself radically transforming her life,

while a remarkable new insight altered her relationship with her father; a practising Catholic priest.
Paperback: 978-1-78535-254-6 ebook: 978-1-78535-255-3

The Ecology of the Soul
A Manual of Peace, Power and Personal Growth for Real People in the Real World
Aidan Walker
Balance your own inner Ecology of the Soul to regain your natural state of peace, power and wellbeing.
Paperback: 978-1-78279-850-7 ebook: 978-1-78279-849-1

Not I, Not other than I
The Life and Teachings of Russel Williams
Steve Taylor, Russel Williams
The miraculous life and inspiring teachings of one of the World's greatest living Sages.
Paperback: 978-1-78279-729-6 ebook: 978-1-78279-728-9

On the Other Side of Love
A Woman's Unconventional Journey Towards Wisdom
Muriel Maufroy
When life has lost all meaning, what do you do?
Paperback: 978-1-78535-281-2 ebook: 978-1-78535-282-9

Practicing A Course In Miracles
A Translation of the Workbook in Plain Language and With Mentoring Notes
Elizabeth A. Cronkhite
The practical second and third volumes of The Plain-Language *A Course in Miracles*.
Paperback: 978-1-84694-403-1 ebook: 978-1-78099-072-9

Quantum Bliss

The Quantum Mechanics of Happiness, Abundance, and Health

George S. Mentz

Quantum Bliss is the breakthrough summary of success and spirituality secrets that customers have been waiting for.

Paperback: 978-1-78535-203-4 ebook: 978-1-78535-204-1

The Upside Down Mountain

Mags MacKean

A must-read for anyone weary of chasing success and happiness – one woman's inspirational journey swapping the uphill slog for the downhill slope.

Paperback: 978-1-78535-171-6 ebook: 978-1-78535-172-3

Your Personal Tuning Fork

The Endocrine System

Deborah Bates

Discover your body's health secret, the endocrine system, and 'twang' your way to sustainable health!

Paperback: 978-1-84694-503-8 ebook: 978-1-78099-697-4

Readers of ebooks can buy or view any of these bestsellers by clicking on the live link in the title. Most titles are published in paperback and as an ebook. Paperbacks are available in traditional bookshops. Both print and ebook formats are available online.

Find more titles and sign up to our readers' newsletter at http://www.johnhuntpublishing.com/mind-body-spirit

Follow us on Facebook at https://www.facebook.com/OBooks/ and Twitter at https://twitter.com/obooks